THE HUMAN–AI DECODER

In a world of AI-complexity, Mario masterfully captures how AI changes work to gain high impact that leads to improved actions. The Human–AI Decoder turns AI aspirations into relevant and real daily choices that make a difference. Anyone using AI for information or efficiency will make better decisions using the decoder because it integrates the human and technology.

—*Dave Ulrich*, Rensis Likert Professor Emeritus, University of Michigan Partner, The RBL Group, University of Michigan

The Human–AI Decoder framework fills an important gap in what AI Singapore have developed. The frameworks helps organisations translate the AI impact on human job roles into actionable next steps – which is key to this AI transformation that is happening now and will only accelerate in 2026 and beyond.

—*Laurence Liew*, Director AI Innovation, AI Singapore

Mario Jacober makes a compelling case for using AI to lift the quality of work we do. He shows how intelligent tools can strengthen judgement, creativity and contribution, reminding us that the real opportunity is human empowerment, not just greater efficiency.

—*Anabel Fall*, Group Chief People Officer, Haniel Group

A clear practical guide to navigating the workforce impact of AI – essential reading for today's leaders.

—*Christian Gswind*, Regional Chief Financial Officer, Gategroup

A powerful and timely guide to the human reality of Artificial Intelligence.

—*Marvin Guggisberg*, Regional Manager APAC, Lufthansa Group

A must-read for HR leaders shaping the workforce in the age of AI. The Human–AI Decoder enables HR to embrace a clear, strategic role in translating AI ambition into workforce reality and from there, to organisational success.

—*Michael Jenkins*, Chief Executive Officer, Expert Humans

A timely and accessible framework for leaders navigating AI's impact on people and organisations. Mario translates a fast-moving field into practical guidance with purpose and precision.

—*Sergio Raja*, Group Head of HR Data Insights,
Zurich Insurance Company

THE HUMAN–AI DECODER

Leading the Human Side of Artificial Intelligence

BY

MARIO JACOBER

emerald PUBLISHING

United Kingdom – North America – Japan – India
Malaysia – China

Emerald Publishing Limited
Emerald Publishing, Floor 5, Northspring, 21-23 Wellington Street,
Leeds LS1 4DL.

First edition 2026

British Library Cataloguing in Publication Data
A catalogue record for this book is available from the British Library

ISBN: 978-1-80686-892-6 (Print)
ISBN: 978-1-80686-889-6 (Online)
ISBN: 978-1-80686-891-9 (Epub)

INVESTOR IN PEOPLE

For Ulyana and Victoria,
whose love and patience held me steady through the long nights and early mornings that shaped this book.

And for my parents,
who gave me the gift of curiosity and the courage to follow it.

And for my brother,
whose quiet support and belief in me have always mattered more than he knows.

CONTENTS

FOREWORD: A LETTER TO MY DAUGHTER

Dear Victoria,

I wrote this book for you and for the generation you are growing up in. You will live in a world where humans and intelligent machines work side by side, a world where decisions move faster than ours ever did and where the meaning of contribution shifts in ways my generation is only beginning to understand. You will step into a future where AI is not unusual or extraordinary. It will simply be part of how life unfolds.

My generation is the last one to know a fully human workforce. We grew up in a time when every decision, every creation and every answer came from a person. Your generation will inherit something very different. You will learn, create and work in an environment where machines are capable, present and woven into everything around you. This is exciting. It also asks for care, clarity and responsibility.

The truth is that none of us knows exactly what the future will look like. Technology is moving too quickly for anyone to predict every turn. But we can shape how we meet it. We can decide what we protect, what we value and what we want the next generation to grow up believing. I wrote this book because I want you to grow up in a future where people still lead the conversation. I want you to live in a world where technology strengthens your confidence instead of limiting it, where your judgement, imagination and courage matter more, not less.

I want you to feel the freedom to question any system, to influence how intelligent tools are used and to know that your voice carries more weight than any algorithm. And I want you to experience a world where organisations build structures that keep humans at the centre of every technological choice.

When you are older and read these pages, I hope you see that this book was not only about work. It was also about people and optimism and responsibility. It was about protecting the human contribution in a time of rapid change. Most of all, it was about you and the belief that your generation deserves a future where technology serves human purpose and never replaces it.

Whatever path you choose, bring your heart, your curiosity and your kindness with you. These are the qualities no machine can copy. They will guide you through every change still to come.

With all my love,
Papa

PREFACE: A CALL TO LEAD THE HUMAN SIDE OF AI

Artificial Intelligence (AI) has shifted from something built quietly into office software to something that now sits in the middle of how organisations function. Tools that once felt like gentle improvements have become systems that influence how work is done and what people are expected to do. Despite this rapid expansion, many organisations still struggle to understand what AI means for the people behind the work.

AI itself is not new. Earlier systems relied on fixed rules and narrow logic. What has changed is the rise of generative, predictive and increasingly autonomous systems that can take on work once handled entirely by humans. They reshape the flow of tasks and adjust the pace of decisions faster than most people are prepared for. AI has become a force that changes how work is created and understood.

Many organisations now find themselves in a moment of uncertainty. They can see AI appearing in areas such as customer service, medical diagnosis, workflow design and content creation. What they cannot see clearly is how this shift touches the human side of work. Technical models describe system maturity, but they leave a gap. They rarely explain how daily work feels when machines begin shaping what people do or how human contribution changes when AI becomes part of the process.

This book aims to provide that clarity. It explains how AI affects real roles, real decisions and real expectations. It also recognises that the people function, traditionally responsible for supporting employees, now has an opportunity to guide how humans and AI work together. HR is positioned in a unique way. It understands people, culture and capability. It can help organisations prepare for the adjustments that come when the shape of work evolves.

At the centre of this book is the human–AI decoder. It gives leaders a clear way to see how AI reshapes tasks and roles and how to respond with purpose rather than guesswork. It helps organisations interpret the shifts they are already experiencing and prepare for what comes next. It also provides a common language built around a classification of the six levels of AI impact, allowing teams to talk about impact with the same clarity and move forward with shared understanding.

This book does not pretend to predict the future. AI is moving too quickly for any blueprint to stay fixed. What the book offers instead is a way to navigate change with steadiness. Leaders will need that clarity as new kinds of work take shape. They will need it just as much as organisations learn, often unevenly, how people and intelligent systems can work side by side.

This book is, at its core, about people. It is about helping them understand what is changing and what still belongs to them. It is about building environments where technology supports human capability rather than overshadowing it. And it is about approaching the future of work with judgement, care and a clear sense of responsibility.

Let us decode AI and shape a future that works for people.

ACKNOWLEDGEMENTS

This book was shaped through ongoing conversations and practical experience. The ideas did not emerge in isolation. They were tested in real settings, challenged in discussion and refined over time.

I am grateful to Michael Jenkins, who encouraged me to write this book. As the author of Expert Humans and Toxic Humans, his perspective and thoughtful challenge contributed to shaping this work.

I would also like to acknowledge the HR Leadership Expert Circle of the Swiss Chamber of Commerce in Singapore. It provided an early forum where ideas could be openly discussed and strengthened. The candour and thoughtful exchanges within that group supported the development of this work.

My thanks also go to the many peers and practitioners across roles and regions who shared their experiences of organisations already navigating change. Their insights grounded this book in reality and ensured that it reflects how work is evolving in practice, not just in theory.

To all of you, thank you for your time, insight and engagement.

AUTHOR'S NOTE

This book begins with a simple truth.

'Artificial Intelligence is reshaping how work happens, yet few people understand its human impact.'

I wrote this book to close that gap. It is for anyone who wants to make sense of how AI is changing work, organisations and society. It is not written only for HR professionals. It is for leaders, teams, educators, technologists, policymakers and individuals who recognise that AI is no longer a distant idea. It is already part of everyday life, often in ways we do not see until the effects are impossible to ignore.

To guide readers through this shift, the book is organised into three parts that build on one another.

Part I explains what Artificial Intelligence (AI) really is, how it developed and where it is heading. It offers the foundation needed to understand why AI has become unavoidable and why the deepest disruption is human, not technical.

Part II introduces the human–AI decoder, a practical approach built on the AI Workforce Impact Model. It shows where AI impacts work, how deep that impact runs and what leaders can do in response. The decoder turns confusion into clarity and gives teams a common language to navigate change across functions and industries.

Part III looks ahead. It explores how roles, structures and organisations may evolve as humans and intelligent systems work together. It examines what organisations must do to be ready for AI, how to prepare people for new expectations and how to build confidence as work continues to change. It also introduces Human-Machine Resources (HMR), a forward-looking view of how HR must evolve to guide the human side of AI and shape a workforce where people and intelligent systems can succeed together.

The insights in these pages come from two decades of leading digital transformations in global organisations and from years spent observing how people adapt when technology becomes part of their daily work. They draw on conversations with senior leaders, researchers and practitioners across industries, as well as on real examples of teams learning to work with new tools and new expectations.

The book is written to be accessible. It uses clear language, relatable stories and practical examples to guide readers through the AI journey. Some examples refer to publicly known situations. Others reflect common patterns that appear wherever AI enters daily work, shaped carefully to protect confidentiality while keeping the learning real and relevant.

My hope is simple. That this book gives readers the clarity, structure and confidence they need to lead the human side of AI with purpose and understanding.

PART I

UNDERSTANDING AI

Every major shift in history begins with a moment when people sense the world around them is changing faster than they expected. AI has brought us to one of those moments.

Part I opens the door to what Artificial Intelligence (AI) truly is, how it has developed and where it is taking us next. It gives readers a clear and accessible starting point for understanding AI's growing influence on work and society. Chapter 1 examines how AI is reshaping organisations and lays out five business-critical challenges leaders are confronted with as the technology moves deeper into daily operations. It also links today's disruption to earlier industrial revolutions and explains why this moment carries a different level of urgency. Chapter 2 brings the technology into focus by explaining its core forms, from machine learning to generative and agentic systems. It presents AI as a practical, human-centred part of modern work. Chapter 3 looks ahead to emerging breakthroughs such as Artificial General Intelligence (AGI) and shows why responsible and transparent adoption will shape how well humans and machines will progress together.

1

WHY AI'S GREATEST IMPACT IS HUMAN

ABSTRACT

Artificial Intelligence (AI) has moved from theory to daily practice. It now shapes how work is done, how decisions are made and how organisations compete for talent, relevance and value. This chapter explains why the current wave of AI differs from past technological shifts and why its deepest impact is human rather than technical. It traces how AI is already transforming tasks, roles and workflows across industries and shows how this mirrors earlier industrial revolutions, where disruption first changed identity and contribution before it changed machinery. What makes the present moment distinct is the speed and breadth of change. AI now influences cognitive and creative work once considered uniquely human. It alters how people judge their own performance, how teams collaborate and how organisations make sense of rapid transformation. Yet adoption is outpacing understanding. Employees feel the effects of AI long before leaders provide the guidance, guardrails or clarity they need. The chapter identifies five business-critical challenges that consistently shape AI's impact, from the tension between efficiency and culture to the growing skills gap, rising expectations for ethical oversight, readiness gaps across the workforce and the human dynamics that fuel resistance or trust. It also challenges persistent myths that limit Human Resources' (HR's) strategic influence at the very moment its role becomes essential. It makes clear that organisations will succeed not by adopting the most technology but by preparing their people to evolve with it.

Keywords: Artificial Intelligence; workforce transformation; human-centred AI; HR leadership; organisational culture; ethical AI; skills and capabilities; human–AI collaboration; AI governance; future of work

AI has shifted from something anticipated to something that shapes daily work. It now sits inside routines, decisions and the flow of ideas. What once felt distant or theoretical is now practical and unmistakably real. The way work gets done is changing, and the way choices are made is changing with it. People feel this shift in the tasks they perform and the expectations placed on them. The influence reaches every level of the organisation, from front-line teams to senior leaders. Companies are beginning to compete and create value in new ways. Across the working day, AI shapes how ideas emerge, how decisions take form and how people learn and grow. Workplaces are becoming environments where humans and intelligent systems operate together. In some areas, tasks are moving towards higher levels of autonomy (World Economic Forum, 2025a).

This is why AI's greatest impact is human. Its effects appear first in how people interpret their value, how they make decisions and how they experience their work. Before job titles change or structures shift, individuals feel the change personally. They sense new expectations, new uncertainties and new questions about where their judgement still matters. Understanding this human impact is the starting point for every meaningful AI transformation.

The central question is no longer what AI can do, but how people choose to work with it. The partnership between humans and intelligent systems should strengthen human contribution rather than replace it. The decisions leaders make will now determine whether organisations fall behind or guide the AI transformation with integrity, inclusiveness and a clear focus on people.

TECHNOLOGICAL PROGRESS RESHAPING THE NATURE OF WORK

A common misunderstanding about AI's workforce impact is the assumption that it replaces entire jobs. In practice, AI begins by transforming tasks, the building blocks of every role, before redefining the role itself. This distinction matters. Most jobs combine repetitive, judgement-based and uniquely human tasks.

AI typically starts by automating the repetitive, rules-based work and gradually moves into more complex cognitive areas (McKinsey & Company, 2025b). Over time, these changes reshape roles in noticeable ways. This is why organisations need to examine the work itself rather than relying on job titles. A title rarely reflects the full mix of tasks inside a role, and many roles share similar patterns of work beneath very different names. Planning for the future therefore depends on mapping tasks and understanding how they are changing. Experience across multiple transformations shows that once the task structure of a role is clear, leaders can see where augmentation supports performance and where human expertise remains essential.

This task-level transformation is already visible across industries. In many organisations, AI handles initial research, summarisation or data preparation. Employees focus on sense-making, interpretation and decision-making. Over time, this division of labour reshapes not only what people do, but how they create value, how they collaborate and how they judge their own contributions. Understanding these dynamics early helps leaders redesign work before disruption forces a reaction. To understand the scale of today's shift, it helps to look at a moment when work was redefined just as dramatically.

BLUE-COLLAR DISRUPTION IN THE INDUSTRIAL REVOLUTION

The First Industrial Revolution demonstrates how technological progress reshapes the nature of work (Schwab, 2016). Emerging in Britain in the late 18th century and expanding during the following decades, it marked the shift from human craft to mechanised production. At that time, artisans, farmers and manual labourers formed the core of the economy. Work was local, craft-based and human in scale. The rise of factories, steam power and organised labour systems changed how work was carried out and showed how quickly established practices can shift when new technologies emerge.

The invention of the steam engine and the rise of mechanised production changed everything. Textile factories replaced hand weavers with mechanical looms, mechanical threshers transformed farming by reducing the need for large rural labour forces and steam locomotives and later combustion engines redefined transportation. Carriage drivers, porters and horse handlers saw their skills become obsolete almost overnight as railways and motor vehicles took over.

History shows that technology rarely eliminates work; it redefines it. Those who adapted moved forward, and those who resisted were often left behind. These disruptions reshaped not only tasks but also identities and livelihoods, revealing a pattern that echoes strongly today: technological change is always human change first.

For many workers, the disruption was not only economic but also personal. Skills that had defined identity and purpose for generations were suddenly devalued. Entire communities were forced to reimagine what contribution meant in a mechanised world. The transition required more than new tools. It demanded a shift in mindset, new ways of learning and stronger social support for workers. These human dynamics mirror the tensions of today's AI era, where the challenge is not simply technological adoption but helping people navigate profound shifts in how value is created and how work is understood. Just as mechanisation redefined the value of physical labour, AI is now reshaping the value of knowledge work in equally profound ways.

WHITE-COLLAR DISRUPTION IN THE AI TRANSFORMATION

While the First Industrial Revolution transformed physical labour, today's transformation is reshaping knowledge work, the foundation of the modern service economy. More than a century separates these two shifts, yet the pattern is similar. What once disrupted factories and workshops is now moving through offices, design studios, consultancies, legal practices, healthcare providers and IT departments. The same force that mechanised manual labour is now altering how cognitive work is performed (Brynjolfsson & McAfee, 2014). The long interval between these waves highlights how technological change repeatedly moves from one domain of work to the next, creating new expectations for skills, roles and organisational structures.

Today's shift is different because it spreads quickly and reaches every layer of work. It touches almost every function at the same time. Earlier waves of change tended to cluster in single industries like textiles, farming or transport, while today's extends seamlessly across sectors.

AI's influence is now felt in every corner of the modern enterprise. It has slipped into the background of countless decisions and creations, often doing in seconds what once demanded long stretches of human focus. In healthcare, it assists radiologists in interpreting complex medical images with greater speed and accuracy. In law firms, AI reviews contracts and case law at a pace no human can match (Richter, 2025). In classrooms, digital tutors adapt content to each student's pace, while in marketing, generative systems produce endless variations of campaigns and creative assets in minutes. Across professions, AI is reshaping tasks at a scale that many organisations are still struggling to understand.

These shifts raise questions about accountability, expertise and what society will value most in human work as intelligent systems grow more capable.

What makes AI distinct from previous technological waves is its general-purpose nature. Much like electricity or the internet, it is not bound to a single function or domain. It can be applied across any process that involves language, pattern recognition or decision-making. Its ability to learn and adapt gives it a reach that many organisations are still trying to understand. Because of this, its impact now reaches every part of the workforce, from operational roles to senior leadership. The AI transformation is not about one tool or system. It is about intelligence becoming part of how work gets done.

A SPEED AND SCALE THAT OUTPACE OUR ABILITY TO ADJUST

What distinguishes this transformation is both its unprecedented speed and its expanding reach into work once considered uniquely human. Industrial revolutions of the past unfolded over decades, giving societies time, often uncomfortable, to adjust. Today, AI technologies can be deployed in weeks or months, transforming workflows almost overnight (Gartner, 2024b). New tools spread with remarkable ease, removing barriers that once kept advanced systems out of reach. Even small businesses can deploy AI at scale without large budgets or specialised teams.

Generative AI has accelerated this timeline even further. What once happened quietly in the back office, such as logistics, accounting or data processing, has moved to the front line. AI now drafts hyper-targeted campaigns in marketing (Inge, 2025), writes software code, answers customer enquiries and summarises legal briefs. Many leaders describe this as watching change happen in real time, a description that feels entirely accurate.

At the same time, AI has moved into areas we once considered purely human, such as reasoning, creativity and design. It can simulate business scenarios, design user experiences and produce full analyses with remarkable speed and consistency. The quality of AI-generated imagery and video can be startling, often indistinguishable from human work (Kramer et al., 2025). The speed and scale of AI now cover tasks that once required whole teams of specialists.

For many knowledge workers, the current shift is direct and noticeable. Embodied and generative AI are beginning to influence creative and cognitive tasks (MIT Technology Review, 2024). Professionals with extensive training and experience are seeing parts of their work automated. The assumption that knowledge work is protected from technological disruption is no longer accurate. No role is entirely insulated, and organisations need to address this transition with clarity, empathy and timely action. When technological capability increases faster than understanding, uncertainty grows and confidence weakens. The gap between what systems can deliver and what people feel prepared to handle is becoming a central challenge of the AI era.

The practical effects of AI appear in day-to-day tasks rather than in strategy documents. They are most visible when teams first encounter new tools in their workflow. In one international services firm, AI applications for drafting client summaries and analysing internal data produced immediate benefits. Reports that previously required several hours were generated in minutes, and employees initially expressed strong support for the tools. Leaders highlighted these early gains and viewed them as indicators that the organisation was progressing as planned.

When AI begins to outpace expectations, the effects surface quickly and reshape confidence across teams.

In conversations with senior managers across different organisations, a similar picture emerges. They describe a widening gap in how people respond as AI tools become part of daily work. Some employees move quickly, confident that the technology fits naturally into their tasks. Others slow down, unsure how their skills will be judged as the balance shifts from individual execution to shared human-machine work. Several managers say they see people holding back, worried that relying too heavily on AI might put them at risk if an output is questioned. Others share the opposite concern and fear they will fall behind colleagues who appear more fluent. As these reactions spread, managers tell me that even evaluating performance becomes harder because the work is changing faster than expectations can adjust.

The speed of routine work rises with AI, but so does the uncertainty surrounding decision-making, quality and accountability. Managers say the practical questions about daily work surface almost immediately. When is it appropriate to use AI? How much human oversight is required for routine tasks? 'Who carries responsibility when a system and a person complete a task together'? Organisations welcome the technology, but people are working inside an environment that has not been fully defined. What these managers describe is consistent with what is happening more broadly.

Technology moves forward at high speed, while the guidance people need follows at a slower pace. In this gap, five business-critical challenges begin to take shape.

FIVE BUSINESS-CRITICAL CHALLENGES IN THE AGE OF AI

Across industries, a clear pattern emerges. Five interconnected challenges rise again and again, shaping how the AI revolution unfolds inside organisations. They shape how people experience change, how leaders make decisions and how teams interpret the pace of progress. They determine whether AI strengthens an organisation or leaves it struggling to keep up. These challenges are not technical footnotes. They reach into how work is organised, how people grow and how culture shifts around new systems that are still unfamiliar. The way leaders respond affects competitiveness, trust, talent and the ability to build lasting value in a world defined increasingly by AI.

Signs of these challenges are already visible. They appear in the way teams experiment with new tools, in the uncertainty that follows when guidance is unclear and in the widening gap between those who move quickly and those who do not. Skills diverge, trust becomes harder to maintain and the pace of learning struggles to match the pace of change. These pressures often build quietly before they reach senior leadership. They begin shaping behaviour and culture even as strategy tries to adjust.

What makes these challenges so significant is their reach across every layer of an organisation. They influence the confidence of frontline employees, the priorities of managers and the focus of senior leaders. They shape how people adapt, how teams collaborate and how organisations respond to ambiguity. Each challenge forces a choice between short-term efficiency and long-term stability, between adopting AI rapidly and adopting it responsibly.

Recognising these challenges is more than an analytical step. It becomes a central task of leadership. How organisations respond will determine whether AI becomes a catalyst for capability, creativity and inclusion or a source of fragmentation, inequity and mistrust. Meeting these challenges requires leadership that is steady, human-centred and prepared to act with clarity.

A closer look at these five challenges reveals the questions now guiding organisational decision-making. In Chapter 5, we return to them through the human–AI decoder to explore how organisations can address each one in practice.

Challenge 1: Balancing efficiency with human-centred culture
The push for greater productivity has found a powerful catalyst in today's intelligent systems. Yet as automation scales, efficiency can come at the cost of empathy. Trust, belonging and purpose erode quickly when people feel replaced rather than valued. Culture also becomes fragile when human connection is treated as an afterthought.

'How can organisations scale automation while preserving trust, meaning and engagement?'

In many AI transformations, leaders focus heavily on cost, speed and output while the human experience becomes invisible. When employees see technology positioned as a substitute rather than a support, engagement drops and resistance grows (Beauchene et al., 2025). Finding the right balance between speed and human connection is essential for long-term performance.

This requires leaders and HR to act as stewards of culture. Empathy, communication and wellbeing should be built into the transformation from the outset. Clear communication, visible leadership support and regular recognition help employees see that they still have an important place in the organisation's future.

Challenge 2: Competing in a skills race fuelled by AI
Across industries, the nature of many roles is shifting as intelligent tools take on more of the routine work. It is speeding up how quickly skills become outdated. Roles are being reshaped as new capabilities emerge, from prompt engineering to algorithmic ethics. Data fluency is rising just as fast. This pace forces organisations to rethink how they develop talent and to move past traditional, step-by-step career paths.

'How can organisations build and evolve talent at a speed that keeps up with AI-driven change?'

The ability to adjust quickly and keep learning has become one of the most important skills in today's economy. Organisations that fail to adapt their skill frameworks will struggle to remain competitive as talent markets shift towards agility and capability depth.

This is not about occasional training or isolated learning events. It requires a continuous learning culture where curiosity, experimentation and adaptability become everyday habits (Nanyang Technological University Business School, 2025). The greatest progress comes when employees can learn at the moment they need it rather than through scheduled sessions. When development is embedded in the flow of work, careers evolve organically rather than episodically. HR's role is to orchestrate this ecosystem so that learning becomes a living system rather than an intervention.

Challenge 3: Upskilling to lead the AI journey

Awareness of AI is no longer enough. Employees and leaders must learn how to use it thoughtfully, ethically and confidently in their daily work (World Economic Forum, 2024). They need to understand not only what AI can do, but where its limits lie and how to challenge its outputs responsibly.

'How can individuals move from awareness to being able to use AI thoughtfully and lead through it?'

Readiness is defined not by technical mastery alone but by judgement. Effective leaders in the age of intelligent systems ask better questions, interpret outputs critically and use insights with accountability.

Upskilling is not only technical. People also need space to practise, explore and build confidence in real work situations. In transformation pilots I have led, low-risk sandboxes where employees explore tools freely, share observations and test their judgement have consistently accelerated adoption. HR enables this transition by creating psychological safety, fostering growth mindsets and making learning a collective, strategic discipline.

Challenge 4: Managing bias, fairness and trust in AI systems

As AI increasingly influences hiring, performance evaluation, learning and promotion, its design and governance carry significant ethical weight. Without careful oversight, algorithms can replicate or amplify historical inequalities (Deloitte, 2021).

'How can organisations ensure AI systems are explainable, fair and trusted by the people they affect?'

Bias in AI is rarely intentional. It often arises from flawed or incomplete data or from assumptions buried in model design. Yet its consequences are real, shaping opportunity, mobility and pay equity. Building trust means being open about how these systems work and who is responsible for their outcomes at each stage. The European Union's AI Act has introduced the world's first risk-based governance framework, setting new standards for oversight and human involvement (European Commission, 2024).

Ethical guardrails cannot be treated as technical safeguards. They require organisational stewardship. HR must play a central role whenever algorithms influence people's decisions, including selection, testing, audit cycles and review. Managers also need to be trained to interpret and challenge AI recommendations responsibly. People will trust these systems when they see that fairness and transparency matter as much as performance.

Challenge 5: Accelerating AI adoption while managing resistance

The move to intelligent systems is as much a human experience as a technological rollout. Fear of redundancy, identity loss or job insecurity can fuel resistance, particularly when change is introduced without transparency or clear direction. People usually do not resist the technology. What they resist is the uncertainty about how it will affect them (Roth, 2025). Successful transformation must therefore be approached as a human transition rather than a systems deployment.

'How can organisations drive adoption while creating a sense of safety, inclusion and clarity for everyone involved?'

Organisations can achieve the strongest results with AI when they bring people in early, pay attention to their concerns and give them meaningful influence over how the change unfolds. Leaders should communicate not only what will change but what will remain constant, helping employees preserve identity and purpose through transition. When people understand why change is happening and how it supports their work, they are far more willing to use new tools.

Empathy-led leadership and HR-led enablement make this possible. Together, they create cultures where technology is viewed as an ally rather than a threat. When leaders are clear and act with empathy, people are much more willing to engage.

✗ ***Executive AI Awareness Pulse Pulse Check (included in Appendix 1) is for leaders seeking to understand*** *leaders seeking to understand where their organisation stands in its AI journey, awareness is the first step towards readiness. To help leadership teams uncover these blind spots, the Executive AI awareness pulse check provides a short reflective exercise developed from real transformation discussions. It provides a structured way for leadership teams to assess how aligned they are on AI's potential, its risks and its expected impact on the workforce. The results can reveal areas of overconfidence as well as areas of underestimation, creating a foundation for more strategic dialogue.*

Beginning a transformation with this kind of structured reflection creates something organisations often lack. It gives people a shared understanding of a shift that cuts across disciplines. It opens the way for honest discussion about priorities, ethical questions and the practical impact of AI on roles and culture. Awareness alone does not deliver change. Yet without it, no real change can start.

AI ADOPTION IS OUTPACING WORKFORCE GUIDANCE

In many workplaces, the tools arrive long before the clarity employees need to use them with confidence. Across organisations I have observed, a growing number of workers use generative or predictive tools informally to assist with tasks such as content creation, analysis or customer response. While this organic experimentation demonstrates curiosity and innovation, it also exposes a leadership gap. Most organisations still lack clear principles that define when and how AI should be used responsibly. Employees are often unsure about which tools are approved, what data can be shared or how their work might be evaluated when assisted by AI. This uncertainty can lead to inconsistent practices and even ethical or legal risk.

Across many organisations, a consistent reality is visible. Employees recognise that AI is becoming part of daily work, yet few imagine it could redefine their own roles until the change is already underway. Many acknowledge its presence without seeing the full implications. Beneath that confidence sits a quieter unease about future relevance, a feeling that appears in almost every workforce discussion. Only a minority of employees feel ready to adapt to AI-driven change (PwC, 2025).

This gap between adoption and preparedness can highlight a deeper organisational issue. People are expected to embrace tools that have not been explained to them, to trust algorithms they did not design and to adjust to changes they did not choose. For HR and business leaders, this is both a challenge and a responsibility. They need to provide the clarity, context and support that help people navigate AI in a fair and human-centred way.

Successful organisations are beginning to respond by creating internal frameworks for AI use. These include principles of transparency, fairness and accountability, clear channels for reporting misuse and mechanisms for learning from experimentation. When people understand the boundaries and possibilities of AI, they engage with it more confidently and creatively. In my view, this alignment of governance with empowerment marks the true beginning of sustainable AI adoption.

In the age of intelligent systems, the advantage won't belong to those who adopt the most technology, but to those who best prepare their people to evolve with it, which we will take a closer look at in Chapter 8 with the workforce readiness.

These dynamics create a clear need for leadership and few functions are as uniquely positioned to fill that gap as HR. The acceleration of AI has moved faster than the systems, guidance and support people need to navigate it. This gap makes the human side of transformation the defining challenge of this moment. The question is no longer whether HR should be involved in AI, but how it will lead.

HR'S RESPONSIBILITY IN AN AI-ENABLED ORGANISATION

AI is quickly becoming the unseen infrastructure of modern work. It sits inside recruiting engines, learning platforms, performance systems and workplace analytics, shaping decisions long before most people realise it is there. As AI moves deeper into the day-to-day operations of organisations, the debate shifts. The question is no longer whether it will influence the workforce. It is how it will be applied and who is ready to guide that transition. Early evidence shows the scale of the shift. More than 60 percent of HR leaders expect to deploy generative AI (GenAI) applications within their functions by 2025 (Gartner, 2025).

This is the moment when HR's responsibility becomes clear. HR stands at the intersection of people, performance and culture. It understands not only the architecture of organisations but also how people learn, grow and adapt within them. That position gives HR the unique ability to shape how AI is introduced, scaled and governed in ways that reflect company values and workforce realities. The transformation ahead is not simply technical. It is deeply human, and it requires the kind of insight HR is designed to provide.

HR is also the function that can interpret what AI means for work at a practical level. It can see how tasks shift, how roles evolve and how teams adjust to new patterns of collaboration. It can identify what can be automated, what should be augmented and what demands a rethinking of skills and career paths. This clarity helps organisations move from reacting to disruption towards planning for it with purpose.

Trust and capability grow from the same foundation, and HR plays a central role in both. Through careful communication, relevant learning pathways and environments where questions can be asked without fear, HR helps people build the confidence they need to work well with AI. Adoption accelerates when employees understand what the tools are meant to do. Confidence often matters more than technical skill.

HR also carries a governance responsibility. AI must serve equity as much as efficiency. HR defines the principles and boundaries that guide how systems influence hiring, promotion, learning and performance. These tools must be explainable, inclusive and aligned with organisational values. Without HR's oversight, organisations risk introducing systems that quietly embed bias or erode trust.

The possibility ahead is a workplace where people and AI strengthen each other rather than work at cross-purposes. HR shapes the guardrails, culture and operating foundations that make this possible. As AI adoption accelerates, the choices made now will influence capability, culture and competitiveness for years to come. Waiting is not a viable option. Leading with intention is.

As organisations step into this new era, another challenge becomes clear. Progress depends not only on new tools but also on the assumptions leaders bring to the work. Some of those assumptions move organisations forward. Others hold HR back at the very moment its guidance matters most.

MYTHS ABOUT HR AND AI

Work itself is changing. Intelligent tools now influence the choices people make, the way tasks move through teams, and the capabilities employees need to grow. Based on two decades of working with HR leaders and transformation teams, I continue to encounter outdated assumptions about HR's role that limit its influence. These myths shape how organisations allocate responsibility, design transformation initiatives and measure success. Addressing them is an essential step before exploring how AI itself functions and evolves.

In practice, the same myths appear across many organisations, and the realities behind them reveal HR's central role in successful AI adoption.

Myth 1: HR should follow, not lead AI

HR ensures that AI strengthens people rather than sidelines them. It brings the human insight, behavioural understanding and organisational context needed to design systems that enhance roles, preserve trust and support culture as work rapidly evolves.

Myth 2: HR cannot create measurable business value with AI

HR creates measurable value by improving retention, accelerating hiring and strengthening workforce capability. These outcomes help organisations place people in the right roles faster, build skills with greater precision and develop a more adaptable and resilient workforce.

Myth 3: AI readiness is all about systems and not the people
Progress depends on trust. People need to believe these systems will help them rather than expose them, and they need to feel confident using them. Human readiness becomes the factor that determines whether organisations advance or remain stuck in resistance, uncertainty and uneven adoption.

Myth 4: AI will make people's decisions more fair by default
AI is not fair by default. It mirrors the data and design choices behind it. HR is essential for embedding ethical standards, ensuring transparent decision pathways and protecting equitable outcomes across hiring, development and performance.

Confronting these myths is more than a matter of redefining HR's role, it is about recognising its strategic authority. HR should co-create how humans and machines collaborate, ensuring transformation is not only efficient but also ethical, inclusive and sustainable with humans at its core.

Together, these insights reveal a deeper truth: AI transformation will succeed only when organisations centre their approach on people. HR is not a peripheral participant in this shift but the function most capable of guiding it with clarity, empathy and strategic intent.

BEFORE WE LEAD, WE NEED TO UNDERSTAND

HR's leadership in an AI-enabled organisation is not an abstract idea. It is a practical responsibility. The decisions leaders make now will shape how people experience intelligent systems, how trust is built and how the culture of work evolves. AI introduces new tools, but it also reshapes identity, contribution and the relationships that define how people understand their work. Leadership in this moment becomes a question of whether the transition helps people succeed or leaves them struggling to keep up.

To guide the human side of AI, leaders first need to understand the technology itself. They need a clear sense of what AI can and cannot do, how it learns, where it fails and why its behaviour changes as it trains on new data. Without this grounding, even the most well-meant strategies can drift into confusion, unrealistic expectations or unintended harm.

When organisations keep people at the centre of AI decisions, they create workplaces where employees and intelligent tools reinforce each other rather than compete. The chapters that follow build on this possibility. They begin by introducing how modern systems work and the principles that shape their strengths and limitations. This understanding becomes essential for every leader responsible for the future of work.

Key Takeaways

- AI is reshaping how work is done and how value is created.
- The deepest disruption is human and organisational, not technical.
- AI's speed and reach exceed those of past technology waves.
- Roles are evolving as tasks shift and skill requirements change.
- AI now influences cognitive and creative work once considered uniquely human.
- Workforce readiness is lagging behind the pace of adoption.
- Five business-critical challenges consistently shape AI's impact across industries.
- Responsible AI requires human oversight and cross-functional governance.
- Persistent myths continue to limit HR's strategic influence.
- HR plays a central role in guiding how people experience and succeed with AI.

2

Evolution of AI

ABSTRACT

Artificial Intelligence (AI) has evolved from early rule-based systems to learning, generative and agentic models that now reshape how work is organised, decisions are made and value is created. This chapter traces AI's historical journey from symbolic reasoning in the mid-1950s to the emergence of machine learning (ML), the rise of generative AI (GenAI) and the first signs of agentic intelligence, showing that today's disruption is decades in the making. The chapter examines key AI technologies currently shaping the workforce, including natural language processing (NLP), computer vision and intelligent automation with practical examples across industries. It examines the recurring cycles of optimism and correction known as AI winters and explores how each wave of progress has redefined the relationship between people and technology. By framing AI as a family of interlinked technologies rather than a single invention, the chapter highlights their combined impact on productivity, creativity and governance across industries. It concludes by introducing the concept of Agentic AI, where autonomous systems collaborate with humans to orchestrate outcomes and transform roles. For readers, understanding AI's evolution provides essential context for responsible adoption, informed decision-making and human-centred workforce transformation in an era of rapid technological change.

Keywords: Artificial Intelligence (AI); machine learning (ML); natural language processing (NLP); Generative AI; Agentic AI; AI workforce impact; computer vision; human–machine collaboration; AI winters; responsible AI

The first time I noticed the power of AI is a moment that has stayed with me. It came during the match between Grandmaster Garry Kasparov and IBM's Deep Blue, a contest that felt both technical and historic. On the screen, the room had fallen into silence as the machine prepared its next move. Kasparov leaned towards the board, certain he recognised the pattern unfolding in front of him. Deep Blue, designed to calculate rather than surprise, chose a move that forced him to pull back, unsettled by something he had not anticipated. It was a small moment in a long match, however it signalled a shift. A system built for a single purpose had revealed something larger. It marked how quickly capability could grow once machines stepped outside familiar rules.

Moments like this seemed rare at the time. They were noticed as curiosities rather than recognised as early signs of a broader transformation. However, the path from that chessboard to today's workplace is more direct than most people imagine.

A system that once powered chess programs now helps executives, drafts policies and reviews vast document sets in seconds. What began in research labs is now embedded in boardrooms and daily workflows. AI is no longer a future disruptor. It has become an immediate force reshaping how work happens, from routine execution to creative generation. Recent industry analyses show that it is already influencing core business processes across sectors, accelerating decision-making and widening the scope of what can be automated or augmented (Accenture, 2025).

Understanding this evolution is essential for anyone shaping how people and organisations adapt to intelligent systems. Leading this transformation requires clarity about what AI has become and why it matters for the future of work.

This chapter traces that progression and explains why this moment represents a genuine shift. It provides a strategic view of how AI is reshaping work rather than a technical explanation of how the systems operate. By following the path from early rule-based programs to today's broadly capable models, the chapter shows why the present moment marks a turning point and why that context matters for managing workforce transformation.

A BRIEF HISTORY OF AI

These early foundations show that today's rapid progress is not sudden but the result of long-running experimentation and quietly advancing intelligence. Fig. 1 makes clear how long this story has been unfolding.

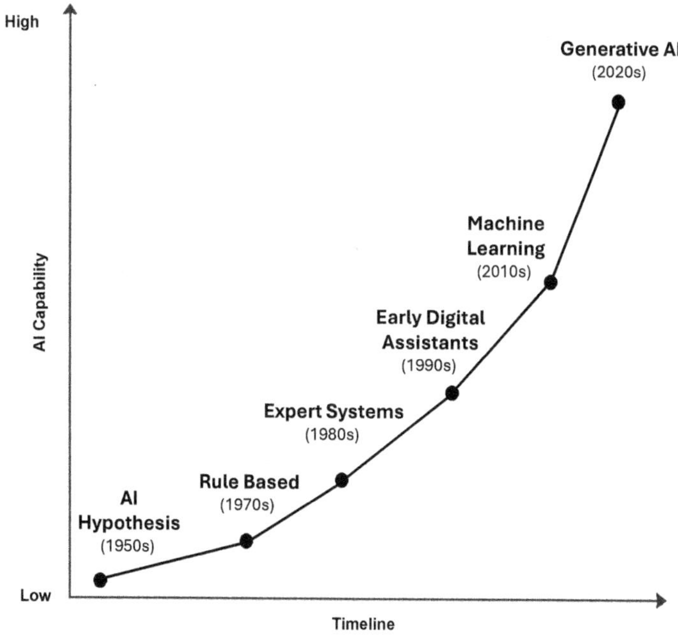

Fig. 1. AI Evolution.

Source: Author's Own Creation.

AI may seem like a modern breakthrough, yet its origins stretch far further back than many realise. To understand its implications for today's workforce, it helps to see how early logic-driven systems were already shaping everyday work long before the current hype cycle.

THE EARLY YEARS OF AI

The term 'Artificial Intelligence' is believed to have emerged in the mid-1950s (Russell & Norvig, 2022), when computer scientists began exploring whether machines could be programmed to mirror elements of human intelligence, an idea that would lay the foundation for what we now call AI.

Early efforts in the 1950s and 1960s focused on symbolic reasoning and rule-based logic. These systems attempted to encode human knowledge in the form of 'if-then' rules-based statements that allowed early programs to solve mathematical equations, play games like chess and engage in basic dialogue (IBM, 2024a). While groundbreaking at the time, these early AI systems lacked flexibility. They couldn't learn from new information, generalise to unfamiliar situations or adapt to environments that didn't follow scripted rules. They were intelligent only in narrowly defined contexts.

By the 1970s and 1980s, AI took a commercial turn with the rise of software applications designed to mimic the decision-making abilities of human specialists. These systems were widely deployed in domains such as medical diagnostics, financial analysis and engineering. Using structured rule trees and domain-specific knowledge bases, these 'Expert Systems' could process inputs and deliver recommendations (Feigenbaum, 1988). However, their intelligence was rigid. If a rule was incomplete or a variable unexpected, the system failed. These limitations, combined with high development and maintenance costs, eventually led to the first of several 'AI winters', which we will further explain a bit later.

WHEN AI WAS ALREADY IN THE OFFICE

While public excitement faded during the so-called AI winters, intelligence continued to move quietly into everyday tools and workflows.

For many office workers in the 1990s, early encounters with intelligent software came through animated on-screen assistants like Microsoft Office Assistant (aka 'Clippy') that appeared during everyday computer tasks and offered tips or suggestions (Microsoft, 2023a). I still remember a colleague in Zurich who swore that Clippy waited for her to get frustrated before offering help. It was the first time many workers felt that their computer was paying attention rather than simply executing commands. Although limited in what they could do, these early digital companions marked one of the first visible attempts to make technology context-aware. They tried to recognise what users were doing, such as drafting a letter or editing a document, and proactively offered help in real time. Sometimes amusing and occasionally distracting, they nonetheless hinted at a future where machines would engage with people more naturally, responding to intent rather than following a fixed set of commands. Beneath their friendly interface, these assistants used simple language-processing rules and decision trees to interpret user input. For many, this represented a first real glimpse of what would later evolve into modern AI. An early effort to bring intelligent assistance into everyday productivity tools. These early systems made human–machine interaction feel more natural, which helps explain why today's AI tools feel familiar. By the early 2000s, invisible AI had already become part of everyday digital life, even if most people did not recognise it at the time.

At the same time, the growth of online search began to transform how people accessed and organised information. Search engines such as Google changed the way knowledge was discovered, introducing ranking logic, pattern recognition and later adaptive algorithms that learned from user behaviour to deliver more relevant results (Google, 2025b). Although not described as AI at the time, these innovations quietly laid the foundations for the algorithmic systems that now shape how we find, filter and consume digital content.

Across industries, I saw enterprise systems begin embedding intelligent capabilities from HR platforms automating workflows to finance and operations systems introducing predictive logic long before it was branded as AI. Financial institutions adopted data-driven monitoring to detect irregular transactions and reduce fraud. Manufacturers implemented predictive models to anticipate equipment failures before they occurred. In logistics and administration, automated workflows started replacing repetitive tasks such as scheduling, approvals and document routing. These systems were rarely marketed as AI, yet their ability to sense, predict and act marked a significant shift towards intelligent business operations.

What made this era important was that AI moved from research environments into real-world use, not through headlines but through intelligent operations, systems that sensed, predicted and acted long before they were labelled as AI. People interact with intelligent systems every day, often without realising it. This quiet normalisation of invisible AI changed how people worked long before most realised the shift had begun.

Today's breakthroughs are built on this long, invisible legacy that has been shaping how we work for years.

THE LEARNING MACHINES ARRIVE

The major shift in AI came during the 2010s, driven by the rise of machine learning (ML), particularly deep learning (Stanford AI Index, 2025). Unlike earlier rule-based systems that required explicit programming, these new models could detect patterns, make predictions and improve over time by analysing vast amounts of data. One key breakthrough was enabling AI systems to learn from experience instead of relying only on predefined logic. This leap was made possible by several converging forces.

Cloud computing made scalable processing power widely accessible. Data storage became cheaper and more abundant, enabling the accumulation of massive datasets. Open-source libraries democratised AI development, while graphics processing units (GPUs) dramatically reduced the time required to train complex models.

As a result, AI began moving into tasks once viewed as distinctly human. It recognised faces in photos, translated language with near-human fluency and personalised digital experiences in ways that quickly reset expectations. This wave of progress was not just a technical milestone but a transformative moment that reshaped how people interacted with technology and redefined expectations on a global scale. For workers, these shifts quietly changed how expertise was expressed, how decisions were made and how digital systems shaped daily tasks.

Leading technology platforms such as Amazon, Netflix, Google and Facebook became prominent examples of ML integration in consumer-facing products and services to drive efficiency, engagement and personalisation (McKinsey & Company, 2025d). Voice-activated assistants became part of everyday life, recommendation engines began shaping what people watched and bought, and news feed algorithms curated digital experiences with increasing precision. Through these developments, AI evolved from an experimental concept into an invisible yet essential layer of the digital world, normalising its presence in daily routines.

What once felt experimental soon became embedded in how people shop, stream, search and socialise. With that normalisation came a profound shift. AI was no longer a concept of the future. It had become a defining force shaping how people live and work. These advances changed what people expected from technology and what they expected from themselves.

THE AGE OF GENAI

The most recent and perhaps most disruptive evolution in the story of AI arrived with the emergence of GenAI. Unlike earlier systems that were primarily designed to classify, predict or recommend based on existing data, generative models introduced a new paradigm with the ability to create. These systems can generate original text, images, music, video and even computer code, blurring the line between machine assistance and creative contribution.

The release of powerful tools such as OpenAI's GPT, Midjourney, DALL·E and other creative platforms marked the public's first real encounter with AI that could write essays, design graphics, compose music or simulate human conversation at scale. The launch of ChatGPT in late 2022 marked a significant turning point, bringing

GenAI into mainstream awareness and sparking widespread fascination and debate (McKinsey & Company, 2024c). The world was suddenly introduced to an AI interface that was conversational, creative and accessible to millions, signalling a new phase in the AI revolution. For the first time, machines were not only automating tasks. They were also contributing to creative and cognitive work once considered uniquely human.

This shift from narrow, task-specific AI to more general-purpose, generative systems represents a critical turning point in the way AI intersects with work. GenAI is no longer confined to invisible back-office functions or technical workflows. It is now writing marketing strategies, generating emails and business reports, assisting in software development, designing user interfaces and even drafting legal contracts. The reach of GenAI stretches across industries, from media and entertainment to law, healthcare, education and beyond.

For the workforce, this represents more than just new tools, as it introduces new dynamics of collaboration, augmentation and even competition. AI is not only helping humans do more but also faster. In many cases, it is challenging what it means to create, to analyse and to decide. Teams are beginning to rethink roles and workflows, asking fundamental questions about what work remains human-led, where co-creation makes sense and where machines may independently take over.

Early enterprise pilots reveal that GenAI introduces new governance challenges as teams balance experimentation with compliance and brand integrity. A HR peer described a pilot where an HR team used a generative tool to draft performance summaries. The outputs were sometimes polished, but occasionally so confidently wrong that managers began double checking every suggestion, which revealed how early convenience can create new forms of oversight. Issues of authorship, intellectual property, bias in outputs and the authenticity of generated content are forcing leaders to establish new rules and guardrails. As the pace of development accelerates, so too does the need for responsible deployment, ensuring these powerful models are used ethically, transparently and with human intent at the centre (Harvard Business Review, 2020).

The age of GenAI is not simply an upgrade in technical capability. It is a redefinition of the relationship between people and machines. They are reshaping how people create, collaborate and define their own value at work.

THE AI WINTERS

Beneath the waves of hype, breakthroughs and massive funding cycles known as 'AI springs', lie moments of deep disillusionment, periods known as 'AI winters' (Mitchell, 2021).

An AI winter refers to a phase in which interest, investment and progress in AI significantly decline. The term 'AI winter' emerged in the mid-1980s in academic and industry discussions, used to describe periods when enthusiasm and funding for the field diminished after a surge of early optimism. Research slows, commercial momentum stalls and the once hopeful narrative around AI becomes shadowed by caution. AI winters are not just downturns in technology. They are moments that expose the difference between what we expect AI to do and what it can actually deliver.

AI winters share several familiar traits. These cycles reflect a recurring gap between ambition and reality, as early promise outpaces the technical and organisational readiness needed to support it.

These winters rarely arrive without warning. The underlying issue is the gap between ambition and actual capability. Early technologies are often oversold, promoted with grand visions that current capabilities cannot yet fulfil. Researchers and developers find themselves constrained by the limits of available computing power or the rigidity of rule-based systems that lack flexibility and learning capacity. When criticism gathers momentum, funding dries up rapidly and talent migrates towards more stable or promising fields. The result is not the end of AI but a pause, a recalibration of expectations and a re-centring of priorities.

Literature on AI's evolution reveals a recurring pattern of AI winters, characterised by familiar cycles of early optimism, rapid investment and eventual correction. The first major slowdown took place in the 1970s, when symbolic reasoning systems struggled to progress beyond experimental problems and enthusiasm began to fade. A second downturn emerged in the late 1980s and early 1990s, when the commercial promise of expert systems failed to meet expectations.

The impact of these winters extended far beyond missed expectations. As excitement cooled, research funding contracted and many promising projects were left unfinished. Talented scientists and engineers drifted into other disciplines, and AI's once-bright image dimmed into scepticism. Yet these quieter years became vital periods of renewal. Out of view, researchers developed statistically grounded methods, including early neural networks and probabilistic modelling, which would later power modern AI.

Understanding the history of AI winters is essential for leaders navigating today's surge in adoption. The field is once again riding a wave of excitement driven by GenAI. The lessons of the past remind us that enthusiasm must be balanced with clarity and readiness. Overpromising invites backlash, while underpreparing risks failure. Responsible progress begins with remembering where we have been and recognising the limits that history continues to reveal.

Could another AI winter lie ahead? While technological advances continue at a remarkable speed, systemic risks remain. The energy demands of large-scale models are under scrutiny, and new computing paradigms that might deliver the next leap have yet to materialise. Without a more human-centred approach to integration, the trust gap between systems and users could widen, slowing adoption and ushering in another pause for reflection.

WHY AI'S HISTORY MATTERS

While the current momentum is strong, history shows that AI is not immune to cycles of optimism and scepticism. Early cautionary signals have emerged in practice. Some organisations that initially reduced call centre staff after adopting GenAI have had to rehire, realising the technology was not yet reliable for full replacement (Dewan, 2025). In the legal sector, well-documented cases have emerged where AI-generated content contained factual errors or 'hallucinations', prompting concern and calls for greater oversight (Opentools.ai, 2025).

Understanding how this technology emerged makes it clear that today's disruption did not arrive overnight. It is the outcome of decades of experimentation, failure, learning and iteration. It also reminds us that each wave of AI, from rule-based systems to ML and now to generative models, has brought both excitement and caution. For HR and business leaders, knowing this history provides perspective. It helps decode AI, set realistic expectations and recognise the long-term trajectory of how machines are evolving as partners in work. Understanding these patterns helps leaders anticipate not just technological shifts, but the human and organisational transformations that follow.

History shows that AI progresses in cycles, rising in moments of discovery and slowing whenever expectations race ahead of capability. The more clearly we see how AI has evolved, the more confidently we can guide its impact on people, work and the organisations that depend on both. With this long journey in view, the next step is to understand what we mean when we talk about AI today.

WHAT IS AI REALLY?

AI is one of the most widely discussed yet often misunderstood concepts. While it is frequently portrayed as futuristic or robotic, the term describes a broad and evolving field of technologies that seek to replicate aspects of human intelligence in machines. Having traced its evolution from early rule-based systems to today's learning and generative models, we can now look at what AI actually means in practice and how it manifests across different forms of work.

In simple terms, AI refers to 'the capability of computer systems to imitate intelligent human behaviour, encompassing activities such as interpreting language, recognising patterns, learning from data, and making judgements based on context' (Merriam-Webster, 2025).

Rather than being a single invention, AI represents a family of technologies that vary in purpose and sophistication. Some rely on clear instructions and predefined rules, while others learn from experience and improve their performance over time. Together, they form a spectrum that ranges from basic automation to advanced self-learning systems capable of analysing complex data and producing human-like outputs.

Some AI systems are designed for narrow functions, such as detecting fraud, processing documents or recognising voices. Others, like GenAI models, are more general-purpose tools that can create text, images and software code with increasing fluency and creativity. Emerging developments, often referred to as Agentic AI and explored later in this chapter, go a step further by managing workflows autonomously, reasoning across systems and executing tasks with limited or no human instruction.

Understanding AI as a connected ecosystem rather than a single force of change is essential. These technologies differ in their technical complexity, purpose and impact on the workforce. For leaders, the challenge is not only to understand what AI is, but to discern which form of AI they are dealing with, how it operates and what it changes about the work people do.

KEY AI TECHNOLOGIES SHAPING THE WORKFORCE

Table 1 summarises the main AI technologies before the chapter explores each one in turn.

Table 1. Current AI Technologies.

AI Technology	What It Does	Workplace Impact
Machine Learning (ML)	Learns from data and improves with experience	Predicts attrition, personalises learning and forecasts performance
Natural Language Processing (NLP)	Understands and generates human language	Powers chatbots, résumé parsing and sentiment analysis
Computer Vision	Interprets visual data such as images and video	Detects defects, monitors safety compliance and enables facial access control

Table 1. (Continued)

AI Technology	What It Does	Workplace Impact
Generative AI (GenAI)	Creates original content from text, images or code	Drafts communications, job descriptions and learning simulations
Intelligent Automation	Automates predefined structured and semi-structured tasks using AI and bots	Processes HR forms, invoices and data from scanned documents
Agentic AI	Autonomously executes end-to-end workflows across systems	Handles entire workflows, monitoring progress and resolving issues with little human involvement

Source: Author's own creation.

AI is not a single system but a family of technologies, each with distinct capabilities and applications. Across the workplace, these technologies are quietly reshaping how work is performed, how decisions are made and how value is created. The sections below outline the main categories of AI technologies influencing today's workforce, with real-world examples that illustrate their practical use.

Machine Learning (ML)

ML is a core branch of AI that helps systems learn from data, recognise patterns and make decisions with minimal human guidance (IBM, 2024b). Unlike traditional programming, which requires every rule to be written out, ML models improve through experience. They learn from large volumes of structured and unstructured information, powering everything from dynamic pricing to predictive maintenance and forming the engine behind many modern digital systems.

Its strength lies in finding connections humans may miss and improving as new information arrives. This makes ML well-suited for fast-changing environments where decisions must adapt quickly. Organisations use it to shift from reacting to events to anticipating them, forecasting outcomes, optimising processes and tailoring customer and employee experiences in real time.

What began as an experimental approach has become a quiet force beneath daily work, guiding predictions and steadily influencing how organisations operate. Financial institutions analyse transaction flows in real time to detect fraud. Retailers refine shopping experiences with recommendation engines, and logistics teams improve delivery routes by learning from traffic patterns, weather and customer behaviour.

Natural Language Processing (NLP)

NLP enables machines to understand and generate human language in ways that feel natural (IBM, 2024c). By blending linguistics, ML and computer science, NLP helps systems make sense of written and spoken communication. This is what allows people to interact with technology through conversation rather than remembering commands or navigating menus.

Modern NLP systems go far beyond keyword matching. They understand context, tone and emotion. They can summarise documents, detect communication patterns and extract meaning from text, helping organisations navigate large volumes of information more quickly and accurately.

These capabilities influence many daily tasks. Customer-service platforms interpret intent and sentiment to help teams resolve issues faster. HR teams analyse thousands of survey comments to identify cultural patterns or detect biased language in job descriptions. Legal departments use NLP to review contracts and highlight exceptions, while clinicians extract essential details from patient notes to support diagnosis and treatment planning.

Language has become a rich source of insight, helping organisations learn from everyday communication.

Computer Vision

Computer vision enables machines to interpret and understand visual information, from images and videos to real-time camera feeds (Gendy & Patel, 2024). It includes object recognition, facial analysis, movement tracking and environmental mapping. These capabilities help systems make sense of the physical world and turn what they see into useful insight or action.

At its core, computer vision relies on deep learning models trained on large datasets of labelled images and video. These models can detect anomalies, follow movement, recognise objects and even infer human emotion. As cameras become more common and computing more powerful, computer vision has become an important tool for improving safety, efficiency and user experience.

Its use is widespread. Manufacturers inspect production lines in real time to reduce defects. Safety teams verify the correct use of protective equipment. Retail stores track inventory or offer cashierless checkout experiences. Security teams rely on facial recognition to manage access, and clinicians use vision-based models to highlight abnormalities in medical scans before human review.

Visual data is now processed fast enough to turn images into practical insight for many organisations.

Generative AI (GenAI)

GenAI refers to models that create new content including text, images, video, music, conversations and software code. Instead of merely analysing existing data, these systems learn from massive datasets and produce outputs that mimic creativity and reasoning. After learning vocabulary, for example, a generative model can write original stories or explain complex ideas in simple language. After learning code, it can write or troubleshoot software functions. These models can also learn artistic styles or scientific patterns and reuse them to generate new designs or solutions (AWS, 2025).

Built on large language models, diffusion models and other advanced neural networks, GenAI can summarise reports, write emails, simulate dialogue, design graphics or generate software prototypes. Its flexibility has transformed how teams communicate, innovate and collaborate with technology.

These capabilities are already widely adopted. Marketing teams create campaign concepts, articles and social-copy variations tailored to audience's style. Legal teams use platforms such as Harvey AI to accelerate research and draft contractual language. Engineers rely on tools like GitHub Copilot to generate code and automate tests. HR teams produce personalised onboarding materials and modular training content at scale, reducing manual work while improving quality.

Machines no longer just analyse information. They now produce it, helping people get more done and work more efficiently.

Intelligent Automation

Intelligent automation combines robotic process automation with AI to create systems that handle both routine tasks and more complex processes requiring judgement. Traditional robotic process automation (RPA) automates predictable workflows such as data entry or document routing. When enhanced with AI, automation can interpret unstructured inputs including emails, PDFs, images or voice recordings, and make decisions based on what it learns (Tupsakhare, 2025).

This integration enables intelligent automation to complete end-to-end workflows that once required human involvement. It is especially powerful in high-volume, compliance-heavy settings where speed and accuracy are essential. These systems do not just execute tasks but adapt as conditions change, learning from new information and improving over time.

Its impact is visible across many functions. Financial services firms use intelligent automation to process loan and insurance applications from start to finish. HR operations rely on it to manage onboarding, background checks and contract creation. Supply-chain teams streamline procurement and invoice matching, while healthcare administrators automate claims processing and diagnostic coding with greater consistency and fewer errors.

Automation has evolved into a system that manages complex processes with increasing precision and adaptability. It now supports many core operational workflows and forms the backbone of routine digital work. Intelligent automation handles structured tasks reliably, but the use of AI to process semi-structured or unstructured information such as documents, emails or conversations is still developing. In practice, progress depends on more than experimentation. It requires careful process design, thoughtful system integration and consistent change management. The technology is mature, yet many organisations remain in the early stages of extending AI-enabled automation across functions.

Agentic AI

The future of AI is not only about better tools or smarter outputs. It is increasingly defined by intelligent systems that can act with purpose, adapt to context and collaborate directly within business processes. This emerging class of technology, known as Agentic AI, represents the current frontier of workforce transformation and marks a turning point in how organisations work, structure teams and define human value (Bain & Company, 2025).

Often referred to as autonomous agents, AI operatives or digital workers, these systems go far beyond traditional automation or even reactive AI assistants. Agentic AI is capable of managing entire workflows from start to finish. It does more than follow user commands. It understands goals, works out the steps, links across systems and carries out the actions independently. These agents are designed to replicate the decision-making and planning abilities once limited to human teams, working alongside employees as collaborators rather than tools. This shift matters because it changes not only who completes the work, but how that work is initiated, coordinated and governed.

Agentic AI introduces a new way of working. Tasks such as coordinating meetings, generating reports, onboarding new hires or handling customer requests are no longer dependent on humans issuing repeated commands to software. Instead, digital agents move autonomously through enterprise systems, connect with applications, monitor progress and resolve issues proactively. They learn from feedback, adjust their workflows and interact with both humans and other digital systems in real time, transforming how work gets done.

WHAT MAKES AGENTIC AI DIFFERENT

Agentic AI represents a significant leap in how AI engages with work. Earlier generations of AI were largely predictive, offering insights based on data, or assistive, responding to user instructions within a defined scope. Agentic AI introduces a new dimension of autonomous goal pursuit. These systems are designed to take initiative, interpret objectives and execute entire workflows without requiring constant human prompting.

Unlike traditional automation or even advanced chatbots, Agentic AI does not wait for a predefined input or scripted path. It begins with an outcome in mind. For instance, instead of being instructed to send a sequence of emails, the agent might be given the goal of 'prepare onboarding of a new employee' and then determine how to complete that task across tools and systems.

Based on my research and analysis of emerging enterprise applications, as well as findings from Deloitte (2025b) and Bain and Company (2025), Agentic AI can be understood through five defining capabilities that go beyond what earlier AI systems could achieve.

First, these systems can interpret high-level goals. Rather than following step-by-step commands, they understand general instructions such as 'generate a sales report' and translate them into concrete actions.

Second, they can orchestrate entire workflows autonomously. Instead of handling one task in isolation, they identify, sequence and complete multiple subtasks ranging from retrieving data to generating content, scheduling meetings or updating internal systems.

Third, Agentic AI operates across platforms. It can interact with HR information systems, collaboration tools, customer relationship management systems (CRMs), email platforms and internal knowledge bases without requiring human mediation at each step.

A fourth capability is dynamic adaptability. These agents detect changes in real time, adjust when information is missing and modify their behaviour to minimise disruptions and manual rework.

Finally, agentic systems communicate proactively. They provide timely updates, raise alerts when something is off track and request clarification when objectives are ambiguous, behaving much like a competent team member.

Taken together, these capabilities show that Agentic AI is not merely an interface enhancement. It is an intelligent actor within the enterprise, bringing autonomy, initiative and contextual understanding to digital work. As it becomes more embedded in organisations, the line between digital worker and human colleague begins to blur, marking a shift towards a workplace where AI is not just a tool but a proactive participant.

Illustrative scenarios help demonstrate how agentic AI could operate in real organisational settings. In sales operations, for example, a digital agent can pull CRM data, cross-reference emails and calendar entries and generate a customised weekly pipeline summary without manual intervention. HR teams could deploy an agent to manage the entire preboarding journey by sending employment contracts, triggering IT and facilities provisioning, guiding new hires through orientation modules and flagging documentation gaps in real time. Customer service teams may rely on an intelligent support agent that triages enquiries, retrieves relevant documentation, queries internal knowledge systems and provides resolutions without the need for tiered escalation. Such an agent can even adjust tone and language in response to customer sentiment. Executives, too, can benefit from these systems. A cloud-based assistant can schedule meetings, summarise project statuses, follow up on action items and recommend responses, offering leaders an always-available support system.

WHY AGENTIC AI MATTERS NOW

For organisations, this evolution presents both transformative opportunities and complex challenges. Success with Agentic AI requires rethinking digital literacy, updating job architectures and embedding new forms of oversight. As roles evolve, HR can help redefine what it means to contribute in a hybrid human–machine workplace.

Agentic AI is no longer theoretical. Parts of it are already in use, and it is evolving quickly. What makes this shift so profound is that it goes beyond simply automating tasks. We are now entering an era of outcome orchestration, where AI does not just assist with isolated actions but can actively manage end-to-end processes with autonomy and purpose. Industry data shows a majority of executives expect AI agents to reshape work roles within the next year (PwC, 2025c).

This marks a clear shift in how people work with technology. AI is no longer just a tool we command but is becoming more like a teammate we collaborate with. And in that shift lies immense potential. Organisations can now scale complex knowledge work not by adding more people but by augmenting the capabilities of the people they already have. It represents a new frontier of productivity, one where intelligence becomes distributed, proactive and deeply embedded in how work gets done.

Agentic AI also intensifies the need for robust governance. These systems act independently, which means accountability, ethical guardrails and transparent decision-making must be built into their design and deployment. Metrics should shift from measuring manual output to evaluating orchestrated outcomes, adaptability and human–machine collaboration.

Perhaps most importantly, Agentic AI forces a re-examination of human value in the workplace. As machines take on execution, uniquely human contributions such as judgement, creativity, empathy and strategic foresight become the most critical assets. In this brave new world, HR must champion a culture that develops these skills, ensures inclusion and builds trust in how digital workers operate.

When organisations adopt Agentic AI with care, they gain more than speed or better decisions. They create the foundations for a future of work that is dynamic, inclusive and unmistakably human.

In short, Agentic AI introduces systems that act on their own rather than waiting for instructions. This is not Artificial General Intelligence, which we explore in the next chapter, but a practical and immediate shift in how work is carried out.

Agentic AI is gaining momentum, yet its maturity inside most organisations remains limited. The underlying capabilities, including autonomous task execution, system integration and contextual decision-making, already exist. What is less developed is the ability to scale these systems across entire operations. Many current applications, such as digital onboarding agents or autonomous scheduling assistants, remain in pilot mode or restricted to a single department. Broader adoption depends on integration, governance and organisational readiness, which are still uneven across industries.

Agentic AI is feasible and advancing quickly, but it is not a standard or turnkey solution. For most organisations, it represents an emerging frontier that requires investment, experimentation and cultural adjustment before it can be used at scale.

Key Takeaways

- AI's current disruption builds on decades of evolution, experimentation and learning.
- Early AI relied on rigid rules; today's systems learn, adapt and generate autonomously.
- Machine learning (ML) shifted AI from automation to prediction and continuous improvement.
- The 'AI winters' remind us that hype without readiness leads to setbacks.
- AI is a family of evolving technologies with diverse functions and workforce impacts.
- GenAI brought machines that create and contribute to knowledge work.
- Knowing AI's history helps leaders separate hype from practical progress.
- AI already powers many everyday tools, often unseen but widely used.
- Ethical use and transparency are essential to build trust and accountability.
- Leaders need to understand AI's impact on people, not its algorithms.

3

THE NEXT INTELLIGENCE

ABSTRACT

The future of Artificial Intelligence (AI) is defined not by faster algorithms but by deeper integration with human work. This chapter explores the next frontier of AI evolution from agentic systems that act with purpose to collective and neuro-symbolic intelligence that blends reasoning, learning and collaboration. It examines how embodied AI and human–machine interfaces will extend intelligence into physical and cognitive spaces, reshaping how organisations operate and people perform. The discussion contrasts today's narrow, task-bound systems with the aspirational concept of Artificial General Intelligence (AGI), outlining both accelerators such as computing power, simulation and global research and barriers including alignment, bias and public trust. By separating myth from reality, the chapter highlights that progress in AI is not only technical but also profoundly human. The question ahead is not how intelligent AI can become, but how responsibly we guide its integration with human work and decision-making.

Keywords: Agentic AI; collective intelligence; neuro-symbolic systems; embodied artificial intelligence; Artificial General Intelligence (AGI); cognitive augmentation; AI governance; AI alignment; Explainable AI (XAI); human-centred innovation

A recent demonstration from XPENG Robotics attracted attention around the world. A humanoid robot walked onto the stage and moved so smoothly and naturally that some people wondered if it was actually a person in a costume. Its steps were steady, balanced and surprisingly lifelike. Soon after the event, they announced that it was preparing to start large-scale production. This showed that the robots were no longer just test models, but machines being built for real use. Many analysts said it was one of the strongest signs that intelligent systems are starting to take on physical and cognitive tasks that used to be done only by humans.

This development mirrors what is unfolding inside organisations. A few years ago, JPMorgan piloted a small digital agent to assist with loan assessments. Today, that limited experiment has evolved into a network of intelligent systems that interpret documents, query other tools, escalate exceptions and propose decisions before a human ever opens the case. The progression is unmistakable. AI is moving from assistive tools to systems capable of acting independently and understanding context.

The next stage is no longer about building stronger algorithms but about creating systems that understand their environment, act with purpose and contribute directly to outcomes. The rise of agentic AI marks the beginning of this phase. These systems operate independently, interpret objectives, adjust to new information and collaborate with human teams (McKinsey & Company, 2025c). They no longer wait for instructions. They take initiative, respond to context and redefine how productivity and responsibility are organised.

One technology leader described how a digital agent inside their company recently completed an internal request that once required three teams. The surprise was not the efficiency. It was the way the system coordinated across tools, identified missing information and paused only to seek clarification before moving ahead. The interaction felt less like software and more like a colleague with a clear understanding of the task.

Agentic AI is a significant step forward, but it is not the end of this evolution. It signals a shift towards deeper collaboration between humans and intelligent systems and points to a future shaped by collective intelligence, transparent decision-making and seamless integration with the physical and cognitive dimensions of work. In this emerging landscape, intelligence will come from connected systems working together and sharing context across the organisation.

These changes carry real consequences for how work is designed. Workflows will become more fluid, decisions more grounded in real-time information and organisations more able to adapt. The outcome depends not only on the sophistication of these systems but on how responsibly they are introduced into daily work and how thoughtfully they support the people who work alongside them.

BEYOND AGENTIC AI

Frontier developments are beginning to push AI beyond individual agents and into forms of reasoning, collaboration and embodied capability that were once out of reach. Table 2 illustrates some of the emerging technologies shaping this frontier and shows how quickly the landscape is evolving.

The next stage emerges when intelligent agents begin to work together and extend what each system can do on its own.

Agentic AI is already reshaping how work happens, yet it remains only one step in a broader evolution. The horizon now extends beyond single agents to a new generation of frontier technologies that deepen reasoning, support richer collaboration and bring intelligence into physical form. The most prominent developments show how rapidly these capabilities are expanding. This section introduces several of these advances, each reflecting a different way in which intelligent systems are taking on functions once associated only with people.

Collective AI

Collective AI builds on the principles of multi-agent systems and represents the next step in distributed intelligence (Riedl & De Cremer, 2025). It moves beyond task coordination to create

Table 2. Future AI Technologies.

AI Technology	What It Does	Workplace Impact
Collective AI	Coordinates multiple AI agents that self-organise and learn in real time	Optimises logistics, crisis response and market simulations
Neuro-symbolic AI	Merges pattern recognition with logical reasoning for explainable intelligence	Enables audit, legal and diagnostic systems with traceable logic
Causal AI	Understands cause-and-effect relationships rather than correlations	Improves planning, diagnosis, workforce analytics and scenario evaluation
Embodied AI	Connects AI to physical or immersive environments where it can sense, move and interact	Drives robotics, VR training, autonomous inspections and device control
Human–AI Integration	Links AI with human cognition through sensors, wearables and neural interfaces	Supports augmented decision-making, memory extension and hands-free workflows
Simulation-Based AI	Trains AI systems in high-fidelity virtual environments and digital twins	Enhances robotics, strategy modelling, forecasting and crisis readiness
Artificial General Intelligence (AGI)	Seeks human-level reasoning, creativity and adaptability	Tackles abstract problems and redefines cognitive work
Artificial Superintelligence (ASI)	Exceeds human intelligence, capable of autonomous reasoning and self-improvement	Could transform innovation and decision-making but raises major ethical and control challenges

Source: Author's own creation.

networks of connected agents and human collaborators that share context, negotiate priorities and adapt their strategies in real time. Instead of relying on central control, these systems generate coherent outcomes through purposeful coordination towards shared goals.

In practice, I have seen early prototypes already managing multiple business tasks across different systems through networks of digital agents. Each agent holds only part of the overall information, yet the network as a whole generates coherent and intelligent outcomes through continuous feedback and adaptation. Together, these agents can achieve outcomes that a single system could not.

This approach could transform the management of complex, interdependent systems such as supply chains, transport networks and financial ecosystems. By enabling distributed decision-making, collective AI supports adaptability, resilience and efficiency, which are qualities that matter for organisations operating in fast-changing environments. As these systems advance, they are likely to evolve into collaborative digital networks that optimise performance and resource use in real time, reducing dependency on human supervision while still requiring ethical oversight and clear accountability.

Neuro-symbolic AI

Neuro-symbolic AI combines two complementary forms of intelligence: the pattern-recognition ability of neural networks and the logical reasoning of symbolic systems (IBM Research, 2024). Deep-learning models excel at identifying correlations in large data sets but often lack interpretability. Symbolic systems, in contrast, rely on explicit rules and reasoning structures, offering transparency but limited adaptability.

By merging these capabilities, neuro-symbolic AI enables machines that can recognise complex patterns, reason through relationships and explain how conclusions are reached. The ability to integrate learning with logic opens new possibilities for decision-making that is both adaptive and interpretable.

This approach matters most in fields where traceability and accountability are essential, such as healthcare, law, auditing and compliance. A neuro-symbolic system can identify anomalies or recommend actions while also showing the reasoning behind its decisions. In doing so, it strengthens trust in automated systems and lays the foundation for AI that supports responsible decision-making in complex and regulated environments. In regulated industries, this clarity is essential because leaders must understand not only what the system recommends but why those recommendations were made.

In one early prototype, a neuro-symbolic model detected anomalies in audit data and explained which regulatory rules informed its conclusions. For teams working in compliance-heavy environments, this combination of reasoning and interpretability offered far greater confidence than unclear model outputs alone.

Advances in reasoning and explainability are only one step. The next involves moving intelligence beyond digital environments into physical settings. This shift introduces embodied forms of intelligence that sense, move and respond within human environments.

Causal AI

Causal AI focuses on understanding cause-and-effect relationships rather than identifying correlations or statistical patterns. While traditional machine-learning models detect associations, causal systems aim to determine why an outcome occurs and what would change if variables or decisions shifted. This distinction becomes crucial in environments where decisions require explanation, justification or the ability to test 'what-if' scenarios.

For organisations, causal AI helps leaders identify the true drivers of outcomes across operations, workforce trends, customer behaviour or risk indicators. Instead of guessing which factors matter most, causal models map the chains of influence that determine how events unfold. This provides a deeper foundation for planning, prediction and responsible automation.

Its relevance extends to domains where high-stakes decisions require traceability, such as financial services, healthcare, compliance and HR. By uncovering causal structures rather than correlations, the technology provides clarity that strengthens trust and improves both transparency and decision quality (Pearl & Mackenzie, 2024).

Embodied AI

Embodied AI refers to AI situated in physical or spatial environments, such as robots, drones, autonomous vehicles or immersive virtual and augmented-reality systems. These machines sense, move and act within the world around them, allowing digital intelligence to operate directly in human contexts. Their defining feature is interaction: they observe, learn from and respond to people and surroundings in real time.

Applications are already visible in hospitals, factories and educational settings. Robotic assistants can support surgical teams, drones can perform safety inspections in high-risk areas and virtual tutors can guide learners through adaptive experiences. Embodied AI links digital intelligence to the physical world, allowing systems to take on tasks that require movement, coordination and real-time response (Lisondra et al., 2025).

Human–AI integration

Human–AI integration explores how technology can interact more directly with human cognition. Advances in wearable sensors, neural interfaces and haptic devices point towards a future in which humans and machines share information seamlessly (Mu et al., 2025). This does not suggest replacement but augmentation with machines enhancing human memory, perception and capability. These interfaces bring AI closer to human cognition, allowing interaction not through screens or commands but through shared sensory and contextual signals.

Such developments raise important questions about autonomy, trust and organisational design. As AI becomes physically embedded in how we live and work, the challenge will be to ensure that its integration strengthens rather than diminishes human agency. Success will depend on designing systems that are safe, transparent and aligned with human values.

Simulation-Based AI

Simulation-based AI trains systems inside detailed virtual environments that reflect real-world conditions. These environments range from digital twins of physical assets to expansive virtual worlds where AI agents encounter dynamic challenges, rare scenarios and ambiguous situations at a speed and scale that physical testing cannot match. By exposing models to millions of simulated situations, organisations can test decisions safely, accelerate learning and improve reliability before deploying systems in live environments.

This approach is already shaping autonomous vehicles, robotics, logistics and factory automation, where performance depends on how well systems handle unexpected events or varied conditions. It is equally valuable for strategy work, allowing organisations to rehearse crisis responses, refine operational workflows and anticipate risks. As simulation fidelity improves, leaders increasingly rely on these environments to refine processes, strengthen resilience and prepare for fast-changing conditions (Liu & David, 2025).

As these technologies mature, they will change which tasks are carried out by people, which are shared with machines and how roles evolve.

Although these examples show different levels of capability, they are all forms of Narrow AI. They operate within defined domains and follow preset goals. Even more advanced systems such as Agentic AI or Collective AI can give the impression of broader reasoning, yet their intelligence remains tied to specific tasks. This stands in contrast to what is often called Strong AI, or AGI, which aims to replicate wide-ranging human cognitive abilities and to learn flexibly across contexts and domains (IBM, 2025b).

Artificial General Intelligence

AGI represents the most ambitious horizon in AI development. Unlike narrow systems designed for specific tasks, AGI would demonstrate broad, human-like cognition with the ability to learn across domains, solve abstract problems and adapt to unfamiliar situations (McKinsey & Company, 2024b). Its potential lies not only in what it could accomplish, but in how fundamentally it would reshape assumptions about intelligence, capability and human–machine collaboration.

In theory, an AGI system could match or exceed human capability not only in speed and scale but in creativity, logic and emotional understanding. It could analyse complex situations, detect subtle patterns across contexts and respond with solutions that integrate reasoning, empathy and experience. The potential of AGI lies in its universality with the ability to learn continuously, transfer insight between fields and interact dynamically with people and environments.

If realised, AGI would represent a major shift for both technology and society. From discussions with technology leaders and researchers, I have seen how this vision already shapes strategic planning and policy debate. It could accelerate progress in science, productivity and innovation and create new opportunities in fields like medicine, climate modelling and global coordination. Yet such power would also bring profound challenges. The arrival of machines capable of independent thought would force a re-examination of long-standing ideas about consciousness, agency and moral responsibility. It would redefine the boundaries between human and artificial capability and challenge the principles that underpin labour, law, education and governance. During a recent AI roundtable, a researcher described how an experimental model generated a novel optimisation technique that none of the team had previously considered. It did not amount to general intelligence, but it offered a glimpse of how emerging systems may begin to operate beyond familiar patterns.

The effects would reach far beyond economics or efficiency. Questions about ownership of knowledge, accountability for autonomous actions and the preservation of human purpose would become central to social debate. Some see AGI as a way to address major global challenges. Others worry that it could become risky if its objectives are not aligned with human values. Either way, AGI represents a mirror through which we must consider what kind of intelligence and what kind of society we ultimately wish to build.

WHEN MIGHT AGI ARRIVE?

The question of when AGI might emerge remains uncertain. Some projections suggest possibilities in the 2040s to 2050s, while others caution it may remain decades further away or prove unattainable. What unites these perspectives is uncertainty, a reminder that technological breakthroughs do not follow predictable timelines even when momentum appears strong.

Optimists see accelerating progress as evidence that the foundations of AGI are already forming. The scaling of data, computing power and model architecture has enabled systems that learn faster, retain context longer and coordinate across multiple tasks. Advances in transfer learning and multi-agent collaboration show early signs of systems that can generalise knowledge between domains, being one of the hallmarks of human-like intelligence. For this camp, AGI is not a sudden leap but the natural outcome of continued exponential improvement.

Pessimists take a more cautious stance. They highlight that current AI models, despite their impressive output, remain fundamentally limited by pattern recognition and lack the grounding that underpins human understanding. They can mimic reasoning but do not truly comprehend cause, consequence or emotion. The gap between performing a task and understanding why it is performed remains wide. Reaching AGI would require breakthroughs not only in computation but in the philosophy of mind, language and learning.

Between these two perspectives lies a more pragmatic view: AGI's timeline will be shaped as much by human choices as by technical capability. Regulation, ethics, funding priorities and public trust will influence how fast or slow progress unfolds. History shows that innovation accelerates when aligned with societal readiness and slows when confidence erodes. The path towards AGI will likely mirror this dynamic, advancing in bursts of discovery punctuated by reflection, caution and recalibration.

Whether AGI arrives in decades, centuries or never, the pursuit itself is already transforming research, policy and industry. It is prompting organisations to rethink what intelligence means, how it can be measured and how humanity defines its role alongside increasingly capable systems (Gartner, 2025).

To understand how we might move towards or away from AGI, it helps to examine the forces accelerating progress as well as the constraints that could slow it down.

Accelerators of AGI Development

The pursuit of AGI has long combined scientific ambition with public speculation. While still beyond current reach, several converging trends suggest a steadily accelerating trajectory towards its realisation. Rapid growth in computing capacity, the emergence of autonomous digital systems, advances in data simulation and the expanding scale of research collaboration are all shaping the conditions for more general, context-aware intelligence (McKinsey & Company, 2025c). Understanding these forces is vital to gauge how quickly we might progress from narrow, task-specific systems to machines capable of reasoning, adapting and acting across diverse domains.

Computer power: The backbone of progress in machine intelligence lies in continuous advances in computational performance. Modern processing architectures and specialised accelerators now support the training of models at scales once considered impractical. Emerging designs inspired by brain-like efficiency, together with the experimental potential of quantum and neuromorphic computing, promise further leaps in capacity and energy efficiency (MIT Technology Review, 2025). These improvements make it possible to explore more complex system designs that support advanced reasoning.

Data and simulation environments: Access to large, diverse and high-quality data remains a cornerstone of AI progress. Combined with sophisticated simulation platforms, from interactive virtual settings to digital replicas of physical systems, AI models can train and experiment in conditions that mimic real-world complexity. Such environments expose learning agents to rare or ambiguous situations, allowing them to test hypotheses, refine decision strategies and build contextual memory across domains, which are capabilities essential to generalised learning.

Collaborative research: AI research today is not confined to isolated labs. Open-source projects, collaborative research by organisations like OpenAI, and AI research hubs in universities are driving rapid iteration and transparency. Cross-disciplinary efforts involving neuroscience, psychology, linguistics and computer science enrich the theoretical and empirical foundation for AGI.

The free exchange of models, datasets and benchmark tools accelerates progress while fostering shared ethical standards and best practices.

Commercial investment and competition: Global competition in AI has led to an unprecedented influx of capital into the field, with tech giants investing billions in infrastructure and foundation models (McKinsey & Company, 2025c). This intense commercial race driven by both innovation ambition and market incentives has transformed AGI from a fringe idea to a central pillar of these tech giants strategy. As organisations seek strategic advantage, the pace of experimentation and model deployment continues to accelerate.

Barriers to AGI Realisation

Despite rapid advances, multiple technical and human factors continue to stand between current AI and general intelligence. Reaching AGI will require more than scale. It will depend on advances in understanding, reasoning and ethical design that today's systems still lack. Many current models still operate through statistical association rather than comprehension, lacking contextual judgement and the capacity for safe, equitable interaction within dynamic human environments. The key obstacles are not solely computational, they are cognitive, ethical and systemic. Overcoming them will require innovation not only in algorithms but also in governance, collaboration and shared human values (Deloitte, 2025a).

Absence of true understanding: Modern systems often excel at detecting patterns but fall short of grasping meaning. They can reproduce correlations but rarely infer causality or apply knowledge flexibly from limited examples, creating a clear gap between imitation and intelligence. Without situational awareness or conceptual reasoning, general cognition remains out of reach. These limitations become especially visible in practical settings. In enterprise pilots discussed by peers, AI systems could summarise complex policy documents flawlessly but failed to answer simple follow-up questions that required real-world understanding, revealing how far current models remain from genuine comprehension and how little data scaling alone can resolve this gap.

Alignment and safety: One of the most pressing challenges in AGI development is the problem of alignment ensuring that an autonomous system's actions are consistent with human intentions, values and social norms. As systems become more capable, unintended behaviours, optimisation errors or misaligned incentives could lead to harmful outcomes. Research into maintaining behavioural alignment with human purpose is still emerging, and the potential risks grow with every increase in autonomy.

Bias and generalisation limits: Systems trained on historical or incomplete data risk inheriting and amplifying existing inequities (Afreen, 2025). While general intelligence would ideally transcend such constraints, its ability to generalise fairly across diverse populations remains uncertain. The representativeness of data, design inclusivity and continuous audit mechanisms will determine whether AI can operate reliably across cultures and contexts.

Interpretability and transparency: The internal reasoning of high-performance models remains difficult to explain, even to their creators. This lack of transparency limits accountability and undermines trust, particularly in sensitive areas such as healthcare, law and finance. Achieving explainable operations will be essential to ensuring that future intelligent systems can be regulated, verified and trusted.

Public trust and regulation: As AI's influence expands, societal unease about surveillance, misinformation, employment and autonomy continues to grow. Incidents of misuse or error can quickly erode public trust. Regulatory responses are accelerating worldwide, yet the resulting patchwork of policies risks constraining innovation while seeking to ensure safety. Building durable confidence will require clear governance, consistent communication and ethical leadership that keep technological progress aligned with public interest.

While the path to AGI is uncertain, its potential to redefine what it means to work, think and create is undeniable. What matters now is how we prepare for the possibility of AGI, not predicting an exact timeline. Organisations should start developing literacy around the ethical, social and operational implications of general-purpose intelligence. HR and business leaders, in particular, should help shape a workforce and policy environment where human potential and machine intelligence can evolve together, safely, responsibly and equitably.

In short, AGI may not be here yet, but the trajectory of AI development is unmistakably heading towards broader autonomy, deeper collaboration and more profound impact. Whether that journey leads to shared prosperity or systemic disruption depends on the choices we make today.

As we look ahead, it is equally important to address the misconceptions that often distort our understanding of AI and influence how people respond to it.

CLEARING UP MISCONCEPTIONS ABOUT AI

As AI becomes increasingly woven into the fabric of modern organisations, so too do the myths and misunderstandings surrounding it. These misconceptions often fuelled by headlines, science fiction or limited exposure shape how people think about AI and in turn, how they respond to it. They can create unnecessary fear, unrealistic expectations or hesitation. To lead responsibly, it is essential to separate fact from fiction and re-centre the conversation around people: what AI changes, what it enables and how humans remain at the heart of progress.

Drawing on practical experience supporting AI adoption, the following are some of the most common misconceptions that still influence how organisations interpret and apply the technology.

'AI replaces humans'

This remains one of the most widespread and anxiety-inducing myths. In practice, AI does not replace people. It replaces specific tasks, especially those that are repetitive, rule-based or heavily data-driven. While this inevitably changes certain roles, it also creates new ones that rely on uniquely human qualities such as judgement, creativity and empathy. The purpose of AI is not to erase human contribution but to augment it. Organisations that see AI as a collaborator in productivity rather than a threat to employment are far better positioned to harness its potential. Much like earlier industrial revolutions, progress will reward those who learn to work effectively alongside intelligent systems. The future will belong to those willing to evolve their roles, skills and mindsets in a world where technology continually redefines how work gets done. Many employees fear replacement rather than augmentation, largely because of inconsistent guidance and limited transparency (PwC, 2025a).

'We still have time before AI really matters'

This is among the most misleading assumptions in today's business landscape. AI is not something that lies far ahead. It is already part of the systems and decisions that shape day-to-day work. From recruitment engines that prioritise candidates, to service bots that resolve inquiries, to predictive analytics that forecast attrition and performance trends, AI quietly influences outcomes across nearly every function. The question is no longer when but how effectively organisations adapt. Those that treat AI as tomorrow's issue risk falling behind today. The most forward-looking companies are already experimenting, learning and embedding responsible AI practices into their operations. They are building literacy, strengthening governance and reshaping workflows to stay ahead. AI already matters. The only question is whether we are ready to lead in its adoption or be led by it.

'AI is a black box no one understands'

While some AI models, especially those based on deep learning, are complex, they are not beyond comprehension. The growing discipline of Explainable AI (XAI) focuses on making these systems more transparent, interpretable and accountable. This is increasingly important as AI takes part in decisions that affect people directly, such as hiring decisions, loan approvals, medical diagnosis and performance evaluation. Without clarity on how conclusions are reached, organisations risk undermining trust and compliance. Explainability helps close this gap, enabling both technical and non-technical stakeholders to understand how AI works and why it makes certain recommendations. Transparency builds confidence, strengthens accountability and ensures that AI supports rather than obscures human judgement. As AI's influence expands, so too must our ability to interpret, audit and challenge its outputs responsibly (Olufunmilayo et al., 2024).

'AI is too technical for most leaders to influence'

This misconception underestimates the human capacity to guide technological change. While engineers and data scientists may design AI systems, it is leaders and teams who determine how they are introduced, governed and experienced across the organisation. Understanding AI doesn't require coding skills. It calls for curiosity, accountability and a willingness to engage with how intelligent systems influence people and performance. Every business function plays a role in ensuring AI is used responsibly. Those who see it as purely a technical issue risk creating a gap between innovation and impact. Influence over AI comes not from technical skill but from vision, empathy and the ability to connect technology with human outcomes. The organisations that will thrive are those whose leaders treat AI as a shared responsibility, one that demands collaboration, adaptability and a human-centred approach to progress.

This shift in mindset prepares us for a bigger question: if leaders can shape how AI is used today, what direction is the technology itself moving towards next?

OUTLOOK OF WHERE IS AI HEADED

As we move beyond the era of Agentic AI, the next stage of AI will be shaped less by advances in computing and more by how people and intelligent systems learn to work together. Progress will not be measured only by processing power or the size of AI models. It will increasingly be defined by the depth and quality of collaboration between humans and machines as they confront complex problems side by side.

The future of work will depend not on how intelligent machines become but on how intentionally we design their partnership with human judgement, creativity and purpose. What lies ahead may include self-organising networks of AI agents, systems capable of higher-order reasoning and adaptive learning, and new interfaces that blend physical environments with cognitive interaction.

Beyond this point sits the theoretical idea of Artificial Super Intelligence (ASI), described in recent academic research as the possibility that future systems could exceed human cognitive abilities across many domains (Zhao et al., 2025). While still hypothetical, it raises important questions about how far we are prepared to extend machine intelligence and how we ensure that any future system remains aligned with human values and collective wellbeing.

The real challenge is not to build more powerful systems. It is to ensure that intelligence, whether human or artificial, stays rooted in shared values. As AI moves from being assistive to becoming more autonomous and embedded in daily life, leadership, governance and responsibility take on increasing importance. The essential question is no longer only what AI can do. It is who we choose to become alongside it.

To lead effectively in this moment, organisations need to move beyond the myths that obscure AI's true nature. AI is not magic and it is not a threat. It is a tool that can expand human capability, sharpen insight and support innovation when used responsibly. Clarity is the first step, because misunderstanding AI does more than slow progress. It risks creating systems that drift away from people, purpose and performance. Research already shows that many employees fear replacement simply because guidance is unclear and communication is inconsistent (PwC, 2025a). The real opportunity is to ensure that the intelligence we build remains a reflection of our best intentions rather than a substitute for them.

The systems we see today, impressive as they are, represent early steps in a longer evolution. What matters now is not predicting when AI might surpass human cognition. What matters is ensuring that each advance reflects the purpose, judgement and values we bring to it. The future of AI will depend on how thoughtfully humans and machines learn, reason and grow together. That choice belongs not to the technology but to the leaders, organisations and societies that guide its development.

The future of intelligence will not be defined by machines alone, but by the choices we make about how they work alongside us.

This is where Part II begins. The next chapters explore how AI reshapes work, roles and organisational design, and how leaders can build a future where people and intelligent systems create progress together.

Key Takeaways

- AI is shifting from assistive tools to autonomous systems that act with context and purpose.
- Agentic AI introduces digital agents capable of independent action and adaptive decision-making.
- Collective AI will create distributed networks where agents collaborate across tasks and domains.
- Neuro-symbolic systems combine learning with reasoning to improve transparency and trust.
- Embodied AI will extend intelligence into physical environments, reshaping daily operations.
- AGI remains speculative but already shapes strategic thinking and long-term planning.
- Advances in computing, data and simulation environments accelerate progress towards more capable AI.
- Alignment, bias and transparency remain essential for safe and equitable deployment.
- ASI raises deep ethical questions about capability, purpose and control.
- The future of AI will depend on how responsibly humans and intelligent systems learn and evolve together.

Part II

DECODING AI

Every transformation reaches a point where understanding the technology is no longer enough. People begin to ask a different set of questions. What is changing inside the work itself? How will my role evolve? What does this shift mean for my team, my organisation and the way decisions are made?

Part II turns the conversation from abstract technology to practical leadership. It equips readers with the tools to decode change, act with intention and prepare their workforce for a future where human and machine intelligence shape progress together.

Chapter 4 explains why organisations cannot navigate AI with scattered assumptions or isolated experiments. It introduces the human–AI decoder, a simple but powerful way to understand how work is changing and how leaders can respond with clarity rather than guesswork. Chapter 5 then puts the decoder to work, showing how to analyse real roles, uncover the shifts happening beneath the surface and match them to the six levels of AI impact. Chapter 6 applies the decoder to the five previously introduced business-critical challenges that shape how organisations experience AI. It shows how the same framework can guide reskilling, build readiness, align human and machine strengths and help organisations move through uncertainty with greater confidence and purpose.

4

THE HUMAN–AI DECODER

ABSTRACT

Artificial Intelligence (AI) is reshaping work in ways people can feel long before organisations know how to describe it. The human–AI decoder offers a simple and human-centred way to understand these shifts and respond to them with clarity. It begins with three guiding questions that help leaders see what is changing inside the work, determine how significant the change is and decide how the organisation should act. The decoder is based on the AI Workforce Impact Model, a framework developed by the author. It examines how tasks, responsibilities, skills, decision-making and human contribution evolve as AI becomes part of everyday work. It then classifies the depth of change through six levels of AI impact, giving organisations a shared language to compare roles and align decisions. The model also translates understanding into practical steps through AI impact actions that guide role redesign, employee support, learning priorities and organisational adjustments that match the scale of the shift. Through real examples, including a call centre scenario, the decoder helps leaders move from early signals to a clear view of AI's influence on the work itself. It demonstrates how organisations can turn understanding into responsible, human-centred action and build a repeatable loop for navigating workforce change as AI advances.

Keywords: Artificial Intelligence; human–AI decoder; AI Workforce Impact Model (AIWIM); impact areas; AI impact scan; impact levels; AI impact actions; workforce transformation; skills evolution; responsible AI adoption

Part I laid the groundwork. It clarified what AI is, how it evolved and why it has become impossible for organisations to ignore. It showed that AI reshapes work long before it reshapes jobs and that these early shifts often move faster than leaders expect. It also revealed something deeper. AI does not only change the tasks people perform. It changes how they think about their contribution, how they see their place in the organisation and how they understand the value they bring to their work.

THE MOMENT THE ROOM FALLS QUIET

The meeting begins with energy. Teams share updates on AI pilots and new features that promise faster workflows and cleaner outputs. There is optimism around the table. People recognise the potential and talk confidently about what the tools can do. Then someone asks the question everyone has been thinking but no one has said aloud:

'What does all of this mean for our people?'

The room falls quiet. Leaders are not hesitating or resisting. They are suddenly aware that, although they can describe the technology, they cannot yet describe the change. They can list capabilities, but not explain how responsibility shifts. They can point to efficiency gains, but not how those gains alter judgement, contribution or identity. The silence reveals a gap that is becoming common across industries: a gap between what the organisation can measure and what its people are beginning to feel.

The changes are already happening. Tasks move faster. Familiar steps disappear. Systems begin anticipating needs that once required human judgement. The pace and pattern of work shift, although the reasons behind those changes are not immediately clear. Employees notice it early. A summary appears before they ask for one. A first draft arrives without being requested. A workflow that once required several actions now takes one. The work continues, but it no longer feels the same.

Recent global findings show that fewer than half of employees feel their organisations communicate clearly about how AI is reshaping their roles, even as they begin to experience the effects directly in their daily work (PwC, 2025b). They sense change before leaders can interpret it. Technology teams understand the system but not the impact on roles. HR sees new skill demands but lacks a shared structure to explain how work is evolving. Executives sense increasing change but cannot quantify its effects.

This is the moment when improvements in speed are no longer enough. Leaders see progress, but cannot describe what that progress means for the people doing the work. They can explain how a tool functions, but not how it shifts value or contribution. They know the organisation is moving differently, but cannot yet explain why the work feels different.

Organisations do not lack information about technology. They lack a clear way to understand what is happening inside the work itself. Efficiency is visible. The human implications are not.

This is where the human–AI decoder begins. It enters at the moment when silence exposes the real issue. Understanding the technology is no longer enough. People need clarity about what AI means for their work, their responsibilities and their future.

WHAT CURRENT FRAMEWORKS MISS

Current research has not lacked ambition in trying to explain how AI affects work. Over the past decade, researchers, consultancies and global institutions have proposed models ranging from automation forecasts to capability taxonomies and job-exposure indices. These studies have positively shaped our understanding of AI's economic and organisational influence, however they share a limitation. They capture the big picture, but they do not reveal how AI alters the work of a role or what that change means for the person whose job is being reshaped.

Many of these frameworks focus on macro trends. Others examine tasks in isolation or map skills at a high level. Some evaluate organisational maturity or technical readiness. Each perspective is important in its own way, but none connects technology, work design and the human experience into a role-level view. As a result, leaders still struggle to answer the most immediate questions employees ask about how their work is changing.

Together, these studies show the scale of change underway and underline why leaders need a clearer and more human-centred way to interpret how AI is reshaping work. Appendix 2 brings these elements together by outlining influential frameworks in the field and showing why leaders need a tool like the human–AI decoder to navigate change with clarity and confidence.

THREE QUESTIONS EVERY LEADER SHOULD BE ABLE TO ANSWER

When the room falls quiet, the agenda shifts. The conversation is no longer about the technology or the performance gains. Leaders realise they cannot rely on technical descriptions to explain what employees are experiencing in their work. The question raised at the table needs a structure that makes the change understandable.

These questions surface in every organisation because they speak to the human reality of changing work. They help leaders see what people need to understand and what actions they must take in response.

How is AI changing work is the first question because it responds to what people notice directly. They see tasks start earlier, finish faster or begin without their involvement. They notice information arriving pre-structured or decisions appearing in forms that once required several steps. The work changes, yet the reason is not immediately clear. People want to understand what the technology is changing inside the role, not the theory behind the system. Until this is understood, nothing else feels stable. Employees need clarity about these shifts.

How big is the impact is the second question because once people recognise that something is different, they look for a way to understand its scale. They want to know whether the shift is limited to a handful of tasks or whether it reshapes their role more broadly. Leaders need the same clarity to make responsible decisions about work design, skills and staffing. Employees need it to understand how their responsibilities may evolve. Without a shared language to describe the scale of change, uncertainty spreads. Teams talk past one another because they lack a consistent reference point.

How should we act is the third question because it determines trust. When people see change and understand its scale, they expect leaders to outline what comes next. They want to know how to adjust, which skills matter and how the organisation plans to support them. Leaders need a structured way to respond so they can align decisions, communicate clearly and avoid improvised reactions that increase confusion.

INTRODUCING THE HUMAN–AI DECODER

These three questions form the core of the human–AI decoder. They provide the structure needed to understand how AI is reshaping work and how people should act in response. Fig. 2 illustrates

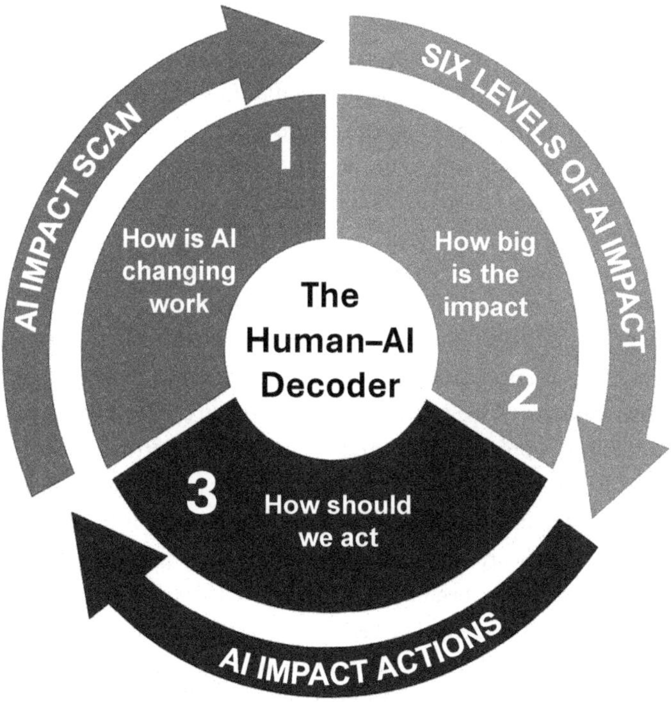

Fig. 2. The Human–AI Decoder.

Source: Author's Own Creation.

this logic, showing how the decoder turns complexity into a pattern that leaders can see, interpret and act on.

The human–AI decoder is the practical tool to decode AI. It is written in straightforward language that leaders, policymakers and employees can use in everyday conversations without feeling overwhelmed by technical terms. It is designed to make complex change understandable. Simple enough for everyday discussions. Grounded in a structure leaders can trust, it helps people see what is changing inside their work. It makes the early signals employees experience visible and creates a shared language for describing what is shifting around them.

Behind the decoder lies a framework built over years of digital transformation and close work with HR peers, business leaders and AI experts. This foundation is the AI Workforce Impact Model, or AIWIM. It gives the decoder its structure, depth and credibility. Readers do not need the full detail of the model to follow this chapter, although a complete explanation is available in Appendix 3 for those who want to explore it.

Put simply, the human–AI decoder is what people use in everyday conversations. AIWIM is what makes those conversations reliable, providing the clarity and structure that sit beneath the surface.

The sections that follow use the three guiding questions to move from early signals to understanding and then to action.

1. HOW IS AI CHANGING WORK?

The first question in the human–AI decoder is 'How is AI changing work?' It matters because the earliest signs of transformation rarely appear in strategy documents or organisational charts. They surface in the tasks people complete and the way their contribution is perceived. They show up in daily work and employees notice them long before the organisation is prepared to describe what is happening.

These signals are often subtle at first. A task that once required focused effort now begins with a suggested draft. A process that previously moved through several steps is completed more quickly. Conversations that demanded manual preparation arrive with the necessary information already compiled. On their own, these changes seem small. Together, they signal a shift in how the role functions and what the organisation expects from the person doing the work.

A simple example makes this clear.

In a global insurance team, a product analyst noticed that the weekly portfolio report, once a two-hour task involving data pulls, manual checks and formatting, now arrived half-prepared. The system fetched the data, flagged outliers and drafted the first version of the commentary for her. Nothing in her job title changed. No one announced a transformation. Yet her morning routine no longer resembled the one she had followed for years. She spent less time assembling information and more time questioning why certain patterns appeared. What initially felt like a time-saving feature was, in practice, the first sign that her role was quietly being redesigned.

Where the First Shifts Appear

These early changes may look scattered, but they are not. They follow a pattern that becomes clear once we look more closely at how work is structured. Every role is made up of several core elements, and AI interacts with each of them in different ways. In the human–AI decoder, these are known as the 'AI Impact Areas'. They show how AI begins to influence tasks, responsibilities, decisions, skills and the value people bring to the work. They also explain why the work starts to feel different before anyone has described the change. Fig. 3 illustrates these five AI impact areas.

The first one appears in 'Automation', the area that describes how tasks change when AI enters the workflow. Once AI takes on routine or structured activities, the work no longer happens in the same order or with the same level of human involvement. Drafts appear before anyone begins typing. Summaries form on their own. Data are organised before someone even opens the file. People describe the work as faster or lighter, although the real change

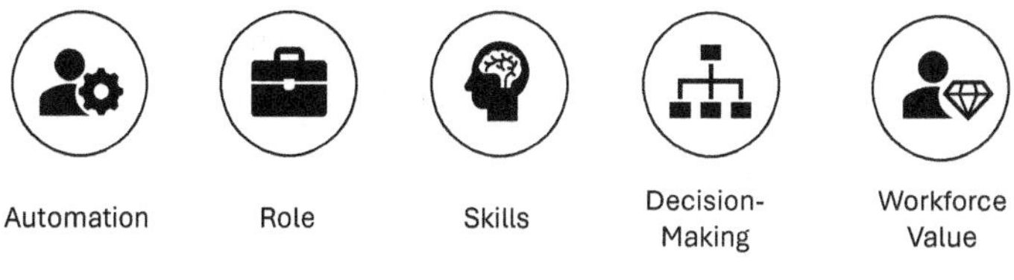

Fig. 3. AI Impact Areas.

Source: Author's Own Creation

lies in how the task is produced. The person becomes the reviewer rather than the creator, often before anyone acknowledges that the nature of the work has changed.

A second shift emerges in the 'Role', the area that shows how the purpose and boundaries of a job evolve. As predictable tasks move to the system, the job begins to lean towards interpretation rather than production. Individuals spend less time collecting inputs and more time understanding what the system has prepared. They handle exceptions, navigate sensitive situations and apply judgement where the technology reaches its limits. Without any formal announcement, the role starts to change. Responsibilities that once defined it fade and new expectations take their place.

The third shift affects 'Skills', the area that captures how capability requirements evolve when AI becomes part of the workflow. Employees find that their existing strengths still matter, but they matter in a different way. Manual proficiency becomes less central. What grows in importance is the ability to evaluate system outputs, identify gaps and redirect errors. People also need to bring context to situations that the AI cannot interpret correctly. They begin asking why an answer appeared, not only how to use it. New skills emerge quietly. Individuals learn to judge system behaviour, refine instructions and monitor inconsistencies. These abilities become essential long before they appear in any formal skill framework.

The fourth shift involves 'Decision-Making', the area that reflects how judgement and authority move between people and systems. As AI becomes part of the workflow, it changes how choices are shaped. Some decisions arrive pre-structured. Others narrow towards a recommended direction. Areas that once depended entirely on human judgement now begin with a system-generated proposal. People learn to assess these proposals, approve them, challenge them or override them. Over time, predictable decisions migrate towards the machine, while decisions requiring interpretation remain with the human. This boundary becomes one of the most important features of the evolving role.

The fifth shift concerns 'Workforce Value', the area that describes how the significance of human contribution changes. When AI handles repetitive or rules-based work, what remains for the human becomes more visible. People notice that moments requiring empathy or situational judgement become more important. They also take responsibility for situations that rely on trust and emotional intelligence. The meaning of the role is no longer defined by volume or speed. It becomes defined by insight, interpretation and the ability to handle complexity. Many employees feel this change most clearly because it reshapes how they understand their own contribution.

These five AI impact areas explain why work begins to feel different before the organisation provides an explanation. Change does not happen in one place. It unfolds across several, often at different speeds and with different levels of visibility. The full rationale behind the impact areas is outlined in Appendix 3 for readers who want a deeper view.

To bring structure to these observations, the human–AI decoder uses the AI impact scan.

Measuring the Change of AI in Work

The AI impact scan works by asking a small set of anchored questions across the five AI impact areas and choosing the answers that best reflect what is happening in the work. These choices reveal how each area is shifting and turn scattered signals into a clearer, more coherent view. The scan helps leaders see the pattern behind what employees experience long before they can fully describe it. It gives the organisation a structured way to move from early observations to insights that can be compared, discussed and acted on. This is the value the AI impact scan provides.

A call centre example shows how the AI impact areas work in practice.

The need for this becomes clear in a call centre where a generative AI assistant has been added to the workflow. At first, the shift appears simple. Responses are drafted automatically, knowledge articles surface instantly and summaries write themselves. Productivity rises and the work feels lighter.

But when supervisors look more closely, they notice patterns that cannot be explained by efficiency alone. Tasks that once defined the job have moved to the system. The purpose of the role has shifted towards handling the complex and sensitive cases. Skill expectations have changed, because the call center agents must interpret system suggestions, manage exceptions and oversee accuracy. Decision-making no longer follows a straight line. Routine choices happen automatically, and humans step in only when judgement or escalation is required. Workforce value for the agent becomes more concentrated in empathy, trust-building and conflict resolution.

The AI impact scan turns these signals into evidence. Recent workplace research shows that task-level changes often accumulate faster than leaders expect, making structured assessment tools essential for understanding how work is shifting beneath the surface (McKinsey & Company, 2025).

It guides leaders through focused questions across the impact areas. These questions show whether AI now completes work that was previously manual. They reveal whether responsibilities have evolved and whether new skills are required. They show if decision authority has shifted. They also indicate whether the role now depends more on human judgement or emotional intelligence. Instead of guessing how the work is changing, the scan makes it visible. It allows organisations to describe the impact clearly and compare roles consistently across teams and functions.

Applying the AI Impact Scan Questions

The picture becomes clearer once these observations can be measured. The scan is the mechanism that turns early signals into a structured evaluation. It begins with a set of guiding questions, shown in Table 3, that help leaders examine what has changed inside the work and how those changes show up across the five AI impact areas.

These questions prompt teams to look at the work closely. They help leaders see whether tasks that were once manual are now completed by the system, whether responsibilities have shifted, whether new skills are required and whether decision authority has moved. They also highlight how the value of human contribution is changing as roles evolve.

To make the results usable, each Area is scored on a simple 0 to 5 scale from 'No Impact' to 'Full Transformation'.

Table 3. AI Impact Scan Questions.

AI Impact Areas	0 – No Impact	1 – Low Impact	2 – Moderate Impact	3 – High Impact	4 – Full Impact	5 – Transformational Impact
Automation	All tasks done by humans	AI supports small or repetitive tasks	AI completes routine tasks; humans review and refine	AI handles most tasks; humans manage exceptions	AI runs core work; humans step in only for complex tasks	AI runs the entire workflow and adapts without human involvement
Role	Role remains the same	Tasks improved or supported by AI; role remains the same	Duties shift or expand as AI supports parts of the work	Role is redefined; humans supervise AI outputs	Most of the role shifts to AI; humans handle oversight and escalation	Original role disappears; humans guide direction and ethics
Skills	No new skills needed	Basic digital or AI skills required	New skills for collaboration and AI oversight are needed	Significant reskilling needed for AI-driven work	New skills needed to oversee and guide AI	Skills shift to system design, ethics and long-term guidance
Decision-Making	Humans make all decisions	AI provides suggestions; humans make final decisions	AI recommends; humans approve or adjust them	AI makes most decisions; humans handle exceptions	AI decides within set boundaries; humans intervene only for complex judgement	AI decides and adapts across the full workflow; humans guide purpose and governance
Workforce Value	Human value remains unchanged	Human value increases through productivity gains	Human value shifts towards creativity, judgement or oversight	Human value rises in supervision and more complex judgement	Human value lies in validating and governing AI-managed work	Human value moves to purpose setting, ethics and long-term accountability

Source: Author's own creation.

Automation

How much of the task execution is done by AI versus humans?

0 – No Impact: All tasks done by humans

1 – Low Impact: AI supports small or repetitive tasks

2 – Moderate Impact: AI completes routine tasks; humans review and refine

3 – High Impact: AI handles most tasks; humans manage exceptions

4 – Full Impact: AI runs core work; humans step in only for complex tasks

5 – Transformational Impact: AI runs the entire workflow and adapts without human involvement

Role

How much has AI changed the purpose or structure of the role?

0 – No Impact: Role remains the same

1 – Low Impact: Tasks improved or supported by AI; role unchanged

2 – Moderate Impact: Duties shift or expand as AI supports parts of the work

3 – High Impact: Role is redefined; humans supervise AI outputs

4 – Full Impact: Most of the role shifts to AI; humans handle oversight and escalation

5 – Transformational Impact: The original role disappears; humans guide direction and ethics

Skills

How much has AI changed the skills required to perform the role?

0 – No Impact: No new skills needed

1 – Low Impact: Basic digital or AI skills required

2 – Moderate Impact: New skills needed to collaborate with or oversee AI-supported tasks

3 – High Impact: Significant reskilling needed for AI-driven work

4 – Full Impact: New skills needed to oversee and guide AI

5 – Transformational Impact: Skills shift to system design, ethics and long-term guidance rather than day-to-day work

Decision-Making

Who makes decisions in the workflow and how?

0 – No Impact: Humans make all decisions

1 – Low Impact: AI provides suggestions; humans decide

2 – Moderate Impact: AI recommends; humans approve or adjust

3 – High Impact: AI makes most decisions; humans handle exceptions
4 – Full Impact: AI decides within set boundaries; humans intervene only for complex judgement
5 – Transformational Impact: AI decides and adapts across the full workflow; humans guide purpose and governance

Workforce Value

Where does human contribution create value in the workflow?
0 – No Impact: Human value remains unchanged
1 – Low Impact: Human value increases through productivity gains
2 – Moderate Impact: Human value shifts towards creativity, judgement or oversight
3 – High Impact: Human value rises in governance and complex judgement
4 – Full Impact: Human value lies in validating and governing AI-managed work
5 – Transformational Impact: Human value moves to purpose setting, ethics and long-term accountability outside the workflow.

Each area is assessed independently, since each represents a different part of how work shifts with AI.

Using the same call centre example, we can see how the AI impact areas are assessed using the AI impact scan questions.

When the scan is applied to the call centre role, 'Automation' stands out immediately. The system now prepares summaries, drafts routine responses, retrieves knowledge articles and handles most predictable queries. What once required manual effort is now completed before the agent begins, placing 'Automation' area at '3 – High Impact'.

As automation moves more routine work to the system, the 'Role' starts to evolve. The job shifts from producing answers to supervising the system that produces them. The agent now focuses on complex or sensitive conversations, manages exceptions and restores trust when the system reaches its limits. What the job represents and how it creates value begins to change. This places the 'Role' area at '3 – High Impact'.

The shift in 'Skills' is just as clear. Communication ability still matters, but the agent must now oversee system outputs, interpret suggestions, manage escalations and refine prompts. These added expectations represent a meaningful evolution in what the job requires and place the 'Skills' area at '3 – High Impact'.

'Decision-making' changes in a different way. Routine choices are proposed by the system, and the agent intervenes only when cases fall outside the system's confidence range. Authority shifts towards automation for predictable scenarios, while humans retain oversight for ambiguous or high-stakes situations. This results for 'Decision-Making' area in a '2 – Moderate Impact'.

All of this reshapes 'Workforce Value'. The repetitive work that once defined the role now sits with the system. What remains is the uniquely human ability to establish trust, read emotional cues, interpret context and resolve conflict. These responsibilities now form the centre of the role, placing 'Workforce Value' area at '3 – High Impact'.

Table 4 shows how these shifts appear in the AI Impact Scan for a call centre example.

When these results are combined, the average of the five scores produces an AI Impact Index of 2.8 for the call centre agent. The

Table 4. Call Centre Example – AI Impact Scan.

AI Impact Areas	Scale	Justification	Score
Automation	High Impact	AI handles most tasks; humans manage exceptions	3
Role	High Impact	Role purpose redefined towards supervising and escalation	3
Skills	High Impact	Significant retraining for AI supervision and empathy-based interaction	3
Decision-Making	Moderate Impact	AI recommends; humans approve in complex cases	2
Workforce Value	High Impact	Human value decreases in routine execution but rises in judgement, empathy and quality control	3
		Total	14

Source: Author's own creation.

calculation is (3 + 3 + 3 + 2 + 3) ÷ 5 = 2.8. The AI Impact Index measures how deeply AI is transforming work. This score becomes the basis for answering the decoder's second question, which examines the AI impact through a formal classification. The scan shows not isolated adjustments but a coordinated shift in how the role functions, how decisions are made and where workforce value now sits.

The next section explores what this level of change means in practice.

2. HOW BIG IS THE IMPACT?

Once people understand how AI is affecting the work itself, the next question follows quickly. They want to know 'How big is the impact?' They want to understand whether the signals they see point to a small adjustment or to something more substantial. Leaders feel this same pressure. They need a way to distinguish between a role that is simply evolving and a role that is being reshaped. Without a clear method, conversations drift into uncertainty and decisions become inconsistent.

The human–AI decoder answers this second question through the six levels of AI impact. The levels give organisations a structured way to describe the extent of the change. They replace speculation with a shared reference point. They help leaders talk about the influence of AI in a way that is grounded, comparable and understood across functions. When people share this foundation, they can align on what the change means and what needs to happen next.

The Six Levels of AI Impact

The impact levels describe how deeply AI has entered the work. They show how far a role has shifted and how much responsibility has moved towards the system. Economic analysis suggests that this redistribution does not happen evenly. Some occupations feel the shift quickly, while others change at a much slower pace, even within the same organisation (J.P. Morgan Global Research, 2025). Patterns begin to emerge once the impact is classified.

Table 5. The Six Levels of AI Impact.

Level of AI Impact		AI Impact Index	Definition
Level 0	**AI-Irrelevant**	0.0–0.5	AI has no meaningful impact; humans do all the work
Level 1	**AI-Supported**	0.6–1.5	AI assists simple tasks; humans still do the core work
Level 2	**AI-Enhanced**	1.6–2.5	AI handles routine tasks to improve work; humans remain in charge
Level 3	**AI-Driven**	2.6–3.5	AI performs most work; humans decide when to intervene
Level 4	**AI-Orchestrated**	3.6–4.9	AI manages end-to-end work; humans provide oversight
Level 5	**AI-Automated**	5.0	AI operates autonomously; humans have minimal or no involvement

Source: Author's own creation.

The classification uses the AI Impact Index as its guide. The ranges in Table 5 make the results easy to interpret. Lower scores reflect roles where AI has a light touch. As the score rises, AI begins to shape daily work more directly. Once the average reaches the mid-twos, the role enters Levels 3, 4 or 5, where AI takes on a more significant share of the activity. These ranges give organisations a clear way to understand the degree of change and compare the impact across different roles.

The earliest point on the scale is 'Level 0: AI-Irrelevant Work', where AI has little or no involvement. Tasks, decisions and judgement remain entirely with the employee. The work looks and feels the same as it always has. Many roles still sit here, especially where AI tools have not yet been introduced or where systems are available but not meaningfully used.

From there, the levels progress as AI takes on a more active role.

The first visible shift appears in 'Level 1: AI-Supported Work'. Here, the role feels supported rather than changed. AI helps with tasks that are easy to generate or retrieve. It proposes drafts, prepares background material and suggests responses. The employee remains at the centre and carries full responsibility, but the shape of daily work begins to shift. The system assists without altering the purpose of the role.

A deeper transition emerges in 'Level 2: AI-Enhanced Work', where the system handles a greater portion of predictable tasks. People begin their day with information the AI has already prepared. They manage exceptions and navigate situations that require emotional or contextual understanding. The job remains, but it functions differently. The role becomes a hybrid of human and system contribution, what can be described as augmented.

Some roles move further into 'Level 3: AI-Driven Work', where AI becomes the primary performer of routine operations. Humans step in when judgement, sensitivity or creative reasoning is required. The role becomes supervisory. Decisions flow through the system. The human monitors performance and intervenes when needed. At this point, the shift is substantial. The design of the job has changed, not just its tasks.

As AI matures, roles may progress into 'Level 4: AI-Orchestrated Work', where systems manage end-to-end workflows. Human involvement becomes selective and focused on governance, assurance or ethical oversight rather than daily execution. People define the principles and boundaries while the system carries out operations. This marks one of the highest levels of impact.

At the outer edge of transformation is 'Level 5: AI-Automated Work', where AI systems operate independently, improve themselves over time and require human input mainly for ethical, strategic or creative direction. Human involvement is no longer tied to execution. It is tied to purpose, values and long-term outcomes.

Together, the levels help organisations determine the degree of change without relying on instinct alone. They clarify whether AI is supporting the work, enhancing it, leading it or driving it. They show when human contribution is still central and when it begins to shift towards guidance and oversight. Most importantly, they give employees a clear sense of where they stand and how their roles may evolve.

A closer look at the call centre example makes this clearer.

The generative AI assistant now handles most routine inquiries. It retrieves information, prepares responses and manages predictable scenarios. The human agent remains essential in situations that require judgement, emotional sensitivity or nuanced interpretation. The work becomes supervised rather than executed fully by the person. With an AI Impact Index of 2.8, the role sits at Level 3: AI-Driven Work, where the shift is substantial, automation takes on a significant share of the work and human oversight remains critical.

The impact levels bring structure to the confusion that often arises when AI begins to change the nature of work. They give leaders an accurate way to describe what they see and offer teams a stable language for comparing roles and functions. At the centre of this approach sits a classification that shows how control, decision-making and execution move between humans and machines. The six levels of AI impact represent distinct points in the evolution of work as AI takes on different responsibilities.

One way to make these levels intuitive is to compare them to how a car becomes more automated with each technological upgrade. Fig. 4 illustrates this progression, showing how control, decision-making and execution gradually shift from humans to machines across the six levels of AI impact.

At the earliest stage, the person drives entirely on their own. Every action is manual. This mirrors work with no meaningful AI involvement, similar to Level 0, where all tasks and decisions remain human only.

The next stage introduces simple assistance. Cruise control keeps the car at a steady pace while direction and judgement stay with the driver. This resembles Level 1, where AI assists straightforward or repetitive tasks without affecting the core flow of work.

A further step adds features such as lane assist or parking sensors. These guide the driver but do not replace them. Responsibility for the journey remains human. This aligns with Level 2, where AI enhances tasks by handling structured activities or providing recommendations while the human directs the work.

Level 0 – AI-Irrelevant

Manual driving – you steer, shift, brake and navigate without any assistance

Level 1 – AI-Supported

Cruise control – car maintains speed, but you control everything else

Level 2 – AI-Enhanced

Lane assist + parking sensors – car warns or guides, but you are driving

Level 3 – AI-Driven

Highway Autopilot – the car drives most of the time, you decide when to engage, exit or intervene

Level 4 – AI-Orchestrated

Full self-driving – the car decides the route and drives end-to-end; you monitor and intervene only if needed

Level 5 – AI-Automated

No steering wheel – car drives and decides direction entirely on its own

Fig. 4. Six Levels of AI Impact (Car Analogy).

Source: Author's Own Creation.

More advanced support arrives with the highway autopilot. The car manages most of the driving under clear conditions, and the driver intervenes only when needed. This reflects Level 3, where AI leads much of the routine work and the human shifts into oversight and exception handling.

At later stages, the person mainly monitors the system as the car navigates on its own. Intervention becomes rare, and the human role moves towards strategic oversight. This corresponds to Level 4, where AI drives entire workflows with limited human direction.

The most advanced stage resembles a vehicle with no steering wheel. The system operates on its own and makes the decisions. The human contributes mainly by defining purpose, boundaries and long-term direction. This matches Level 5, where AI functions fully autonomously, improves itself over time and relies on human input for ethical, strategic or creative guidance rather than operational control.

Together, the levels give organisations a clear and consistent way to understand how AI impacts work. They show how a role moves from being fully human-led, to partially shared, to largely driven by AI system. They help teams recognise which stage they are observing and what each stage requires in terms of design, support and capability.

Once the scale of change is clear, the next question naturally follows. People want to know what the organisation intends to do. Leaders need to understand which choices are appropriate for the level of impact they are seeing. A detailed explanation of the AI Impact Levels that underpin this understanding is included in Appendix 5 for readers who want to explore the full model.

The next section shows what this level of impact means in practice and how organisations should respond.

3. HOW SHOULD WE ACT?

Once the scale of change is clear, the final question becomes unavoidable. People want to understand 'How the organisation will act'. Leaders want to know how to align their actions with the level of impact they have identified. A clear response matters, because uncertainty grows quickly when employees see their work evolving but cannot see how the organisation intends to support them. The human–AI decoder answers this question through the AI impact actions. These actions provide a structured way to move from understanding to execution and allow leaders to act with clarity and responsibility.

The AI impact actions translate the six levels of AI impact into decisions that shape how work evolves. They help leaders redesign roles, support employees, adjust learning priorities and adapt organisational structures. They also provide employees with a clear view of what will happen next and how their contribution continues to matter. Each action reflects responsibilities that emerge as AI becomes more capable and as work moves from human-led to hybrid or AI-led patterns.

Understanding the AI Impact Actions

AI changes work in ways that require a deliberate and coordinated organisational response. As roles shift, leaders need to understand not only what is changing and how significant the change is, but also how the organisation should act. The AI impact actions are part of the human–AI decoder that turns insight into direction. They show how to redesign work, how to support people through transition and how to reshape structures so that humans and intelligent systems can contribute effectively together. Fig. 5 visualises these actions and the role they play in helping leaders move from understanding to action.

The first area of response focuses on 'Workforce Models', which concern how the work itself is organised. As AI becomes part of daily operations, organisations must determine which activities remain in human hands, which move to the system and which require shared execution. At early stages of change, integrating new tools may be enough. As impact deepens, the design of the job

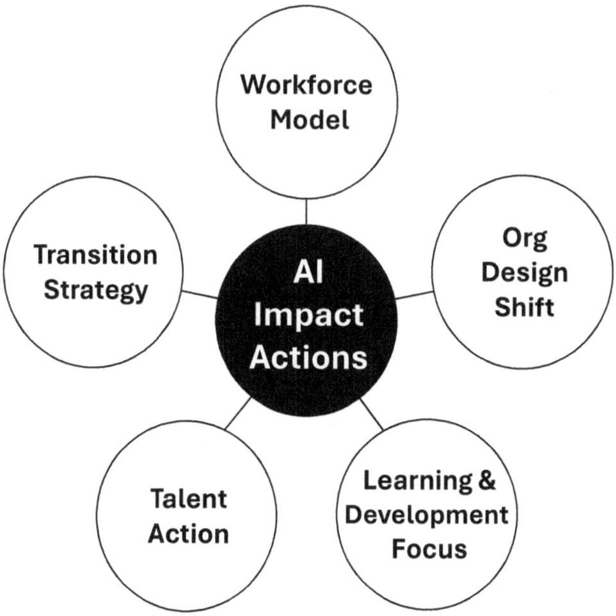

Fig. 5. AI Impact Areas.

Source: Author's Own Creation.

shifts. People move from direct execution towards responsibilities centred on judgement, oversight and guidance. The structure of the work must reflect the scale of the change.

A second area is shaped by 'Transition Strategy', which guides how employees move from the current version of their work to what comes next. Early adjustments may require only light shifts in tools or processes. As AI takes on more responsibility, employees begin to need new capabilities or redefined roles. At more advanced stages, some may transition into adjacent or newly created positions that reflect the organisation's evolving needs. These transitions require thoughtful planning and clear communication so that people understand how to adapt and where they fit.

A third area is defined by 'Talent Action', which focuses on how organisations support people as their roles change with AI. At the early levels, employees remain in place and build the skills needed to work confidently with new tools. As AI takes on more predictable tasks, roles evolve and employees learn to understand system outputs and focus on the higher-value work that remains. At deeper Levels of impact, people shift into oversight roles where they supervise system behaviour, manage exceptions and protect quality. When AI replaces an entire role, Talent Action guides how employees are redeployed or how transitions are handled with respect and clarity. At the highest levels, people move into strategic and ethical roles where they shape how AI is used in the organisation. A responsible approach preserves employability wherever possible and sustains trust as work continues to evolve.

A fourth area is defined by the 'Learning and Development Focus'. AI changes which capabilities matter most. Early in the transition, employees need confidence in working with new tools. As AI becomes more capable, they need skills for interpreting system outputs, resolving exceptions and applying judgement when the system reaches its limits. At advanced stages, learning shifts towards governance, ethical oversight and the ability to ensure that AI operates within organisational expectations. Learning must evolve in step with the work.

The final area concerns 'Organisation Design Shift', which describes how structures evolve as AI alters how work is performed.

Reporting lines, decision rights and governance mechanisms must adapt to match new workflows. Some approval steps disappear as systems handle predictable work. New oversight roles emerge. At higher levels of impact, organisations benefit from governance bodies that monitor AI performance, evaluate risk and ensure accountability. Structural changes must reflect where human involvement remains essential and where the system now carries primary responsibility.

How the AI Impact Actions Unfold Across the Six Levels of AI Impact

As organisations move through the six impact levels, the AI impact actions shift from maintaining continuity to enabling deeper transformation. They follow a predictable pattern as the level of impact increases. Table 6 shows how the response evolves across all six levels of AI impact.

Level 0 reflects work that remains entirely human-led.
Tasks follow familiar routines, and structures stay stable. The workforce model stays as it is, with a focus on building basic digital readiness rather than redesigning work. Talent decisions centre on retention because roles remain intact. Learning emphasises foundational digital skills, and organisations maintain traditional structures while preparing gently for change.

Level 1 introduces the first wave of AI assistance.
AI begins to organise calendars, draft simple text and support daily tasks, increasingly entering white-collar and business functions. The workforce model shifts towards a digitally supported environment, and the transition strategy focuses on introducing early forms of AI augmentation. Roles do not change, so the focus is on retaining and upskilling. People learn how to use AI tools with confidence, and organisations start to automate simple workflows that remove friction.

Level 2 marks a move towards hybrid human–AI work.
AI handles predictable tasks and frees up time for more meaningful work. The workforce model becomes hybrid, and the transition strategy focuses on role evolution. Talent actions emphasise

Table 6. Overview AI Impact Actions by Level of AI Impact.

Level of AI Impact	Workforce Model	Transition Strategy	Talent Action	L&D Focus	Org Design Shift
Level 0	Maintain Traditional Workforce	Build Digital Readiness	Retain	Build Digital Skills	Maintain Traditional Structures
Level 1	Build Digitally Supported Workforce	Introduce AI Augmentation	Retain & Upskill	Learn AI Tools	Automate Basic Workflows
Level 2	Move to Hybrid Workforce	Drive Role Evolution	Reskill within Role	Work Effectively with AI	Redefine Roles
Level 3	Adopt a Supervisory Workforce Model	Integrate AI into Workforce	Transition & Reskill	Oversee AI Systems	Streamline Structures
Level 4	Establish Governance Workforce	Strengthen AI Governance & Oversight	Redeploy or Phase Out	Manage AI Responsibly	Establish Governance Bodies
Level 5	Develop Meta-Human Workforce	Lead Ethically & Strategically with AI	Reposition	Guide AI Purposefully	Rebuild Around AI-First Models

Source: Author's own creation.

reskilling so people can understand AI outputs, handle ambiguity and apply judgement. Learning priorities shift towards working effectively with AI, and teams begin rethinking how tasks are shared. Organisation design starts to adjust as roles blend human strengths with system-driven efficiency.

Level 3 represents a clear shift towards AI-driven execution.
AI takes on most operational work, and human contribution moves into oversight, orchestration and exception handling. The workforce model becomes supervisory, with the transition strategy centred on integrating AI into day-to-day operations. Talent actions focus on reskilling into oversight and quality assurance roles. Learning shifts from performing the work to supervising the system that performs it. Organisation structures begin to streamline as responsibilities migrate from doing the work to governing it.

Level 4 signals AI-orchestrated processes.
AI manages entire workflows from start to finish. Traditional roles may disappear or merge into governance and assurance functions. The workforce model becomes governance-oriented, and the transition strategy focuses on strengthening oversight. Talent actions often involve redeployment or responsible role phase-out when tasks no longer require human execution. Learning shifts towards responsible AI management, fairness and accountability. Organisations begin establishing governance bodies and introducing roles dedicated to compliance, trust and algorithmic risk.

Level 5 sits at the highest point of the model, where AI operates independently.
Human contribution concentrates on ethical, strategic and creative leadership. The workforce model becomes meta-human, with work centred on guiding purpose, values and intent rather than executing tasks. The transition strategy shifts towards leading ethically in AI-first environments. Talent actions involve repositioning people into roles that shape organisational direction and long-term principles. Learning focuses on steering AI purposefully. Organisation design evolves towards AI-first structures supported by teams responsible for maintaining cultural integrity and ethical alignment.

Together, the AI impact actions create a structured and humane pathway for workforce evolution.

They help organisations respond proportionately to the degree of change: preserving stability where AI's impact is light, redesigning roles and skills as the impact grows and embedding governance and leadership when AI becomes the dominant driver of work. Across all six levels, a consistent pattern emerges. As AI expands its capability, work moves from execution to interpretation, from interpretation to supervision and from supervision to strategic leadership.

The goal is not automation for its own sake. It is to guide people through these shifts with clarity, fairness and care. As organisations use the human–AI decoder across teams and functions, the accumulated evidence will refine these levels further and keep the framework relevant as the nature of work continues to evolve.

Recent research on human–AI teams shows that clearly defined roles, transparent oversight boundaries and well-designed collaboration protocols are essential for building trust and preventing confusion (Hemmer et al., 2025). These Actions help make that possible. They give organisations a predictable and people-centred way to understand what is changing, how extensive the change is and what support employees will need as their roles evolve.

The call centre offers a clear view of how the AI impact actions guide the shift from human-led work to human–AI collaboration.

As the generative AI assistant is introduced, the change is visible almost immediately. Routine customer questions, once handled entirely by the call center agent, are now resolved by the system in real time. The assistant retrieves information, drafts responses and prepares summaries. What looks at first like a simple efficiency gain soon reveals a deeper shift in how the work itself is structured.

The first sign of this shift appears in how 'Workforce Models' evolve. The centre can no longer rely on the traditional structure in which agents handle every question end-to-end. As AI becomes more capable, the role changes. The system manages predictable conversations, while humans focus on the moments that require judgement, empathy or creative problem-solving. The model moves from pure human execution to a hybrid pattern in which the system takes the lead on volume and humans ensure quality and trust.

As the work changes, leaders should guide people through the transition. This is where 'Transition Strategy' becomes essential. Agents cannot be left to navigate these shifts on their own. They need clarity about how their responsibilities are evolving, what is expected in the new environment and when they remain essential. They also need support in building confidence with the system. When the transition is thoughtfully managed, employees understand where they fit and how to grow.

The introduction of AI also forces clear decisions about talent in the call centre. 'Talent Action' becomes essential as routine enquiries are handled by the system and human work shifts towards judgement, empathy and exception management. At the early stages, agents stay in their roles and learn to use AI-generated drafts, suggestions and summaries. As AI begins to resolve predictable cases on its own, some agents are reskilled to take on the more complex conversations that require context and emotional nuance. Others move into oversight roles where they monitor AI responses, guide escalations and ensure that the system behaves in line with service standards. A smaller group may transition into areas such as service quality, trust monitoring or AI performance review when frontline volume declines. Each of these decisions must be handled with clarity and care so that employees see a future for themselves as the environment changes.

As these shifts take place, learning must keep pace. The 'Learning and Development Focus' begins with digital readiness. Agents learn how the system works and how to collaborate with it. As the role evolves, learning expands towards skills in exception handling, judgement and ethical oversight. In later stages, the focus moves towards governance, bias detection and the ability to ensure that automated responses remain aligned with organisational expectations. This progression allows employees to stay effective and confident as the work transforms.

Finally, the change in workflow requires the organisation itself to adapt. The 'Organisation Design Shift' becomes visible when the call centre can no longer operate with the same layers of supervision or the same division of responsibilities. Some approval steps disappear because the system handles predictable work. New oversight roles emerge to monitor AI performance, ensure fairness and manage high-stakes customer interactions. At higher levels of AI maturity, the centre builds formal governance around system behaviour, allowing humans to guide purpose, standards and boundaries while the AI manages execution.

Taken together, these AI impact actions show how a single role can be redefined without losing its human core. The call centre does not eliminate work. It redistributes it. AI manages routine interactions and scale. Humans focus on empathy, complexity and judgement. With the right actions in place, the centre becomes faster, more reliable and more supportive of its people. It demonstrates how an organisation can guide transformation rather than simply react to it. A fuller explanation of the AI impact actions and how they support the model can be found in Appendix 6.

A People-Centred View of the AI Impact Actions

AI may change systems and structures, but employees feel the shift long before charts or score ranges appear in a slide deck. They notice when familiar tasks begin to move faster, when routines quieten, when tools start to anticipate what they need. The human–AI decoder was created to make these moments understandable. It gives organisations a way to interpret the early signals of change and turn them into actions people can trust.

For employees, learning is often the first sign that the organisation intends to invest in their future. It tells them they will not be replaced without warning or expected to catch up on their own. When learning is continuous and built into daily work, it reassures people that they can grow with the change. It restores a sense of momentum at a time when work may feel unfamiliar.

Talent decisions shape the emotional core of any transformation. Employees want to know that their roles are not being redefined in the dark. They want to understand what will happen if their tasks shift or if automation reaches deeper into their daily routines. When reskilling, redeployment or transitions are handled with honesty and clarity, employees see that the organisation takes their future seriously. Trust is built in these moments, not through grand statements, but through the fairness of each decision.

Workforce models influence the experience people live every day. They determine how teams collaborate, how responsibility is shared and how much agency employees retain in a changing environment. When organisations explain these models clearly, employees understand how AI fits into their work and where their strengths continue to matter. It reduces fears of replacement and replaces them with a grounded sense of contribution.

A thoughtful transition strategy helps employees make sense of the journey. Uncertainty grows when communication is vague or when decisions arrive without explanation. Employees need to hear what the change means, why it is happening and how they will be supported along the way. When leaders take the time to explain the path forward, employees stay engaged even when the pace of change accelerates.

The final piece is the organisation design shift. Structural changes often feel distant until they touch daily workflows, reporting lines or expectations. Employees want to understand the purpose behind these adjustments. When organisations explain how new structures protect fairness, accountability and human judgement, people see that these shifts are not about removing humans, but about creating the conditions for them to thrive in an AI-enabled environment.

Taken together, a people-centred view of the AI impact actions reinforces the purpose of the human–AI decoder. It ensures that the transformation is not happening around employees but with them. It brings clarity, dignity and a sense of place within the future that is being built. And it keeps people at the centre of every decision as work continues to evolve.

CONSIDERING THE INFLUENCING FACTORS

In addition to the AI impact actions, the model includes a set of influencing factors that help organisations interpret the impact of AI and shape their response with more nuance. These factors guide leaders in refining decisions based on elements such as scale, readiness and risk. They make it possible to tailor the response to the

Table 7. Influencing Factors.

Factors	What It Measures	Why It Matters	How to Use It	Human–AI Decoder Link
Headcount Exposure	Number of employees in the impacted role(s)	High scale means high disruption potential or ROI	Prioritise roles with both high AIWIM scores and large headcounts	Combine scores to build Impact × Scale heatmaps
Skill Transferability	Ease of moving existing skills to new roles	Low transferability increases transition cost and effort	Identify roles that need intensive reskilling or redesign	Supports Talent Action for lower skill reuse to redesign or phase out
Time to Reskill	Effort and duration to prepare for a new role	Affects viability, sequencing and cost of transformation	Feed into reskilling timelines and workforce planning	Guides Transition Strategy redeployment priority when combined with high impact levels
Employee Readiness	Confidence and mindset towards AI adoption	Determines ease of change and risk of resistance	Use insights to guide communication and change plans	Act as a modifier for roles with mid-range impact scores (1–3)
Organisational Dependency	Degree to which role/process is business-critical	Some high-impact roles cannot be replaced easily due to operational reliance	Flag these for staged implementation, controls or fallback layers	Align Workforce Model to inform rollout pacing and governance
Ethical Intelligence	Ethical, transparent and socially responsible operation of AI-enabled roles	Promotes fairness, accountability and alignment with organisational values	Flag roles or systems with ethical or reputational risk for added oversight and governance	Tie to decision-making and workforce value to uphold trust, integrity and responsible AI

Source: Author's own creation.

organisation's context and ensure that change remains both effective and humane.

The influencing factors include headcount exposure, skill transferability, time to reskill, employee readiness, organisational dependency and ethical intelligence. Each one offers insight that helps leaders refine priorities, allocate resources and manage transformation risk. Table 7 brings these factors together, offering a clear view of the conditions that amplify or moderate AI's impact.

These factors do not replace the AI impact actions. They enhance them to help organisations calibrate decisions so that workforce strategies remain aligned with values, expectations and operational realities.

⚒ ***Influencing Factors Check*** *(included in Appendix 4) is a practical tool that works alongside the human–AI decoder to refine workforce planning and talent decisions. While the decoder identifies how deeply a role is affected by AI, the influencing factors provide the context needed to interpret that impact with nuance. These factors act as 'reality checks', enabling leaders to adjust for scale, risk and human factors before finalising workforce strategies.*

With the AI impact actions and influencing factors in place, the human–AI decoder brings the three guiding questions together into a clear and complete picture. The organisation can now see what is changing inside the work, understand the scale of that change and identify the steps needed to support employees and redesign work responsibly.

These recommendations provide a high-level guide for aligning AI's workforce impact with thoughtful, human-centred action. They help leaders connect diagnosis with execution so responses are proactive, consistent and grounded in a simple and adaptable model. Each path reflects the level of disruption the workforce is experiencing, while still allowing room to account for an organisation's unique context, culture and readiness.

At its core, the human–AI decoder provides a structure for navigating complex change while keeping people at the centre. It is broad enough to support enterprise-wide transformation and flexible enough to apply to a single role. The most effective approach is to start where the impact is most visible and build from there, using the decoder to connect insight and action one role, one use case and one decision at a time.

MAKING SENSE OF THE AI IMPACT

By this point in the human–AI decoder, the organisation has moved through the three questions that matter most. It has seen how AI is changing the work itself, understood the scale of those changes and identified how to respond.

How is AI changing work?
The AI impact scan shows what is shifting inside the work.
How big is the change?
The six levels of AI impact reveal how big the shift is.
How should we act?
The AI impact actions guide what leaders should do next, with influencing factors fine-tuning the response to real-world context.

Together, these steps give organisations a simple, human-centred way to understand and lead AI-driven change. The decoder turns scattered signals into a clear picture, helping leaders act with confidence and helping people understand what the future means for their roles.

AI will keep evolving, and these same questions will return with every new tool or use case. The human-AI decoder provides a structured way to revisit the three guiding questions that matter most, helping organisations move from uncertainty to clarity and from reaction to preparation.

The next chapter brings the decoder to life, applying it to real roles and using it as a practical playbook for navigating workforce change.

Key Takeaways

- Leaders and employees feel the impact of AI early, often before anyone can describe what is changing.

- The human–AI decoder provides a clear method for understanding how work evolves with AI.
- The first question asks 'How AI is changing the work' itself, focusing attention on what people experience every day.
- The second question asks 'How big is the impact' using the six levels of AI impact to classify the scale of change.
- The third question asks 'How the organisation should act' and is answered through the AI impact actions and influencing factors.
- The human–AI decoder is based on the AI Workforce Impact Model, described in Appendix 3.
- The AI impact areas reveal how tasks, responsibilities, skills, decisions and human contribution begin to shift.
- The six levels of AI Impact give teams a shared language for interpreting change and aligning decisions.
- The AI impact actions explain how to redesign work, support people, adapt learning and organisational structure.
- The decoder creates a repeatable loop that helps organisations respond to AI-driven change with clarity, responsibility and confidence.

5

THE SIX LEVELS OF AI IMPACT

ABSTRACT

Artificial Intelligence (AI) is entering the workforce in uneven, often unpredictable ways. Leaders see signs of change, yet many struggle to understand what those changes mean for people, roles and organisational design. This chapter introduces the human–AI decoder as a practical playbook for translating early disruption into clear, human-centred decisions. It shows how the decoder works across six levels of AI impact, ranging from fully human work to roles now shaped by near or full autonomy. Through examples drawn from coaching, HR operations, underwriting, clinical diagnostics, legal services and multilingual communication, the chapter illustrates how tasks, skills, decision-making and human value evolve as AI moves deeper into the workflow. The six levels provide a consistent language for describing how work is changing and for comparing patterns across roles, functions and industries. They reveal the tipping points where AI shifts from assisting tasks to orchestrating and ultimately performing the work independently. The chapter explains why Levels 3, 4 and 5 require particular attention, as these are the points where work design, capability building and ethical oversight must accelerate. Rather than treating AI as a technology rollout, the decoder reframes it as a workforce design opportunity. It helps leaders see where AI genuinely adds value, where work must be redesigned, and where guardrails or new human capabilities are needed. By following the decoder's three guiding questions, leaders can move from uncertainty to intention, ensuring that AI strengthens the workforce instead of sidelining it.

Keywords: Human–AI decoder; AI workforce impact; autonomy levels; workforce transformation; AI-driven work; AI-orchestrated work; responsible AI; reskilling; job redesign; human–machine collaboration

A casual conversation with a Regional CEO revealed how unprepared many leaders feel about AI's impact on the workforce. When I told him I was writing a book about AI and explained what it was about, the discussion shifted. The instant he heard it focused on the human–AI decoder, he leaned forward. His focus sharpened. 'That is exactly what we need', he said:

> **'We have fifteen thousand employees and do not yet share a way to make sense of the impact. A common language is needed to describe what is changing. Could you run a session for our regional leadership team in Singapore?'**

His reaction showed something deeper than curiosity. It revealed the gap many leaders feel but rarely admit. Leaders see AI everywhere. What they struggle with is making sense of what that presence actually means. The need is not to describe what AI can do, but to translate its impact into decisions people can trust and act on.

This chapter uses the human–AI decoder as a playbook to meet that need. It shows how the decoder works when applied to real examples across the six levels of AI impact. Each example reveals a different pattern of change, from roles that remain fully human to those moving towards greater autonomy. Together, they demonstrate how leaders can recognise how AI is changing work, understand the depth of that change and respond with intention rather than uncertainty.

Chapter 4 introduced the human–AI decoder as a structured way to understand how AI reshapes work. It explained how the decoder helps leaders examine where AI is touching work, how deep that influence runs and what it means for the people who experience it. That chapter showed how the decoder operates through a single example. This chapter builds on that foundation and shows what happens when it is applied across many different roles, industries and functions.

Each example in this chapter illustrates one of the six levels of AI impact. These levels give leaders a clear and consistent way to describe how work is changing, compare patterns across different roles and functions and understand the type of transformation taking place. They turn broad, often confusing shifts into something leaders can see, name and act on. They make AI's impact measurable and comparable, whether the change is light augmentation or a move towards greater autonomy.

The human–AI decoder builds on this structure by reframing AI not as a technology rollout but as a workforce design opportunity. It helps leaders see where AI genuinely adds value and where it reshapes roles. It also shows where new skills, guardrails or ways of working between people and intelligent systems are required. The combination of the human–AI decoder and the six levels of AI impact gives organisations a practical and reliable foundation for making informed decisions with the AI impact actions about how work should evolve.

The decoder moves through a simple progression that leaders can recognise and apply:

1. **How is AI changing work?**
   → Run the AI impact scan
2. **How big is the impact?**
   → Map to the six levels of AI impact
3. **How do we act?**
   → Set the AI impact actions

These guiding questions turn broad disruption into clear, human-centred choices. They help leaders move from noticing change to understanding it, and from understanding to acting with purpose. They show that the human–AI decoder is not only a way to classify AI's impact but a way to design responses that strengthen culture, capability and trust. The influencing factors are not reviewed in the examples, because they are organisation-specific and depend on each company's unique context, risks and readiness.

✗ ***Human–AI Decoder Playbook*** *(included in Appendix 5) offers leaders and teams a straightforward way to see how AI is changing a role and what to do in response. The examples in this chapter were created using this playbook, which can be applied individually or used in workshops to guide discussion, alignment and practical decision-making.*

HUMAN–AI DECODER IN ACTION

The six examples that follow show how the human–AI decoder applies across different industries and functions, tracing the progression from human-led to fully autonomous work.

Each example highlights how AI reshapes tasks, decision-making and human value along the six levels of AI impact:

Level 0 – AI-Irrelevant Work: 'Executive Coach' – a profession defined by empathy, trust and human presence, where AI has little or no role in the core interaction.

Level 1 – AI-Supported Work: 'HR Administrator' – supported by chatbots and workflow tools that automate routine queries while humans handle sensitive issues and decisions.

Level 2 – AI-Enhanced Work: 'Insurance Underwriter' – working alongside AI systems that analyse data and assess risk, freeing professionals to focus on complex judgement calls.

Level 3 – AI-Led Work: 'Healthcare Diagnostic Specialist' – where AI leads image analysis and diagnostics, and clinicians validate results and ensure ethical integrity.

Level 4 – AI-Orchestrated Work: 'Contract Analyst' – overseeing governance, compliance and risk as AI platforms autonomously review, approve and manage contracts.

Level 5 – AI-Automated Work: 'Translators and Interpreters' – a field transformed by generative AI, where language translation and interpretation are performed almost entirely by intelligent systems.

Together, these use cases trace the full spectrum of workforce transformation under AI from work that remains inherently human to roles now redefined by full automation.

An interesting pattern emerged during early research and stress-testing of the human-AI decoder.

Most roles impacted by AI were clustered at Levels 2 and 3, revealing where many organisations find themselves today on the AI Impact Level Curve, which will be further explored later in this chapter. These middle levels represent the current AI frontier, where work is shifting from simple assistance to meaningful augmentation and early forms of autonomy. Levels 4 and 5, while less common now, point to what is coming next and are likely to expand as capability advances.

The first use case guides the reader through the human–AI decoder step by step to build familiarity with its structure. The scenarios that follow use the same playbook outlined in Appendix 5. They may feel familiar at times and that is intentional. The consistency shows how easily the decoder can be applied to any role once the pattern is understood. The chapter closes with the AI Impact Level Curve, which brings these examples together and shows where the most significant shifts in work tend to occur across the six levels of AI impact.

EXECUTIVE COACH (LEVEL 0 – AI-IRRELEVANT WORK)

The first scenario applies the human–AI decoder to an Executive Coach, a role that sits at Level 0 and remains entirely human-led. This example shows how the decoder works when AI has little or no influence on the work itself. It also demonstrates the starting point of the model before any automation, augmentation or workflow change begins.

1. How Is AI Changing the Work?

Running the AI Impact Scan

The human–AI decoder always begins with a simple guiding question: How is AI changing the work?

The clearest way to answer it is to look directly at the role as it is performed.

Picture a coaching session. A client leans forward, searching for the right words. The coach waits, giving space for whatever comes next. No prompts appear. No automated voice chimes in. The work unfolds in small moments that rely entirely on human presence and emotional understanding.

Around the edges of the session, AI lends a quiet hand. A transcription tool captures the conversation. A summariser helps record key themes and actions. A digital assistant schedules the next meeting or sends the follow-up notes. The tools are present, yet they never enter the dialogue.

This leads to the real question: 'How much is AI actually touching the role, and does the Executive Coach need to change because of it?' The tools support the flow of work, but they do not guide it, reshape it or influence the relationship between coach and client.

This is where the AI impact scan becomes useful. It gives a structured way to answer the question. It does not focus on what AI might do one day but looks at what AI is doing in the role today. By moving through the scan questions AI impact areas, leaders can see the full picture and judge how much, if at all, AI is transforming the work.

Automation

The first area we examine is 'Automation'. AI is present, but only in the background. A digital assistant sets up the meeting. A transcription tool captures the conversation. A summariser helps record key themes, actions and reflections. These systems support the work, but they do not enter the dialogue. They do not question, reflect or sense emotion.

Score: 1 – Minor Impact. AI supports small or repetitive tasks.

Role

The next question is the 'Role' itself. Has the purpose of coaching changed. It has not. Coaches still create psychological safety, ask difficult questions, hold silence, reframe thinking and interpret subtle non-verbal cues. AI has not touched any of that.

Score: 0 – No Impact. Role remains the same.

Skills

Next come 'Skills'. The skills that matter most are the same ones that have always mattered: empathy, listening, intuition and timing. A coach may use a digital tool to simplify notes, but nothing about the craft requires new AI capability.

Score: 0 – No Impact. No new skills needed.

Decision Making

'Now Decision-Making' follows. In a coaching session, every choice comes from the coach. Which question to ask. Whether to challenge or invite. Whether to pause or redirect. AI does not whisper suggestions or propose options.

Score: 0 – No Impact. Humans make all decisions.

Workforce Value

Finally, we look at 'Workforce Value'. This is where the truth becomes unmistakable. Clients do not work with coaches for efficiency. They work with them for connection, insight and trust. These qualities cannot be replicated by a system. The entire value of the interaction remains human.

Score: 0 – No Impact. Human value remains unchanged.

When each Area is evaluated, the scores fall into a simple pattern: 1, 0, 0, 0, 0. Together they total 1. Dividing that number by 5, the number of AI Impact Areas, produces an AI Impact Index of 0.2. The calculation confirms what we had already assumed, only now in a clear and structured way. AI supports the administrative and organisational tasks around the session, but the centre of the work, the part that depends on human presence, understanding and connection, remains fully and unmistakably human.

2. How Big Is the Impact?

Mapping to the Six Levels of AI Impact

With the scan complete, the decoder asks its second question: How big is the change?

For the Executive Coach, the AI Impact Index sits at 0.2. When mapped against the decoder's impact level ranges, Level 0 covers scores from 0.0 to 0.5. The comparison is immediate. A score of 0.2 falls comfortably inside this band, placing the Executive Coach in Level 0 - AI-Irrelevant Work.

This classification matters because it separates roles that are being reshaped by AI from those that remain rooted in human capability. Level 0 represents work grounded in qualities that technology cannot replicate. It confirms that AI is not entering the core of the craft and that coaching depends on something that cannot be automated at this moment in time.

In this case, the Executive Coach reflects this baseline state. The integrity and value of the role rest on uniquely human skills, not on technical substitution. While peripheral AI tools may add convenience, the essence of coaching remains untouched. The work is still defined by human connection, and no system can replace that yet.

The levels give leaders a precise way to speak about this. Instead of saying, 'AI does not affect coaching', they can say, 'Coaching is a Level 0 role. AI sits only at the administrative edges.' That clarity prevents overreaction and protects what should remain human.

3. How should we act?

Setting the AI Impact Actions

Once the level is clear, the final question becomes practical: How should the organisation act?

The AI impact actions for Level 0 clarify if the role is being transformed at all and show how to respond when the answer is no. They reveal where AI has influence and where the work remains entirely human.

Workforce Models

In this context, the coaching role sits in a traditional human-only model. AI plays no part in delivering outcomes. That absence is not a limitation. It is an accurate reflection of how the work creates value.

Transition Strategy

No formal transition is required. Digital readiness is enough. Tools like secure video platforms, digital journaling spaces or AI-assisted transcription can support convenience, but they do not replace the core interaction. They widen access and efficiency without touching the heart of the practice.

Talent Action

The appropriate talent action is retention. The role remains fully intact, and employees continue performing the work as they always have. Development follows existing pathways, with no new skill requirements introduced by AI. Coaching continues to rely entirely on human presence and judgement.

Learning and Development Focus

Learning should focus on building digital skills that support, not substitute, the work. Coaches can strengthen their awareness of how technology shapes confidentiality, presence and connection in digital environments. The aim is to use technology to enhance the relationship, not recreate it.

Organisation Design Shift

No structural redesign is necessary. The coaching role can continue as it is while becoming more connected to leadership, wellbeing and cultural development strategies. Integrating coaching into these areas reinforces its human-centred contribution.

Strategic Summary

The Executive Coach represents a form of work built on empathy, trust and understanding. These qualities define its value and remain beyond the reach of AI. Digital tools may simplify administration, but they cannot reproduce the authenticity of conversation or the insight that emerges only through human connection.

At the same time, the landscape is beginning to shift. New AI-powered coaching platforms are emerging, including tools such as Coachvox AI (2025), which can simulate elements of coaching dialogue and reflective interaction to support leadership and personal development. These systems are becoming increasingly capable and will continue to evolve, gradually entering parts of the coaching ecosystem and adjacent people-focused roles. Their emergence signals that even deeply human professions may not remain untouched forever. Some tasks may eventually be supported or augmented by intelligent assistants that help with preparation, structure or follow-up.

This is where the human–AI decoder becomes essential. It provides a structured way for people and organisations to build awareness and foresight, helping them see which parts of the role can be supported by digital tools and which parts must remain human to preserve integrity and meaning. It guides leaders to understand where AI genuinely adds value and where the work depends on qualities that cannot be automated.

Level 0- AI-Irrelevant confirms that some roles continue to rely entirely on human judgement, emotion and presence. The strategic priority is not automation. It is amplification. Use technology to extend reach and reduce friction, but preserve the deep human essence that defines coaching excellence. The human–AI decoder gives leaders the clarity to reach that conclusion with confidence rather than assumption. It shows that responding to AI does not always mean redesigning the work. Sometimes it means acknowledging what only people can do while preparing thoughtfully for what may come next.

HR ADMINISTRATOR (LEVEL 1 – AI-SUPPORTED WORK)

1. How Is AI Changing the Work?

Running the AI Impact Scan

Imagine an employee reaching out with a simple question.

An employee logs into the HR portal late at night, unsure about leave entitlements or benefits eligibility. Instead of waiting for office hours, a virtual assistant appears with an instant response. A chatbot explains policy basics, confirms rules and offers links to the right resources. The query is resolved in seconds, long before a human ever needs to step in.

The HR Administrator sees these exchanges happening in the background. AI is now the first voice employees hear for predictable questions. Chatbots answer common enquiries. Self-service tools guide people through straightforward tasks. Automated workflows trigger confirmations and route requests. Yet the moment a question becomes emotional, sensitive or ambiguous, the HR Administrator steps in to provide judgement, fairness and context.

Seeing this, the key question becomes clear. How much is AI actually touching the role, and does the HR Administrator need to adapt because of it. To answer that, we turn to the AI impact scan, which shows the true extent of AI's influence and reveals how much of the work is changing and how much remains human.

The first area we examine is 'Automation'. AI handles predictable and repetitive tasks such as answering standard queries and routing simple requests. It reduces administrative load, but does not touch judgement or discretion.

Score: 1 – Minor Impact. AI supports small or repetitive tasks

The next question is the 'Role' itself. The purpose remains unchanged. The administrator still manages employee needs, ensures compliance and provides support. The only shift is in workload distribution. AI takes the simple tasks so HR can focus on interactions that require interpretation and empathy.

Score: 1 – Minor Impact. Tasks are improved or supported by AI, but role remains the same.

'Skills' come next. Basic digital fluency is helpful. Administrators benefit from training in monitoring chatbots, validating data and understanding automated workflows. Yet the core skills of empathy, communication and fairness remain unchanged.

Score: 1 – Minor Impact. Basic digital or AI skills required.

'Decision-Making' follows. Humans decide every meaningful outcome. They interpret policy nuances, manage exceptions and handle emotionally charged situations. AI provides information but does not decide.

Score: 1 – Minor Impact. AI provides suggestions and humans make final decisions.

Finally, we look at 'Workforce Value'. AI improves speed, but human value still comes from fairness, trust and emotional understanding. Employees turn to HR Administrators when they need support, care or thoughtful guidance. AI cannot provide that.

Score: 1 – Minor Impact. Human value increases through productivity gains.

The pattern is clear: 1, 1, 1, 1, 1. The total is 5. Dividing by 5 yields an AI Impact Index of 1.0. AI assists with routine tasks, but the heart of the role still relies on human judgement, clarity and care.

2. How Big Is the Impact?

Mapping to the Six Levels of AI Impact

With the scan complete, the decoder asks its second question: How big is the change?

An AI Impact Index of 1.0 places the HR Administrator within Level 1: AI-Supported Work. Level 1 covers AI Impact Index from 0.6 to 1.5, confirming that AI supports the work by improving efficiency in repetitive areas while leaving control and ownership with people.

This classification matters because it distinguishes between roles that are beginning to benefit from automation and those that are being structurally reshaped. In Level 1 roles, technology acts as a helpful assistant. It increases speed and accessibility, but it does not alter the nature of the craft. The HR Administrator continues to guide employees, resolve exceptions and interpret policy with fairness and sensitivity.

This clarity helps leaders avoid overstating the shift. Instead of saying, 'AI is changing HR', they can say, 'HR Service is moving into Level 1. AI covers routine questions. Humans handle what matters most.'

3. How Should We Act?

Setting the AI Impact Actions

The AI impact actions for Level 1 reveal how to support the role as AI becomes a helpful extension rather than a threat. They clarify what should evolve and what should remain human.

In a Level 1 role, everything begins with the idea of 'Workforce Models', because this is where the shape of the work becomes visible. For the HR Administrator, the model shifts into a digitally supported one. AI handles the predictable questions and the simple workflows, answering what can be standardised and routing what can be automated. The human role does not diminish. It becomes more focused. Administrators remain responsible for interpretation, fairness and the relational moments that shape the employee experience. Technology lightens the load. People carry the meaning.

From there, the next consideration is the 'Transition Strategy', and here the tone matters as much as the tools. The move into AI augmentation works best when it is gradual and transparent. Chatbots should be introduced as helpful assistants that improve access, not as quiet replacements for human interaction. Employees need to know when they are speaking with a system and when they can reach a person who will listen, interpret and care. Clear pathways preserve trust as automation grows around the edges of HR work.

Attention then turns to Talent Action, because Level 1 work is not about redesigning roles but about strengthening them. Retention remains the priority. HR Administrators continue to be essential and the focus shifts to development rather than replacement. Digital upskilling in areas such as system navigation, data accuracy and simple AI-supported tasks helps them work more efficiently. As administrators become more comfortable with these tools, they improve the quality and speed of their work while maintaining full responsibility for decisions and service delivery.

Effective adoption also depends on the 'Learning and Development Focus'. Learning becomes the bridge between technology and human connection. Targeted training helps administrators use AI tools effectively while preserving the qualities employees rely on most. Empathy, consistency and fairness matter even more as digital systems take on routine tasks. Teaching HR teams to balance speed with care reinforces trust in both the technology and the people behind it.

Finally, there is the Organisation Design Shift, which at Level 1 requires only subtle adjustments. The simplest and most effective change is to automate basic workflows so that routine queries move through AI tools and HR teams can focus on the work that needs thought, conversation and context. Case-by-case support, conflict resolution and fostering a healthy workplace culture remain firmly with humans, where they belong. Keeping human oversight visible ensures that credibility does not erode as automation becomes more common.

Strategic Summary

The HR Administrator is an example of work that becomes stronger through AI assistance without losing its human core. Productivity rises, but the role remains people-centred. Employees still rely on HR for reassurance, guidance and fairness. The strategic priority is to build digital confidence and strengthen the partnership between humans and AI so that automation amplifies, rather than diminishes, human connection in the employee experience.

At the same time, new AI capabilities are emerging in HR. Virtual assistants are improving. Predictive analytics are beginning to shape workforce insights. These developments signal that Level 1 roles will continue to evolve. Some tasks may eventually move into deeper automation. Others will remain human because they depend on discretion, empathy or emotional context. For the HR Administrator, this means that the initial AI use case is only part of the story. Additional AI tools may begin influencing different tasks across the role, from case management to employee sentiment analysis or even basic policy interpretation. Each new use case should be assessed with the AI impact scan, one AI impact area at a time. The combined scores give a clearer picture of the overall impact on the role. It is this total impact, not any single tool, that determines which AI impact actions are appropriate and how the role should evolve over time.

This is where the human–AI decoder becomes essential. It gives leaders a structured way to track these shifts and understand which parts of the work can be supported by technology and which must remain human. It helps organisations prepare for what is coming without undermining what still needs people.

Level 1 - AI-Supported confirms that AI is present, but human connection continues to define outcomes. The goal is not to redesign the role. It is to elevate it. Strengthen human capability, build digital awareness and ensure that technology supports the work rather than reshaping its purpose.

INSURANCE UNDERWRITER – LEVEL 2: AI-ENHANCED WORK

1. How Is AI Changing the Work?

Running the AI Impact Scan

Imagine the start of an underwriting day.

A new customer file arrives, yet the underwriter does not begin with a blank screen. Instead, an AI system has already scanned the documents, extracted relevant details, checked for inconsistencies and produced a preliminary risk score. Patterns that once required hours of manual review are now surfaced instantly. The underwriter reads the output, pauses and begins to work. The human role has not disappeared. It has shifted.

AI is now woven into the first steps of underwriting. It processes large volumes of applications, identifies anomalies and highlights unusual patterns. It provides predictive indicators that sharpen attention and speed up early assessment. When a case becomes unusual, ambiguous or sensitive, the underwriter steps in. Judgement, context and ethical reasoning remain firmly in human hands.

Seeing this, the key question becomes clear. How much is AI actually changing the work and what does that mean for the future of underwriting. To answer that, we turn to the AI impact scan, which shows the true extent of AI's influence and reveals how much of the work is changing and how much remains human.

The first area we examine is 'Automation'. AI now handles early-stage processing such as document review, data ingestion and risk flagging. It reduces manual effort and increases throughput, but it does not take responsibility for the final decision.

Score: 2 – Moderate Impact. AI completes routine tasks and humans review.

The next question is the 'Role' itself. The purpose of underwriting remains the same, yet daily tasks have shifted. Manual data handling has faded. Interpreting AI outputs, validating model recommendations and resolving exceptions have become central to the role.

Score: 2 – Moderate Impact. AI causes expansion or shift in duties; role continues largely as before but includes new responsibilities.

'Skills' come next. Underwriters now require data literacy, statistical reasoning and the ability to read AI-enabled tools with confidence. Skills in ethical evaluation and model interpretation complement traditional expertise in risk and judgement.

Score: 3 – High Impact. Significant reskilling for new tools or roles required.

'Decision-Making' follows. AI influences early assessment but does not decide. Humans exercise authority, interpret context and manage exceptions. AI shapes what is seen first, but humans control the outcome.

Score: 2 – Moderate Impact. AI recommends while humans review and approve.

Finally, we look at 'Workforce Value'. The contribution of the underwriter has shifted from manual processing to higher-order reasoning, contextual interpretation and relationship management. Clients and regulators continue to depend on human judgement, not machine output.

Score: 2 – Moderate Impact. Human value shifts towards creativity, judgement or oversight.

The pattern is clear: 2, 2, 3, 2, 2. Together they total 11. Dividing by 5 produces an AI Impact Index of 2.2. AI enhances efficiency and depth of analysis, but the core responsibility still rests with human expertise, ethical discernment and contextual understanding.

2. How Big Is the Impact?

Mapping to the Six Levels of AI Impact

An AI Impact Index of 2.2 places the Insurance Underwriter in Level 2: AI-Enhanced Work. Level 2 spans AI Impact Index from 1.6 to 2.5, confirming that AI handles structured tasks and supports complex analysis while humans remain responsible for interpretation and decision-making.

This classification matters because it marks a turning point. AI is no longer just a convenience tool. It has become a cognitive assistant capable of shaping the early direction of the work. The underwriter operates within a hybrid environment where human judgement and AI precision combine to produce better insight, accuracy and consistency. Human contribution now lies in contextual reasoning, ethical oversight and the nuanced understanding of cases that do not fit expected patterns.

This clarity helps leaders avoid overreacting or underreacting. Instead of saying, 'AI is taking over underwriting', they can say, 'Underwriting is moving into Level 2. AI informs the work. Humans define it.'

3. How Should We Act?

Setting the AI Impact Actions

For a Level 2 role, the strategic objective is to strengthen human–AI collaboration while maintaining accountability and trust in decision outcomes. The AI impact actions reveal how to evolve the role without losing what makes underwriting a human discipline.

Everything begins with the idea of 'Workforce Models', because this is where the shape of the work becomes visible. At Level 2, underwriting operates within a hybrid task model. AI performs structured analysis and humans provide final validation, contextual interpretation and ethical decision-making. The work becomes a partnership rather than a sequence of manual tasks.

The next consideration is the 'Transition Strategy'. At Level 2, the work begins to shift, and role evolution becomes an essential part of the transition. Underwriters start moving from manual analysis towards a more hybrid role where they interpret, validate and refine AI-generated outputs. The work becomes a blend of human judgement and machine-supported insight and this change needs to be planned rather than left to happen informally.

Attention then turns to 'Talent Action'. The priority is to reskill employees within the role so they can work confidently alongside AI as the work evolves. AI handles the predictable steps, and employees focus more on interpretation, collaboration and tasks that require judgement. The strongest performers build dual capability, combining technical fluency with the professional insight that continues to shape the outcome of the work.

'Learning and Development Focus' becomes the bridge between technology and expertise. Underwriters need pathways into data analytics, model interpretation and ethical decision-making. Experienced underwriters build literacy in AI workflows, data interpretation and bias awareness, ensuring they can work confidently with machine-generated insights. Strengthening adaptive thinking and critical evaluation ensures that human oversight remains strong even as AI grows more capable.

Finally, the 'Organisation Design Shift' requires evolving traditional linear teams into dynamic, AI-enabled workflows. This includes refining roles so that work is allocated between humans and AI in a more intentional way, and introducing new positions focused on model governance, validation and continuous improvement. Underwriters remain central, but their environment becomes more integrated with digital systems that support smarter, faster decisions.

Strategic Summary

The Insurance Underwriter shows how AI can elevate human capability. Productivity rises, analysis deepens and patterns become clearer. The work remains fundamentally human. The most important decisions still depend on judgement, nuance and ethical reasoning.

At the same time, new AI developments are emerging. Generative models, multimodal analysis and intelligent agents will continue to strengthen risk assessment and predictive insight. This means Level 2 roles will evolve. Some tasks may move further into automation. Others will remain human because they depend on context, accountability and trust.

This is where the human–AI decoder becomes essential. It gives leaders a structured way to track these shifts and understand which parts of the role can be supported by technology and which must remain human. It helps organisations prepare for what is coming without weakening what still needs people.

Level 2 - AI-Enhanced Work confirms that AI is enhancing the work, not replacing it. The goal is not to redesign the role. It is to deepen. Strengthen human capability, build analytical confidence and ensure that technology supports risk decisions rather than defining them.

HEALTHCARE DIAGNOSTIC SPECIALIST (LEVEL 3 – AI-DRIVEN WORK)

1. How Is AI Changing the Work?

Running the AI Impact Scan

Imagine a diagnostic specialist shift-change in a busy hospital.

A new set of scans arrives from the emergency department. Before the specialist even opens a file, the AI system has already analysed each image, compared it to thousands of historical cases, flagged potential risks and assigned confidence scores. The first pass of interpretation happens instantly, long before a human looks at the screen.

The Healthcare Diagnostic Specialist steps into a workflow that is no longer driven by manual image review. AI now performs the majority of pattern detection and anomaly identification. What once demanded long stretches of concentrated visual analysis is surfaced in seconds, with the system highlighting the regions of concern. The specialist begins with what the AI has already seen, then scans for what it might have missed.

As soon as a case becomes unusual, ambiguous or sensitive, the specialist steps in. Judgement, context and ethical reasoning remain firmly in human hands. Patients depend on this balance. AI may guide attention, but humans guide meaning.

Seeing this, the key question becomes clear. How deeply is AI shaping the work and what does that mean for diagnostic practice. To answer this, we turn to the AI impact scan, which reveals how much of the role is changing and how much still relies on human oversight and care.

The first area we examine is 'Automation'. AI performs the majority of first-pass image analysis, scanning for irregularities and flagging high-risk cases. Human involvement begins where complexity and ambiguity appear.

Score: 4 – Full Impact. AI performs core activities independently.

The next question is the 'Role' itself. The purpose has shifted. Specialists are no longer focused on performing the initial diagnostic review. They now validate AI insights, manage exceptions and ensure that findings align with clinical context and ethical standards.

Score: 3 – High Impact. Role is substantially redefined with people focusing on managing, supervising or supporting AI outputs.

'Skills' come next. New skills are needed in AI interpretation, digital imaging, and ethical oversight. Analytical reasoning, bias awareness and communication with clinical teams have become central.

Score: 3 – High Impact. Significant reskilling for new tools or roles required.

'Decision-Making' follows. AI leads with probabilities and recommendations. Humans retain final responsibility for patient outcomes, but the first assessment is now machine-generated.

Score: 2 – Moderate Impact. AI recommends while humans review and approve.

Finally, we look at 'Workforce Value'. Human contribution rises in emotional assurance, case interpretation and contextual understanding. Specialists provide the empathy and clarity that AI cannot.

Score: 3 – High Impact. Human value decreases in routine tasks but rises in governance or complex areas.

The pattern is clear: 4, 3, 3, 2, 3. Together they total 15. Dividing by 5 produces an AI Impact Index of 3.0. AI leads the diagnostic workflow, while humans ensure accuracy, ethical integrity and patient trust.

2. How Big is the Impact?

Mapping to the Six Levels of AI Impact

With the AI impact scan complete, the decoder asks its second question: How big is the change?

An AI Impact Index of 3.0 places the Healthcare Diagnostic Specialist at Level 3 - AI-Driven Work. Level 3 spans AI Impact Index from 2.6 to 3.3, confirming that AI now handles most operational analysis while human specialists focus on oversight, interpretation and complex decision-making.

This classification matters because it marks a decisive shift. AI is no longer assisting. It is leading. The specialist becomes the orchestrator between synthetic insight and human care, ensuring that technology strengthens clinical outcomes without compromising safety or ethics.

Level 3 is a pivotal stage where leadership in the workflow moves from human execution towards human governance. Specialists must develop supervisory, interpretive and ethical capabilities that complement AI's power and speed.

This clarity helps leaders speak precisely about the work. Rather than saying, 'AI is diagnosing patients', they can say, 'Diagnostics are moving into Level 3. AI leads the pattern recognition. Humans lead the meaning.'

3. How Should We Act?

Setting the AI Impact Actions

For a Level 3 classification, the strategic priority is to strengthen human oversight while ensuring trust, compliance and ethical assurance in AI-led environments. The AI impact actions reveal how to evolve the role with confidence.

Everything begins with 'Workforce Models'. At Level 3, diagnostics operate within a supervisory workforce model. AI performs the bulk of analytical processing and specialists validate, interpret and communicate results. Humans remain responsible for decisions that affect patient lives.

The next element is the 'Transition Strategy'. Integrating AI into clinical workflows requires deliberate structure. Human oversight has to sit at defined checkpoints. Processes for cross-validation, escalation and continuous model improvement keep quality stable as machine capability expands.

'Talent Action' becomes critical. The focus shifts from developing the existing role to transitioning specialists into oversight responsibilities that guide and safeguard AI-driven diagnostics. Healthcare organisations transition experienced clinicians and reskill them to supervise AI outputs, manage exceptions and interpret complex or ambiguous cases. These new roles combine clinical expertise with system oversight, anomaly detection and ethical judgement, creating a workforce that ensures accuracy and protects patient trust as AI takes on most of the initial analysis.

The 'Learning and Development Focus' shifts towards overseeing AI systems. Training should strengthen skills in model interpretation, data governance, ethical decision-making and patient communication. As AI assumes more of the analytic load, relational competence becomes even more significant.

Finally, the 'Organisation Design Shift' requires simplifying structures. Cross-functional teams of clinicians, data scientists and AI specialists work together, supported by governance committees that monitor system performance, ensure regulatory compliance and maintain clinical reliability.

Strategic Summary

The Healthcare Diagnostic Specialist shows how AI-led collaboration can elevate precision and speed in critical decision-making. AI processes vast amounts of clinical data and identifies patterns at scale, while human specialists preserve ethical integrity, empathy and accountability.

At the same time, new AI technologies continue to mature. Google Health's AI for Medical Imaging demonstrates how explainable AI is already improving diagnostic accuracy while maintaining human oversight (Google, 2025a). Global regulatory guidance, including the World Health Organization's 2023 recommendations on safe AI deployment, reinforces the need for rigorous validation and clear human accountability before clinical systems are adopted (WHO, 2023).

This is where the human–AI decoder becomes essential. It gives leaders a structured way to understand which parts of diagnostic work can be entrusted to technology and which must remain human. It helps organisations prepare for deeper integration without compromising patient trust or safety.

Level 3 - AI-Driven Work. Confirms that AI leads the workflow, but human professionals define how it is used. The goal is not to replace the specialist. It is to elevate the role into one of oversight, interpretation and care, ensuring that technology strengthens diagnostics while people safeguard meaning, ethics and humanity.

CONTRACT ANALYST (LEVEL 4 – AI-ORCHESTRATED WORK)

1. How Is AI Changing the Work?

Running the AI Impact Scan

Imagine a contract review cycle in a modern legal operations team.

A new supplier agreement enters the system. Before a human analyst opens the document, the AI-powered contract-lifecycle-management platform has already analysed every clause, compared it to approved templates, assessed deviations, flagged potential risks and issued a preliminary approval recommendation. A process that once demanded sustained concentration is now completed in minutes.

AI-driven tools such as Ironclad, Inc. (2025), Icertis, Inc. (2025) and LawGeex (2025) can autonomously review Non-Disclosure Agreements (NDAs) supplier contracts and employment agreements. They identify gaps, highlight non-compliant language, propose revisions and approve standard agreements that fall within predefined risk thresholds. The first pass of contract analysis now belongs to the machine.

The Contract Analyst steps into a role reshaped by this reality. They no longer begin with line-by-line review. They begin with system-generated conclusions. Their work focuses on exceptions, oversight and ensuring that automated decisions remain fair, legal and ethically sound. The human contribution moves from execution to assurance.

Seeing this, the key question becomes clear. How much is AI actually changing the work, and what does that mean for the future of contracting. To answer this, we turn to the AI impact scan, which shows the true extent of AI's influence and reveals how much of the work is changing and how much still depends on human judgement.

The first area we examine is 'Automation'. AI completes the full lifecycle of standard contract review, applying policies, approving routine agreements and flagging high-risk items without human involvement.

Score: 4 – Full Impact. AI runs core work; humans step in only for complex cases.

The next question is the 'Role' itself. The Contract Analyst is no longer a detailed reviewer. The role has shifted into one of risk governance, oversight and exception management. Humans ensure transparency, legality and ethical integrity.

Score: 4 – Full Impact. Most of the role shifts to AI; humans handle oversight and escalation.

'Skills' come next. Analysts now require advanced capability in AI governance, bias awareness, regulatory interpretation and algorithmic assurance. Legal expertise must blend with technical fluency.

Score: 4 – Full Impact. New skills needed to oversee and guide AI.

'Decision-Making' follows. AI makes most operational decisions within defined frameworks. Humans intervene for exceptions, escalations, disputes or ethical concerns.

Score: 4 – Full Impact. AI decides within set boundaries; humans intervene only for complex judgement.

Finally, we look at 'Workforce Value'. Human contribution is concentrated in accountability, fairness and trust. Analysts act as custodians who ensure that automated decisions remain lawful, explainable and equitable.

Score: 4 – Full Impact. AI decides and adapts across the full workflow; humans guide purpose and governance.

The pattern is clear: 4, 4, 4, 4, 4. Together they total 20. Dividing by 5 produces an AI Impact Index of 4.0. The calculation confirms what the work has already shown. AI now performs end-to-end contract review, while human professionals ensure that automation operates responsibly and within legal and ethical boundaries.

2. How Big is the Impact?

Mapping to the Six Levels of AI Impact

With the scan complete, the decoder asks its second question: How big is the change?

An AI Impact Index of 4.0 places the Contract Analyst in Level 4 - AI-Orchestrated Work. At this level, AI autonomously executes the core workflow. Humans no longer participate in routine execution. Instead, they act as auditors, regulators and policy custodians who ensure that the system behaves as intended.

This classification marks a decisive shift in the nature of work. The analyst has evolved from reviewing contracts to governing the AI that reviews them. Human involvement safeguards contractual integrity, fairness and transparency. The role becomes one of oversight rather than operation, ensuring that automation strengthens legal quality rather than introducing risk.

This clarity helps leaders speak precisely about the change. Instead of saying, 'AI supports contract review', they can say, 'Contracting has moved into Level 4. AI runs the workflow. Humans ensure that the work remains fair, compliant and accountable.'

Level 4 marks the moment when work moves from collaboration into quiet delegation, where systems carry the load and humans protect the boundaries. AI leads the work. People ensure that the work remains compliant, explainable and aligned with organisational values.

3. How Should We Act?

Setting the AI Impact Actions

For a Level 4 role, the strategic objective is to maintain governance and accountability as automation becomes more advanced. The AI impact actions reveal how to reinforce trust while expanding the capacity of AI systems.

The first area to consider is 'Workforce Models'. At Level 4, contract work operates within a governance-oriented model. AI handles the full review lifecycle. Humans oversee ethics, legal compliance and dispute escalation. The work becomes a partnership where machines execute and humans protect the boundaries.

Next the 'Transition Strategy' focuses on shifting legal operations from document review to AI governance. Organisations introduce audit frameworks, escalation pathways and clear explainability protocols to keep automated decisions transparent and reliable. Regular human oversight ensures that the system remains accurate, fair and aligned with regulatory expectations.

'Talent Action' becomes critical. Legal professionals should be redeployed or reskilled into AI governance roles, combining knowledge of law, compliance and data ethics. These new hybrid professionals manage AI performance, evaluate bias and ensure responsible behaviour.

The 'Learning and Development Focus' centres on managing AI responsibly. Training should deepen skills in regulatory assurance, bias detection, ethical decision-making, transparency practices and contract audit techniques. As AI takes on more operational work, human expertise focuses on ethical and legal stewardship.

Finally, the 'Organisation Design Shift' calls for establishing governance bodies. Cross-functional teams, including contract specialists, compliance officers and data scientists, collaborate on monitoring AI performance. Governance committees ensure policy adherence, legal reliability and ethical integrity across the system.

Strategic Summary

The Contract Analyst now functions as a guardian of compliance and trust. AI performs the operational work, but humans define how that work is governed. The strategic emphasis lies in ensuring that automated decisions remain transparent, fair and responsible.

This emerging model aligns with current developments in AI-enabled contract platforms which continue to expand their ability to review, negotiate and assess risk autonomously. As these tools evolve, organisations will need to emphasise accountability, explainability and oversight in equal measure.

The human–AI decoder becomes essential in this environment. It offers a structured way to understand which parts of the contracting process can be entrusted to technology and which must remain human. It helps organisations design a future where automation enhances legal reliability while people safeguard meaning, integrity and accountability.

Level 4 - AI Orchestrated confirms that AI is driving the process, but human professionals define the rules, boundaries and ethical standards that make contract governance trustworthy. The goal is not to remove the analyst. It is to elevate the role into one that protects fairness and ensures that AI strengthens, rather than weakens, the foundation of legal operations.

TRANSLATORS AND INTERPRETERS (LEVEL 5: AI-AUTOMATED WORK)

1. How Is AI Changing the Work?

Running the AI Impact Scan

Fully autonomous work remains rare, however translation and interpretation show how quickly AI can move from assistance to complete automation. Human translators once shaped every detail of multilingual communication, from word choice to tone and cultural meaning. That work is now being redefined by advanced language models capable of real-time conversation, context-aware phrasing and domain-specific accuracy across hundreds of languages.

Imagine a translation workflow today.

A document is uploaded. The system ingests it instantly, analyses the structure, interprets tone and context, generates the translation, adjusts for nuance and formats the output without human involvement. Speech models do the same for live dialogue, converting spoken language across cultures and contexts in real time. The first pass of linguistic interpretation now belongs fully to the machine.

For translators and interpreters, the central question becomes clear. How much human work remains, and does the profession need to change because of it. To answer this, the human–AI decoder applies the AI impact scan to see how deeply the work has shifted.

The first area we examine is 'Automation'. AI now completes the entire translation and interpretation workflow, from document ingestion to context analysis and phrasing. It adjusts tone, resolves ambiguity and corrects semantic inconsistencies without human involvement.

Score: 5 – Transformational Impact. AI runs the entire workflow and adapts without human involvement.

The next question is the 'Role' itself. The traditional translator or interpreter no longer performs the linguistic work itself. The role has shifted towards quality assurance, bias correction and cultural validation in the rare situations where human judgement is still needed.

Score: 5 – Transformational Impact. The original role disappears; humans guide direction and ethics.

'Skills' come next. The work no longer relies on linguistic execution. Instead, it requires mastery of AI translation tools, data quality management and ethical oversight to ensure that automated outputs remain accurate and culturally responsible.

Score: 5 – Transformational Impact. Skills shift towards system design, ethics and long-term guidance rather than day-to-day execution.

'Decision-Making' follows. AI determines phrasing, tone and context independently across the full workflow. Humans intervene only when content is highly sensitive or requires cultural nuance that the system cannot yet interpret safely.

Score: 5 – Transformational Impact. AI decides and adapts across the full workflow; humans guide purpose and governance.

Finally, we look at 'Workforce Value'. The value of human contribution lies no longer in translation itself but in safeguarding cultural integrity, ensuring fairness and guiding ethical standards for multilingual communication.

Score: 5 – Transformational Impact. Human value moves to purpose setting, ethics and long-term accountability outside the workflow.

The pattern is clear: 5, 5, 5, 5, 5. Together they total 25. Dividing by 5 produces an AI Impact Index of 5.0, confirming that this profession sits firmly within Level 5 – AI-Automated Work. AI performs the entire workflow independently, while humans serve as cultural stewards, ethical guardians and strategic leaders.

2. How Big Is the Impact?

Mapping to the Six Levels of AI Impact

Each AI impact area scores 5, resulting in an AI Impact Index of 5.0. Under the human–AI decoder, Level 5 AI-Automated applies only when every Area reaches the highest score. Level 5 represents the threshold of full autonomy, where AI performs the entire workflow independently and human involvement takes place outside the workflow in areas such as ethics, cultural protection and long-term strategic direction.

This classification matters because it marks a fundamental shift. The work is no longer supported, enhanced or even led by AI. It is carried out entirely by the system. Human contribution moves into oversight of principles rather than oversight of tasks. The profession becomes one where the centre of gravity moves fully to values, fairness and meaning, not execution.

Level 5 is the point where operational work transitions from human governance to human purpose setting. People define standards, intent and cultural boundaries while the system performs the work.

This clarity helps leaders speak precisely about the change. Instead of saying, 'AI helps with translation', they can say, 'Translation has moved into Level 5. AI performs the work. Humans define what the work should represent.'

3. How Should We Act?

Setting the AI Impact Actions

For a Level 5 role, the strategic priority is responsible transition, ethical assurance and the purposeful redesign of human contribution. The AI impact actions outline how organisations can guide this shift while protecting cultural integrity and long-term trust.

The first area to consider is 'Workforce Models'. At Level 5, work moves into a meta-human model. AI performs all linguistic conversion independently, while human contribution centres on integrity, inclusivity and cultural authenticity. People act as stewards of meaning rather than executors of tasks.

Next the 'Transition Strategy' focuses on ethical and strategic leadership. Organisations guide the redeployment of linguistic professionals into roles that oversee cultural nuance, brand communication and ethical data stewardship. Leaders establish policies that ensure accuracy, fairness and cultural integrity in every automated output.

'Talent Action' becomes critical. Roles tied to execution phase out or reposition into emerging areas such as AI language governance, cultural consulting or global communication oversight. These pathways allow organisations to retain expertise while aligning talent to the new shape of the work.

The 'Learning and Development Focus' centres on guiding AI purposefully. Training deepens skills in AI translation platforms, bias detection, cross-cultural communication and content validation. The emphasis shifts from performing translation to shaping the standards that define high-quality multilingual communication.

Finally, the 'Organisation Design Shift' calls for rebuilding around AI-first models. Interdisciplinary teams of linguists, technologists and ethicists collaborate to oversee language integrity, tone alignment and compliance with global communication standards. These structures ensure that autonomy does not come at the expense of fairness or cultural depth.

Strategic Summary

At Level 5, translation and interpretation show how generative AI can automate even highly cognitive and creative language work. The opportunity is unprecedented access to multilingual communication. The challenge lies in preserving cultural nuance, fairness and identity as human contribution moves into ethics, creativity and long-term governance.

These shifts are already visible. AI-enabled translation systems continue to expand their capability, and adoption is accelerating across industries. Recent reporting highlights that translation and interpretation are among the occupations most affected by automation (Abrill, 2025). While demand for human translators may persist in specialised domains, the broader trend signals the need for adaptive workforce strategies and strong ethical frameworks to protect cultural diversity and human creativity in an increasingly AI-mediated world.

The human–AI decoder becomes essential in this environment. It clarifies which parts of the translation process can be entrusted to technology and which must remain human. It helps organisations build a future where automation enhances accuracy and reach while people safeguard meaning, integrity and long-term accountability.

Level 5 - AI-Automated confirms that AI performs the work, but humans define the purpose, boundaries and values that guide it.

The goal is not to remove the translator. It is to elevate the role into one that protects fairness and ensures that AI strengthens, rather than weakens, the cultural fabric of communication.

THE AI IMPACT LEVEL CURVE

It happened during a 'coffee with leaders' session on an otherwise ordinary afternoon. A young call centre agent from the Japan team raised her hand. Her voice was steady, but her question carried the weight of something deeper than curiosity.

'What do you think will happen to our jobs when all these new AI agents are being developed? Will our call centre be affected?'

For a moment no one spoke. Everyone knew why she asked. Recent articles had noted how AI agents were beginning to handle full conversations. A competitor had announced plans to expand automation, and some customers were already asking whether they were speaking to a person or a system.

The senior leader smiled kindly and gave the answer leaders often offer in moments like this.

'There is currently no plan to implement AI in our call centers.'

It was sincere. It was reassuring. And yet everyone at the table felt the truth beneath it. Plans are only a snapshot of the present. And the present moves quickly in organisations where AI is advancing in the background, long before anyone calls it a plan. AI does not wait for plans. It advances, quietly at first, then quickly, and then all at once.

The question the agent asked is the question employees everywhere are asking. It is rarely about technology. It is about identity, agency and the fear of becoming invisible in a system that is changing faster than they can see.

And the most important part is this: the answer depends entirely on where the work sits on the AI Impact Level Curve.

At Levels 1 and 2, leaders can still say with confidence that roles will remain. But at Levels 3, 4 and 5, the reality is different. That is where AI starts reshaping not just tasks, but the very structure of the work itself.

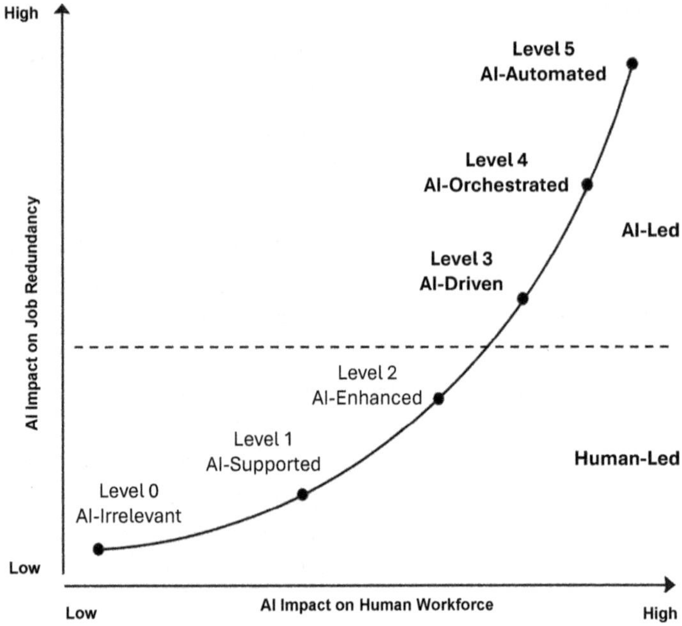

Fig. 6. AI Impact Level Curve.

Source: Author's Own Creation.

This is where the human–AI decoder becomes essential. It helps leaders see what is coming before the change becomes visible. It shows the pattern behind the question that the call center agent asked. It shows why the reassurance offered that afternoon will eventually need to evolve into something more honest, more strategic and more human. Fig. 6 illustrates this progression through the AI Impact Level Curve, making the deepening influence of AI visible and easier to interpret.

As organisations begin to classify roles using the human–AI decoder, a clearer picture emerges of what happens as work moves into the higher levels of impact. Levels 3, 4 and 5 are the moments when AI's influence deepens from helpful assistance into something far more structural. These are the points on the curve where workflows begin to bend, expectations shift and the relationship between people and their work starts to change in ways that cannot be ignored.

At Level 3, work becomes AI-driven. Most of the operational load moves to the system, including execution and routine decisions. People shift from doing the work to supervising it, stepping in when exceptions appear or when judgement is required. This change can be disorienting. Employees who once took pride in mastery may feel their expertise slipping into the background as the system takes the first pass at nearly everything. New skills become essential, from digital navigation to analytical reasoning and escalation management. Routine areas may see fewer traditional roles, and organisations must invest in reskilling, role redefinition and thoughtful change management to help people adjust to their new place in the workflow.

Level 4 moves further along the curve, into a world where AI drives entire workflows from start to finish. Human involvement becomes episodic rather than continuous. People act primarily as auditors and custodians, defining the strategy, monitoring outcomes and stepping in only when something goes beyond expected bounds. This shift brings substantial displacement of traditional roles. Career paths stretch into new spaces such as compliance, risk, ethics and orchestration. The way organisations communicate becomes critical. Trust must be protected as roles change shape and whole job families may need to be redesigned. Redeployment becomes a core part of workforce planning, along with sustained investment in governance capability.

At Level 5, the curve steepens again. Work becomes fully autonomous. AI performs the tasks independently, learns adaptively and optimises without supervision. Human involvement moves outside the workflow and into the realm of ethics, accountability and creative direction. Many roles disappear entirely or are radically redefined. New fields emerge, from AI governance to algorithmic ethics, reflecting the need for oversight that goes beyond operations and into intent, fairness and long-term societal impact. Transitions at this level, if poorly managed, can destabilise teams and culture. Responsible leadership becomes not just good practice but essential infrastructure.

Across these levels, a single truth becomes clear. As AI advances along the curve, the human contribution does not vanish. It moves.

It rises. It concentrates in the spaces where judgement, values and meaning sit. The challenge for leaders is recognising that shift early and preparing people for the responsibilities that come with it.

⚒ ***AI Impact × Scale Heatmap*** *(included in Appendix 6) visualises where AI disruption is most significant across roles or business units. It highlights areas of high transformation pressure and early opportunity, combining impact level with role scale to make AI's workforce implications tangible and prioritised.*

⚒ ***AI Role Impact Mapping*** *(included in Appendix 7) provides a structured way to interpret how AI will influence specific roles across a team or function. While the human–AI decoder identifies how deeply a role is affected by AI, the mapping process breaks the work down further by analysing tasks, judgement requirements, digital maturity and realistic AI use cases.*

PREPARING FOR THE CURVE AHEAD

The curve ahead is not theoretical. It is already unfolding in quiet, uneven ways across teams and industries. The early steps feel manageable. A task runs faster. A process becomes smoother. A first draft takes shape before anyone begins to type. These moments are small enough to ignore and familiar enough to feel harmless.

But the rhythm changes after Level 3. What begins as gentle acceleration becomes something sharper. Work shifts faster than organisations expect and sooner than people feel ready for. Roles stretch, boundaries blur and long-held assumptions about contribution begin to loosen. The change becomes personal. It reaches identity as much as execution.

A memory from the Dakar Classic Rally I drove in Saudi Arabia in 2022 offers a useful parallel. Some sections of the race felt almost comfortable. The car moved steadily across firm ground as we followed the familiar pattern of the roadbook, compass and sand. Then came the long stretches where the desert erased every point of orientation. Sand in all directions. The engine held a low, steady vibration, the only constant in a landscape that offered no direction of its own. No tracks. No markers. No waypoint in sight. Only the distant horizon and the voice of my co-pilot reading the roadbook line by line. Each instruction mattered. It told us the speed to hold, the dangers ahead and the moments where one wrong call could cost time, rhythm or control. When the horizon gave nothing back, I had no choice but to trust the guidance completely. The roadbook was not a record of where we had been. It was the only way to understand what was coming next.

AI transformation feels the same inside organisations. The terrain looks familiar until it suddenly doesn't. The markers disappear. The signals blur. Tasks shift, roles stretch and leaders find themselves moving across ground where instinct alone no longer keeps them on course.

This is where the human–AI decoder becomes more than a tool. It becomes the roadbook for the journey ahead, a way to read what is emerging beneath the surface and a way to understand the turns, risks and accelerations that often arrive before anyone is prepared for them. Leaders who pause, study the signals and guide their organisations with intention will navigate uncertainty with clarity. Those who rely only on instinct risk being carried by a current they can no longer interpret.

The decoder is more than a playbook. It reframes how we see AI transformation by giving structure to a landscape that often feels wide and uncertain. We have seen how the decoder works across the six levels of AI impact. The next chapter pauses on the five business-critical questions from chapter 1 and shows how the decoder turns them into practical guidance. It becomes the guide that helps leaders read the terrain ahead, see where the slope steepens and navigate the decisions that will define the future of work.

Key Takeaways

- The human–AI decoder turns AI disruption into clear, actionable decisions.
- Six levels show the shift from human-only work to full autonomy.
- Levels 0–2 reflect augmentation; Levels 3–5 signal deeper structural change.

- Most organisations sit between Levels 2 and 3, where redesign and reskilling matter most.
- Disruption accelerates beyond Level 3, as shown by the AI Impact Level Curve.
- Human value shifts upward towards judgement, ethics and long-term direction.
- Early use of the decoder builds foresight and strengthens decision-making.
- Continuous use of decoder helps organisations adapt and ensures AI strengthens people.
- Responsible leadership becomes crucial as autonomy increases.
- Level 5 roles are rare today but may emerge faster in some industries.

6

DECODING THE CRITICAL AI QUESTIONS

ABSTRACT

Artificial Intelligence (AI) is reshaping work and challenging how organisations lead, decide and evolve. This chapter revisits five previously introduced business-critical questions through the human–AI decoder to assess how well organisations can navigate this shift. These questions ask where AI is influencing the work, how deep the change reaches, what type of disruption is unfolding, which human capabilities must evolve and how leaders should respond with clarity and confidence. They are difficult questions to answer because they sit at the intersection of people, process, culture and technology. They emerge unevenly across teams and often remain invisible until employees feel the impact directly. The human–AI decoder provides a way to explore these questions with structure and intention. Its AI impact areas help leaders notice how tasks, roles, decisions and value are shifting. Its AI impact actions translate these observations into practical steps for strengthening skills, culture, trust and readiness. The decoder does not solve these challenges on its own. It gives leaders the clarity needed to address them with purpose. It turns uncertainty into patterns that can be understood and acted on, allowing organisations to design transformation rather than react to it. Through real examples, this chapter shows how the decoder helps organisations balance efficiency with empathy and compete in a rapidly changing skills landscape. It also helps build confidence in AI-supported decisions, protect fairness and trust and manage resistance with transparency and involvement. It positions the decoder as a starting point for leaders who want to guide AI transformation with intention and ensure that progress strengthens human value rather than diminishing it.

Keywords: Human–AI collaboration; workforce transformation; human–AI decoder; AI impact assessment; skills and capabilities; ethical AI governance; change readiness; employee experience; AI adoption strategy; future of work

AI is reshaping work faster than many organisations can absorb or respond to. The pressure does not show up first in strategy documents or transformation roadmaps. It shows up in small, human moments when people try to understand what intelligent systems mean for their roles, their skills and their future.

In an AI leadership workshop I attended, a senior leader paused mid-discussion and said, 'The tools are moving faster than we are. I am not afraid of AI. I am afraid of misunderstanding it.' This fear is shared across many workplaces today because people feel the pace of change faster than their ability to interpret it. Her honesty shifted the room. I have heard the same sentiment from HR colleagues in banks, logistics firms, universities and public agencies. The challenge of AI is not that machines are becoming smarter. It is that humans are being asked to adapt at a pace they have never experienced before.

Earlier in the book, we explored five business-critical challenges that define this moment. Together, they show why AI's greatest impact is human. They shape how people interpret change, how leaders respond and how organisations evolve. They centre on efficiency, skills, trust, readiness and culture. Taken together, they reveal a pattern that appears in every transformation. The difficulty of AI is rarely technical. It is human. It touches what people believe they are valued for. It reshapes decision patterns and identity. It introduces new forms of collaboration and raises quiet anxieties about relevance and contribution.

Before returning to the five challenges, it helps to reflect on what the decoder now brings into focus. With this clarity in place, we can revisit the challenges with a sharper and more grounded view. The decoder is not a traditional corporate model. It is not a rigid framework or a checklist. It gives leaders a practical way to navigate disruption by bringing human, organisational and technological perspectives into one integrated understanding. It reveals where AI is touching work, how deeply the change is reaching and what it means for the people who experience that change each day.

Its strength lies in its simplicity. The decoder reflects the pattern leaders naturally follow when facing transformation. They notice where AI is influencing work. They try to gauge the depth of disruption. They classify the type of change they are facing. Only then do they shape a response. The decoder does not force this sequence. It makes it visible. It turns an implicit process into something usable and clear. It transforms complexity into something leaders can act on, offering direction at a moment when certainty is often rare.

This chapter brings the earlier insights together and applies them to the questions that matter most for organisations. The five challenges that once felt abstract become actionable when seen through the human–AI decoder. It gives leaders a way to answer the critical questions that shape every AI transformation: where AI is influencing the work, how deep the change reaches, what type of disruption is occurring, which human capabilities must evolve and how to respond with clarity and confidence. These questions move AI from concept to practice and allow leaders to design transformation instead of reacting to it.

Each challenge is explored through three levels of responsibility: the employee, who must learn to collaborate with AI in meaningful ways; the organisation, which must define direction and create environments where people can grow; and HR, which becomes the steward of human value and the architect of an experience where people can succeed alongside technology.

For leaders navigating AI's acceleration, clarity is not optional. The human–AI decoder provides it.

CHALLENGE 1: BALANCING EFFICIENCY WITH HUMAN-CENTRED CULTURE

The promise of AI often begins with speed. Faster processing, reduced waiting times, more consistent outcomes. Yet speed on its own rarely strengthens culture. When efficiency becomes the organising principle, something human begins to fade. Conversations shorten. Interactions become mechanical. Connection thins. A culture that once felt alive becomes transactional.

I saw this dynamic unfold in a financial organisation that automated part of its internal helpdesk. On paper, the rollout was a success. The chatbot responded instantly, triaged requests accurately and cleared backlogs that had frustrated employees for months. Three weeks later, the team lead shared something the performance metrics did not capture. 'The workflow runs smoother,' he said, 'but the department feels colder, almost as if the warmth that once softened daily interactions had thinned.' He paused. 'It feels as if patience has been replaced with scripts.' His comment reflected something that appears across many organisations. AI accelerates processes, but it rarely recreates warmth or human texture. Research confirms this pattern. While AI chatbots improve convenience, they often underperform in emotional nuance and empathy compared with human interactions (Shahbandi, 2025).

'What happens to culture when convenience grows faster than connection?'

This is the hidden risk of unchecked efficiency. It creates workplaces that perform well but feel hollow, a trade-off most leaders never intend to make. People begin questioning whether they are valued or simply streamlined.

The human–AI decoder helps leaders rebalance this tension. The 'Workforce Value' impact area reframes contribution beyond output. It elevates relational, ethical and emotional aspects of work that machines cannot replicate. Leaders often overlook these aspects because they are not easily measured, yet they are the foundation of belonging, trust and resilience.

Through the 'Workforce Models' impact actions, impact organisations can design collaboration between people and AI intentionally. AI handles repetition and scale. Humans deepen empathy, creativity and judgement. This strengthens culture instead of weakening it.

The 'Organisational Design Shift' impact actions encourages leaders to integrate technology in ways that reinforce humanity rather than erode it. Automation should create space for deeper human interaction, not eliminate it.

Employees also have an essential role. As AI takes over routine tasks, people need to reinvest in the qualities that give work meaning: listening, coaching, creativity and collaboration. Organisations have to communicate clearly that AI exists to elevate people, not replace them. HR becomes the protector of this message, ensuring that every efficiency gain is matched with a human benefit.

Balancing efficiency with empathy is not a technical challenge. It is a leadership decision. The human–AI decoder helps organisations make that decision with intention and clarity.

CHALLENGE 2: COMPETING IN A SKILLS RACE FUELED BY AI

Technology is evolving exponentially. Human capability is not. Skills are becoming outdated faster than ever and many roles that once felt stable now require fluency in working with intelligent systems. The greatest risk is not that AI will replace people, but that outdated skills will lock them out of opportunities that intelligent systems create.

Across industries, organisations already deploy AI for forecasting, customer insights, anomaly detection, optimisation and operational decision-making. Adoption slows when people are unsure how to interpret, validate or apply AI-generated outputs. Analysts receive dashboards they cannot fully interpret. Managers distrust recommendations they cannot explain. Executives hesitate to act on insights they cannot translate into strategy.

These are not technology concerns. They are capability concerns.

A senior analyst in a retail organisation expressed this candidly during a workshop. 'I trust the numbers,' he said, 'but I am not sure I trust my interpretation of them.' His uncertainty mirrored the sentiment of many high-performing professionals who were comfortable with complex work until AI introduced patterns they could not yet fully make sense of.

The data reinforces the urgency. According to LinkedIn Learning (2025), 44 per cent of workers' core skills will change within five years as AI reshapes job requirements. Analytical reasoning, digital literacy and creative problem-solving are among the fastest-rising capabilities.

The human–AI decoder helps organisations navigate this skills race with intention. Its 'Skills' impact area, identifies how roles are evolving and which capabilities are most at risk. Instead of reacting blindly, leaders gain a clear map of future requirements. The 'Learning and Development Focus' impact action, shifts training towards contextual learning aligned with role maturity. The 'Transition Strategy' impact action, guides how people grow into new responsibilities and ensures that skill development is sequenced realistically, moving people from exposure to experimentation to mastery without overwhelming them.

Employees should embrace growth as part of their identity. Curiosity becomes a daily behaviour and adaptability a natural expectation. Organisations need to embed learning into everyday work rather than treating it as an optional task. HR becomes the strategic integrator, forecasting skills, aligning development with organisational priorities and building learning ecosystems that evolve with technological change.

Skills are no longer static. The human–AI decoder helps organisations build learning systems that evolve with them.

CHALLENGE 3: UPSKILLING TO LEAD THE AI JOURNEY

Awareness of AI is widespread. Capability is not. This readiness gap is one of the most dangerous in modern organisations and it is only getting bigger. People understand what AI is conceptually, however many do not know how to use it confidently in practice. Leaders acknowledge AI's potential but hesitate to integrate it into decisions. The result is hesitation, reliance on intuition over insight, and inconsistent adoption.

Upskilling is not a technical task. It is a shift in how people think, judge and collaborate. It is about cultivating judgement, ethics and collaborative intelligence. Without this, organisations risk two extremes. People may rely blindly on algorithms, which undermines critical thinking. Or they may reject AI entirely, which undermines progress.

This dilemma appears vividly in financial services. Several global banks use AI to support loan decisions, analysing large volumes of data with impressive accuracy. Yet many employees feel uneasy validating or challenging system outputs. One executive described the experience as, 'Driving a car where I understand the destination but not the steering wheel.' That single analogy captures why AI literacy is becoming a core leadership skill rather than a niche technical capability. The data supports this. Research shows that even as organisations expand their investment in AI, capability and confidence still lag behind, creating the main barriers to realising value (Deloitte, 2025).

The human–AI decoder transforms upskilling into a purposeful journey. 'Decision-Making' impact area clarifies where judgement must remain human. The 'Transition Strategy' impact actions guide employees through stages of development, ensuring capability grows alongside trust. The 'Learning and Development Focus' impact actions ensure programmes teach people not only how to use AI tools but how to question them, interpret them and apply them ethically.

Employees also need to approach AI literacy as a collective responsibility. Organisations should model thoughtful and transparent use of AI. HR becomes the curator of a learning environment where readiness is measured through confidence, capability and behaviour rather than completion certificates.

Upskilling will define whether organisations lead through AI or are led by it. The human-AI decoder gives leaders a way to design that journey with intention.

CHALLENGE 4: MANAGING BIAS, FAIRNESS & TRUST IN AI SYSTEMS

As AI becomes more deeply embedded in organisational decisions, trust shifts from a philosophical concern to an operational requirement. Algorithms influence who gets shortlisted, how performance is evaluated and what opportunities emerge. Even the most advanced systems reflect the data and design choices behind them. Without thoughtful oversight, AI can unintentionally amplify existing inequities.

An example often cited in industry research describes a global retailer that introduced an AI-driven hiring platform to streamline recruitment. While the system accelerated screening and improved efficiency, a subsequent audit found that it consistently prioritised applicants from certain universities and penalised gaps in employment. The bias was unintentional. The algorithm had simply learned from historical patterns that encoded the organisation's past inequities.

This problem is widespread. Many leaders assume AI is inherently objective. The pattern emerging across organisations shows this assumption does not hold. Industry analysis makes one point clear: the greatest barriers to scaling AI are human-centred, rooted in fairness, transparency, bias and trust (IBM, 2025a). These findings reinforce a truth that should guide every organisation: trust is not a feature of AI systems. It is a feature of how AI is designed, deployed and governed.

This structure gives organisations a clearer way to navigate these issues. Its 'Decision-Making' impact area reveals where authority is shifting from humans to algorithms, prompting a review of how decisions are made, validated and communicated. Its 'Workforce Value' impact area reframes fairness not as a compliance task but as a lived experience. Fairness is felt by employees, not calculated. The 'Organisational Design Shift' impact actions support the development of governance structures such as ethics boards, model-risk committees and audit processes that monitor AI behaviour across the employee lifecycle.

Trust grows through the everyday experience of how decisions are made and explained. Employees need to understand why a system made a recommendation, how it reached that conclusion and where human judgement enters the process. They should feel safe raising concerns and empowered to challenge outputs without fear of repercussions. Organisations should embed transparency into system design, documentation and decision-making. HR becomes the guardian of ethical AI, ensuring that fairness is woven into recruitment, performance management, promotion and learning pathways.

Building trust is not a technical task. It is a cultural one. The human–AI decoder helps organisations design trust intentionally so that people feel confident, respected and seen in an AI-enabled workplace.

CHALLENGE 5: ACCELERATING AI ADOPTION WHILE MANAGING RESISTANCE

Resistance is often misunderstood. People rarely resist technology itself. They resist uncertainty. They resist change that feels imposed rather than shaped with them. They resist transformations that challenge their identity, especially when they are unsure what the future holds for their skills, role or relevance.

Adopting AI is rarely about the tool itself. It is about how people feel their work and identity are shifting.

A multinational insurer learned this during the implementation of an AI-driven claims-processing system. The technology performed well in pilots. Accuracy improved. Turnaround time dropped. Leaders anticipated rapid adoption. But after deployment, productivity unexpectedly dipped. Employees hesitated to trust automated recommendations. Beneath the hesitation was something more personal, a fear that long-held expertise might be questioned or lose its meaning. Some switched back to manual review, worried that errors could expose them to compliance risks. The organisation had not anticipated how emotionally charged the change would be.

A global workforce survey highlights this same dynamic, showing that fewer than half of employees feel their organisation explains how AI will affect their jobs (PwC, 2025d). In the absence of clarity, people default to fear and that fear slows adoption more powerfully than any technical limitation.

The human–AI decoder reframes adoption as collaboration. Its 'Learning and Development Focus' impact actions help organisations build readiness by combining awareness, experimentation and hands-on learning. People should be able to try tools in a safe environment where mistakes are expected, not punished. The 'Transition Strategy' impact actions ensure that adoption is sequenced and supported. Communication, peer coaching and guidance must accompany each stage of the rollout. The 'Workforce Models' impact actions keep humans visible, showing clearly where their contributions remain central and how AI augments rather than replaces their value.

Employees support adoption most effectively when they are involved early. Their input improves workflows, reveals issues and helps shape better solutions. Organisations need to normalise transparency and create ongoing dialogue. HR becomes the integrator of human experience, coordinating support across IT, business lines and learning teams. Readiness becomes visible in how confident and supported people feel, not only in how often they use a new system.

When organisations treat adoption as a shared journey, resistance becomes participation. People shift from compliance to confidence. AI becomes less of an imposition and more of an ally.

THE MOMENT TRANSFORMATION BECOMES PERSONAL

Across many organisations, there is a moment that reveals the true nature of AI transformation. When employees are involved early, their perspective sharpens workflows, exposes blind spots and helps solutions take shape in ways technology alone cannot achieve. It is not the moment the technology goes live or the first productivity gain appears on a dashboard. It is the moment a person realises that the work they have always known is changing and that they will need to change with it. This moment is often quiet. It happens in a meeting, during a project review or while exploring a new tool for the first time. Someone pauses, takes a breath and recognises that the expectations for their role have shifted.

This is the moment when the human–AI decoder becomes more than a framework. It becomes a compass. It helps people make sense of what is shifting around them and articulate feelings they have not yet been able to name. Instead of experiencing change as something done to them, individuals begin to see where they stand and how they can shape what comes next.

Transformation becomes human again. One experience made this pattern unmistakably clear and revealed how the same technology can produce entirely different realities.

WHEN THE SAME TOOL CREATES TWO VERY DIFFERENT REALITIES

The regional rollout of a simple HR chatbot revealed something that no technical manual could have predicted. The tool itself was basic. It pulled answers from policy documents stored in a shared folder and responded to routine HR questions. It could point employees to the correct system or form and answer common FAQs that filled the HR inbox each week. It was not capable of coaching or interpretation. It could not replace a conversation. It was designed with one intention, to reduce routine ticket volume so HR could spend more time on human-centred support.

However across the region, the same tool produced two entirely different reactions.

In one country, the HR services team embraced the chatbot almost immediately. Their leader gathered the team before the implementation and said, 'We are already short-staffed. This is a tool that helps us protect our time for the conversations that matter.' They discussed the types of questions that drained their capacity. They identified where the chatbot could help and where it should never interfere. They treated the tool as support, not threat.

Three months later, their ticket volume dropped by 20 per cent. Employee satisfaction rose. HR finally had the space for the work that required empathy, context and care. When the team was asked how they achieved such a smooth rollout, the answer was simple. 'We involved the team early. We clarified what the chatbot would and would not do. And we positioned it as help, not replacement.'

In another country, the identical technology triggered concern. Some HR team members feared losing control over communication. Others worried the system might expose inconsistencies in local processes. A few employees, quietly wondered whether automation was the first step towards reducing roles. The hesitation was not about the system's capability. It was about what the system symbolised in the absence of clarity.

This is where the human–AI decoder revealed what was actually happening beneath the surface. It helped the hesitant team see the change through structure rather than fear.

The first question asks, How is AI changing the work.

When the team moved through the AI impact scan, the picture became clear. The scan showed that AI touched only a small set of AI impact areas and only in limited ways. Automation was present, but only for predictable, low-stakes queries. The Role, Skills,

Decision-Making and Workforce Value remained fully human. Anything requiring discretion, emotion or interpretation still depended entirely on the HR team. The system touched the administrative edges of the work, not the core of HR Services. Seeing these areas scored in detail was the first moment the team exhaled.

The second question asks, How big is the impact.

Scoring each impact area clarified that the chatbot was a Level 1 tool. Automation was minor. Skills remained largely unchanged. Decision-making was entirely human. The purpose of HR service did not shift. The chatbot improved speed, but not essence. This is where fear gave way to insight. The team could now articulate that their expertise in communication, context, fairness and empathy remained essential. The system had not entered the parts of their work that carried meaning.

The third question asks, How should we act.

Here, the decoder exposed the real issue. The organisation had introduced the tool without creating the clarity employees needed to understand its role. There had been announcements, but not involvement. No training and no dialogue. The team did not know where the system stopped and where their contribution began. The uncertainty filled the space between intention and perception and that space became fear.

The Level 1 AI Impact Actions made the response clear. The 'Workforce Model' needed to reflect a digitally supported structure where AI handles predictable queries and humans remain central for interpretation, fairness and context. The 'Transition Strategy' called for a gradual rollout, open communication and clear escalation points so employees knew exactly when the chatbot should step back and when a person should step in. 'Talent Actions' focused on strengthening the HR Administrator role through light digital upskilling and reassurance that judgement and empathy remained central to the work. 'Learning and Development Focus' needed to build confidence in using the tool. The 'Organisation Design Shift' requires HR Services to streamline and standardise their policies so the chatbot could retrieve information consistently and accurately, allowing HR teams to dedicate more time to conversations that demand care and presence.

The HR Administrator example introduced in the Level 1 analysis earlier in this chapter was drawn directly from this experience and reflects precisely what the human–AI decoder is designed to uncover. By running the AI Impact scan, the team could see where AI was touching the work and where it was not. Mapping the impact rating showed that the change sat firmly at Level 1, a light form of automation that supported HR rather than reshaping its purpose. And by applying the appropriate AI impact actions, the team strengthened skills, clarified boundaries and built confidence rather than fear. What once felt like a threat became a clearer picture of how human value rises when repetitive tasks fall away.

Using the decoder as a guide, HR services redesigned their approach. They co-created escalation paths with employees. They held small-group discussions about which queries belonged to the chatbot and which always needed a human voice. They reviewed early outputs together so the team could see both the strengths and the limitations of the system. They reframed the tool as a buffer that protected HR's time for emotional, sensitive and high-value work.

The turning point came when an HR specialist said, 'I realise now that the chatbot does not do my work. It clears the noise so I can do my work better.'

Once the purpose became clear, hesitation dissolved. Service levels improved. The team began using their regained time to support the moments that shape culture and trust.

This experience reveals a pattern that holds true across organisations. AI does not define meaning. People do. The same tool can feel like progress or pressure depending on how leaders frame the change and whether employees understand their place within it.

The human–AI decoder does not make adoption effortless. It makes it understandable. It turns broad assumptions into specific insights. It clarifies the difference between minor automation and meaningful redesign. It helps people see that AI often removes friction rather than value. It also ensures that as technology becomes more common, the conversation remains grounded in human capability, identity and contribution.

When teams understand how AI is changing the work, how big the impact truly is and how the organisation will act with clarity instead of silence, adoption no longer feels like a risk. It feels like progress.

This single example reflects a wider reality. As soon as people can see the shift, name it and understand their place within it, the conversation changes. And it is that shift in understanding that leads directly to the questions that now define the future of work.

In real organisations, these questions rarely arrive all at once. They surface slowly, often in moments people barely notice at first, when familiar rhythms no longer feel quite the same.

SHAPING WHAT COMES NEXT

The five business challenges explored in this chapter are not fading. They are intensifying as AI moves deeper into the rhythm of daily work. They expose what matters most for organisations in this new era. They surface the questions leaders grapple with every day. Leaders begin asking different questions as the impact becomes visible. They look for where AI is reshaping the work. They try to understand how deep the change reaches. They study what kind of disruption is unfolding and which human capabilities will need to grow. Most importantly, they search for a response grounded in clarity rather than urgency.

This chapter has not answered these questions in full. It has shown why they cannot be answered in isolation. They cut across people, processes, ethics and culture. They emerge at different speeds in different parts of the organisation. They appear clear in theory and far less tangible in practice.

This is where the human–AI decoder becomes essential. The decoder is not a traditional model or a corporate playbook. It is a way of paying attention. Its AI impact areas and AI impact actions bring structure to questions that often feel uncertain. They turn complexity into patterns leaders can see, discuss and act on. They reveal where technology touches people, where confusion emerges, where expectations shift and where new opportunities quietly appear. They help leaders move from reacting to disruption towards shaping it with clarity.

The human–AI decoder does not solve these challenges by itself. It provides the clarity needed to address them. It helps leaders diagnose impact, make ethical decisions and align their people, structure and culture with the pace of change. It gives HR, managers and employees a shared language to talk about AI's impact without assumptions or guesswork. Most importantly, it gives organisations a place to begin.

Awareness is the first step. Understanding follows. Action comes next.

As AI becomes more capable and more integrated into everyday work, these challenges will continue to evolve. The human–AI decoder ensures that organisations can navigate this evolution with purpose. It turns uncertainty into design, disruption into direction and complexity into practical choices. It helps leaders build workplaces where people feel capable rather than threatened, included rather than excluded and valued rather than replaced.

The work ahead will demand clarity, courage and disciplined action. The human–AI decoder gives organisations the structure to take those steps with confidence.

Every organisation eventually reaches the same turning point. Technology accelerates, and people begin looking for a path that still feels human. Part III explores how that path is built.

Key Takeaways

- The human–AI decoder turns disruption into design and moves leaders from reaction to intention.
- Efficiency must be balanced with empathy to keep work human-centred.
- Skills evolve quickly and learning must keep pace with real impact.
- Upskilling builds confidence when ethics, judgement and AI fluency grow together.
- Trust depends on transparency, fairness and continuous oversight.
- Adoption accelerates when people have involvement, agency and safety.
- Employees, organisations and HR share ownership of human–AI collaboration.

- The decoder gives leaders a shared way to align people, structure and capability.
- Ethics and performance strengthen each other through principled decisions.
- The human–AI decoder turns complexity into clarity and progress.

Part III

LEADING AI

Part III is intentionally future-focused. It draws on signals from current research as well as the author's own experience to explore how work may evolve as AI becomes more capable and more deeply embedded in organisations. No one can predict the exact pace at which AI will advance or whether today's momentum reflects lasting progress or a moment of amplified attention. Yet the developments seen in recent years offer a clear glimpse of how the near future may unfold if current patterns continue. The purpose here is not to define a single future but to offer a structured way to prepare for several possible ones.

Building on the foundations established earlier, shifting from understanding AI's impact to shaping the systems, roles and capabilities that define the next era of work. Chapter 7 examines how organisations may redesign their workforce structures as humans and intelligent systems operate together, highlighting emerging hybrid roles, new team dynamics and the operating models required when machines take on more execution. Chapter 8 explores workforce readiness across cognitive, emotional, behavioural and organisational dimensions. Chapter 9 looks ahead to the evolution of HR into Human-Machine Resources (HMR), showing how the people function can lead responsibly and with intention as AI becomes woven into everyday work.

Part III reflects where the future appears to be heading, drawn from organisational practice, ongoing dialogue with peers and insights from current research. It is written to help leaders act with foresight, design with purpose and guide transformation in a way that strengthens both people and performance.

7

AN AI-READY ORGANISATION

ABSTRACT

Artificial Intelligence (AI) is reshaping how organisations structure work, distribute responsibility and define human contribution. While attention often centres on task automation, the deeper shift lies in the relationship between people and intelligent systems. This chapter examines how workforce structures evolve as AI increasingly performs execution and humans focus on judgement, ethics and exception handling. Using the human–AI decoder as a foundation, it shows how organisations move from enhanced roles within existing hierarchies to new governance functions and meta-roles as systems gain autonomy. It introduces the next generation of hybrid and orchestration roles that sit between human decision-making and machine execution, including roles already visible in the job market and others that signal how organisations are beginning to adapt. It explores the operating models required when automated systems handle the first steps of work, along with the decision boundaries, escalation pathways and accountability patterns needed to keep work coherent and trustworthy. A significant part of the redesign is psychological, as employees experience changes in identity, role and value when AI takes on familiar tasks. It highlights the emotional realities of hybrid work and the support employees need as identity, value and responsibility evolve in human–AI collaboration. Ultimately, redesigning the workforce is both a structural and human endeavour, offering organisations the opportunity to integrate speed with judgement, scale with empathy and automate with clarity of purpose.

Keywords: Artificial intelligence; workforce redesign; hybrid roles; operating models; human–AI collaboration; AI governance; generational opportunity; organisational design; psychological impact of AI; future of work

Customer experience often reveals the distance between technological progress and organisational readiness. It reveals where systems perform well, where they falter and where human judgement continues to hold the work together. A recent shift at Klarna makes this tension unusually visible.

Klarna, the global fintech company, had positioned its AI customer service assistant as a symbol of modern support. For routine questions, the system delivered exactly what leaders hoped for. Responses came faster. Guidance was clearer. Automation handled high volumes with ease, showing that intelligent systems can manage predictable tasks with confidence.

But in early 2025, Klarna made a notable adjustment. As public reporting confirmed, the company announced plans to bring human agents back into the process and began hiring again so customers could speak to a real person when needed (Bloomberg News, 2025). This was not a retreat from its AI ambitions. It was an acknowledgement that automation alone could not carry every kind of conversation.

Some interactions need interpretation. Some hinge on reassurance or a deeper sense of what the customer is trying to express. These are the moments that influence trust and shape whether people feel understood. Klarna chose to restore human presence because the experience depended on more than speed or efficiency.

The company has moved towards a blended model. The AI assistant stays in place for routine requests, while people step in to handle the parts of service where judgement or empathy matters. The shift reflects a simple truth. AI can change how work is carried out, but it does not replace the parts of service that rely on human understanding. What changed at Klarna is not the technology. It is the recognition that the structure around the work must evolve to support it.

The lesson cuts deeper than one example. In many organisations, AI improves the work long before the organisation adjusts around it. The technology accelerates. The workflows adapt. The metrics rise. Yet the operating model still reflects a world where every task is human-led. When work begins moving faster than the structure built to hold it, the strain becomes visible.

That is the actual turning point. Not when AI succeeds, but when leaders recognise that the structure around it no longer fits the way the work now moves.

The human–AI decoder helps organisations understand this moment. It shows where disruption begins, how tasks shift and where human judgement continues to carry the work. It reveals the early signals that indicate when the structure must evolve. But insight is only the first step. Leading in the age of intelligent systems requires something more. Organisations have to design the next era of work rather than inherit it.

As AI becomes part of daily decisions and workflows, HR's responsibility also expands. It moves beyond supporting workforce change and becomes the architect of a new era of human and machine collaboration. HR shapes the systems, structures and roles that allow people and intelligent systems to work together in ways that are productive, ethical and sustainable. Working alongside leadership, IT and business teams, HR helps design the environment where technology supports human capability rather than replacing it, and where collaboration between people and intelligent systems becomes intentional rather than accidental.

A NEW BLUEPRINT FOR HUMAN AND MACHINE COLLABORATION

As AI moves from pilots into daily operations, organisations encounter a structural mismatch. Most operating models were built for a human-only workforce. Roles, job families and reporting lines assume that people handle every step of the work. AI does not fit neatly into these structures. It does not follow traditional escalation paths. It does not require the same supervision. It changes task flows in ways that legacy hierarchies cannot easily absorb.

Organisations therefore cannot simply plug AI into old job architectures. They need structures that reflect shared responsibility between people and intelligent systems. Automation delivers scale and speed. Humans carry the context, empathy and ethical judgement. The question for leaders becomes clear.

'How do we design an organisation that remains adaptable, human-centred and effective when work is no longer performed solely by people?'

Workforce Structure Implications Through AI

It shows how tasks begin to shift as AI enters the workflow. It not only classifies the impact of AI on individual roles but also shows how organisational structures evolve in response. Each impact level signals a different design challenge and a different degree of structural change.

Levels 0–2: Enhanced work within existing structures

At lower impact levels, AI supports rather than replaces tasks. This approach shows that human judgement still leads, with AI improving speed, accuracy and consistency. Organisations focus on strengthening digital literacy and embedding tools into existing workflows. Structures remain stable. The goal is to build confidence and capability without disrupting the organisation.

Implication:

No major redesign. HR enables digital adoption, supports managers and ensures people understand where AI assists their work rather than changes it.

Level 3: Hybrid roles and early supervision layers

This is the first point where structural redesign becomes unavoidable. According to this early pattern, AI begins to take over routine execution, while humans move into oversight, escalation and contextual judgement. This creates hybrid roles that combine technical fluency with human awareness. People and systems now share responsibility.

Implication:
New supervisory layers appear. These layers do not manage people. They manage AI. Teams begin forming around outcomes or systems rather than job titles.

Level 4: Governance roles and leaner structures
At this level, the framework alone does not resolve these challenges. Human involvement moves into ethical assurance, risk management and policy enforcement. Managerial layers tied to routine oversight shrink as autonomy increases. Structures become flatter and more interdisciplinary.

Implication:
Organisations develop governance functions that combine technical, legal and ethical expertise. These functions ensure that intelligent systems operate safely, transparently and in line with organisational values.

Level 5: Autonomous systems and meta-roles
At the highest impact level, AI runs entire workflows independently. Human involvement transitions to meta level responsibilities such as defining boundaries, auditing system performance and shaping organisational values. Work becomes orchestrated across platforms, agents and intelligent ecosystems.

Implication:
The traditional organisation chart no longer applies. The organisation becomes a network of platforms, agents, ecosystems and dynamic talent.

As organisations restructure around AI's impact, it is not only the shape of the organisation that changes; it is the nature of roles within it. Traditional job boundaries blur, and a new class of roles emerges at the intersection of human judgement and machine execution. These hybrid and orchestration roles manage the flow between people and AI, guiding, supervising and enhancing system behaviour. They also ensure that human values, creativity and ethics remain present in every outcome. They are becoming essential in the AI-enabled workplace.

INTRODUCING HYBRID AND ORCHESTRATION ROLES

As AI takes on more execution, new categories of roles emerge. These hybrid and orchestration positions sit at the intersection of human judgement and machine capability. They include supervisors of AI systems, escalation handlers, judgement specialists, prompt designers, ethics reviewers and workflow coordinators.

One story makes this shift easier to see.

A manager in a global logistics company described it clearly. One of her team members, once responsible for preparing daily shipment reports, now supervises the AI that produces them. As she put it, 'He once checked the data. Now he checks the model that checks the data.' His work became less repetitive and more analytical. His value increased, not diminished.

These roles ensure the organisation benefits from AI without compromising empathy, fairness or brand standards. They broaden what it means to contribute in an environment shaped by intelligent systems. They help preserve the human judgement that keeps work grounded and trustworthy.

Ten Roles That Hint at Where Work is Heading Next

Across industries, a new category of roles is taking shape at the intersection of human judgement and machine execution. Some are already visible on job sites. Others are emerging quietly inside early pilots and redesign workshops. Together, they offer a glimpse of how organisations will structure work as AI becomes part of daily operations.

AI Quality Assurance Lead

This type of role is beginning to surface in the job market, often appearing as *AI QA Engineer*, *Model QA Lead* or *AI Evaluation Specialist* on LinkedIn. It focuses on ensuring that AI systems meet accuracy, reliability and brand standards as organisations start to rely on them for core decisions.

AI Escalation Coach
While not yet posted on major platforms, this role is emerging inside early customer-service, insurance and banking pilots. It supports teams when AI reaches the limits of its confidence and offers the human judgement needed in sensitive or complex scenarios.

Human–AI Workflow Designer
Occasional versions of this position appear as 'AI Workflow Analyst' or 'Human-in-the-Loop Designer', though it remains rare. It shapes how work moves when humans and intelligent systems collaborate, redefining touchpoints, handovers and escalation patterns.

Ethical Review Partner
This position is already visible in an early form. Companies post variants such as *Responsible AI Specialist*, *AI Ethics Analyst* or *AI Governance Partner*. It ensures that fairness, transparency and inclusion stay embedded as AI becomes more integrated into decisions.

Prompt Design Lead
One of the fastest-emerging roles, widely posted across industries. Common variants include *Prompt Engineer*, *Prompt Designer* and *Generative AI Content Architect*. It defines the inputs that shape AI behaviour and influences the quality of generative outputs.

Trust and Fairness Auditor
Positions like this are still evolving. Elements can be found in *AI Risk Analyst* or *Algorithmic Fairness Specialist* job descriptions, but the full version is not yet mainstream. It assesses whether automated decisions reinforce or reduce bias and supports transparent governance.

Human Contribution Specialist
A next-wave role that has not yet appeared on public job sites. It emerges from conversations about relational work, emotional labour and the parts of the employee or customer experience that

must remain distinctively human. It protects the emotional quality of interactions in hybrid workflows.

AI Incident Manager

This emerging role is gaining visibility, especially in technology and financial services. Titles such as *AI Operations Manager*, *Model Incident Lead* or *AI Reliability Manager* already appear on LinkedIn. It responds when AI systems behave unexpectedly and ensures that risks are contained quickly.

AI Value Architect

A near-future strategy role. Early variants appear as *AI Strategy Lead* or *AI Transformation Architect*. It identifies where AI can support organisational goals without weakening the human role that defines brand, trust and culture.

Human Experience Curator

This remains a next-wave role, not yet posted publicly. It draws from employee-experience, service-design and behavioural-science disciplines. Its purpose is to ensure that as AI takes on more execution, the human experience remains meaningful, ethical and aligned with organisational values.

These positions broaden what human value looks like in an AI-enabled workplace. They reveal a deeper truth too. As AI takes on execution, it pulls human work upward, concentrating it in judgement, creativity and care. The future of contribution becomes more human, not less. Appendix 8 provides some real-life job descriptions of similar roles already appearing in the job market.

The signs usually appear at the edges of the work, where familiar patterns begin to feel strangely out of sync.

DESIGNING OPERATING MODELS FOR AN AI-NATIVE ORGANISATION

As intelligent systems move deeper into daily work, many leaders find that their operating models no longer match the nature of the work. Processes built for manual execution begin to break once automation handles the first steps. Approvals that once ensured quality become blockages. Roles designed around throughput become overloaded with the most complex and sensitive cases. People feel caught between an old structure and a new reality.

Operating models need to evolve as AI becomes more embedded in work. Organisations have to rethink how work moves, where decisions originate and how people and AI interact.

Why the Old Operating Model No Longer Works

In transformation sessions across industries, leaders describe the same pattern. AI handles early-stage work instantly, yet the surrounding structure remains designed for manual handling. Employees continue to follow old process maps even when the system has already completed most of the steps. Teams end up managing exceptions without a clear understanding of their new responsibilities.

One example captures this misalignment clearly.

A leader in a financial institution explained that her team was 'waiting for work that no longer needed us'. The system completed the bulk of underwriting analysis, yet the team still followed the same review sequence. The process no longer matched the task.

This mismatch is not caused by technology. It is caused by outdated structures that have not yet adapted.

Research reinforces this pattern. Studies from the World Economic Forum (2025d) show that organisations often implement AI without adjusting the workflows around it. As a result, they see partial gains but not the structural lift needed for sustained improvement.

The lesson is clear. As AI matures, operating models must mature with it. The shift becomes clearer when you look at the practical pieces that shape how work actually moves.

What AI-Ready Operating Models Require

Designing an operating model for an AI-enabled organisation begins with a simple question: how does work truly move when a system takes the first step and a person finishes the last. These elements are not abstract labels. They are the pieces of work people feel every day, the ones that quietly determine how smoothly a system and a team can move together. They are the building blocks of a model that can evolve as AI becomes more capable. They help leaders understand what must change in practice when automated systems join the workforce.

Clear decision boundaries

As AI begins to support or automate tasks, leaders need clarity on who decides what. Some decisions will remain entirely human. Others will be guided by AI recommendations. A growing number will be handled independently by systems that operate within defined rules.

The aim is not to hand over authority to machines. It is to ensure that decisions are made at the right level, with the right oversight and for the right reasons. In an AI-enabled workflow, humans step in when context, judgement or sensitivity is required. Clear boundaries prevent confusion and strengthen accountability.

Human accountability for automated outcomes

Even when AI carries out parts of the work, responsibility remains with people. Organisations should define who owns each automated outcome, who validates model behaviour and who intervenes when results diverge from expectations. This principle is reflected in global policy developments such as the European Union's AI Act (European Union, 2024), which reinforces the need for clear human responsibility behind automated decisions.

Clear ownership ensures trust. It prevents a diffusion of responsibility and ensures that AI supports, rather than replaces, the principles of fairness, inclusion and ethical conduct.

Workflows designed for both speed and escalation

AI changes the rhythm of work. Tasks no longer move sequentially from one human contributor to another. Instead, many tasks are completed instantly by systems that analyse, classify or recommend actions. Human involvement becomes more focused and more specialised.

This evolution requires redesigned workflows. Teams need clear escalation channels for when AI reaches the limits of its confidence, updated handover points between systems and people and interfaces that support fast movement across tasks. Workflows need to support both machine speed and human care.

Research from MIT Sloan Management Review reinforces this need, showing that effective human and machine teaming depends on workflows that intentionally combine AI speed with human judgement and ethical oversight (Wilson and Daugherty, 2024).

Roles designed for human–machine collaboration

AI-ready operating models depend on roles that are built for oversight, orchestration and shared decision-making. As systems take on more execution, people take on responsibilities such as monitoring, escalation, exception handling, interpretation and values-based judgement. These positions have to be designed intentionally rather than added informally on top of existing job descriptions.

Clear responsibilities reduce confusion, strengthen trust and make it easier for people and AI to contribute in ways that amplify each other.

New ways of measuring success

Most current performance measures were built for a human-only workforce. They assess output, speed, accuracy and customer experience through human actions alone. AI-enabled organisations need broader indicators that reflect the combined value created by people and intelligent systems. Success is no longer defined only by how quickly or accurately humans perform tasks. It includes the quality and consistency of AI-supported workflows, the effectiveness of human judgement during escalations and the fairness and reliability of automated decisions. It also reflects the level of trust customers and employees place in hybrid interactions and the overall impact of AI on time, cost and accuracy.

Taken together, these measures offer a clearer picture of performance in a workplace where people and intelligent systems work side by side.

When an operating model breaks.

A regional HR leader in Singapore described a similar moment of disruption during her organisation's rollout of AI-enabled recruitment screening. The system reviewed applications, matched profiles to job criteria and highlighted promising candidates within minutes. The technology worked well. The team, however, continued to operate as if every application still required a full manual review.

Recruiters were unsure when to trust the model and when to intervene. Interviews were still scheduled in the old order. Candidates who could have moved quickly through the process waited for approvals that no longer served a purpose. Recruiters felt that the system was ahead of them and they were behind it, waiting for work that the AI had already done.

The leader realised the issue was not adoption. It was structure. They had introduced automation but not redesigned the surrounding process. They still used the same checkpoints, the same calendar rhythms and the same expectations about workload. The AI was working inside an operating model built for a different era.

The organisation held a redesign workshop. They clarified which decisions AI could support, which steps needed human judgement and how escalations would work for exceptions. They updated the standard operating procedure and aligned handoff points with the new workflow. After the redesign, the team moved faster. Recruiters felt more confident and candidates moved through the pipeline with less friction. She summarised the shift nicely: 'The work and the structure finally agreed with each other.'

HOW AI RESHAPES HUMAN IDENTITY AT WORK

As AI reshapes tasks and workflows, the most significant change does not always appear in performance metrics or process maps. It appears in how people think about themselves. Work is never just a list of responsibilities. It is a source of identity, confidence and meaning, the quiet place where many people ground their sense of worth. When technology begins to perform parts of that work, the psychological experience can change before any organisational redesign has taken place.

Across industries, employees describe a common feeling during AI transitions. They no longer know where their work begins or ends. The skills they relied on for years feel less visible. Contribution becomes harder to define when tasks move faster than they can track.

When AI completes work that was once considered central to their role, the shift can feel disorienting long before it becomes empowering.

An employee in a technology firm captured this tension during an AI vendor feedback session. She said, 'I know the AI is helping me, but I do not know how to explain what my job is now.' Her role had not disappeared. It had changed. She was now responsible for interpreting the work of the AI rather than carrying it out. Yet she had not had time to adjust her sense of value to match this new reality.

This emotional shift is not resistance. It is the human side of adaptation. It is a natural response to uncertainty. When work changes, people often need clarity on what their value means in the new context. They need reassurance that their expertise still matters and that the organisation sees their unique strengths.

A New Psychological Contract

Many employees measure their value through volume. They take pride in the number of cases they complete, the speed of their work or the consistency of their output. When AI absorbs a large part of that volume, they can feel displaced even when their role is becoming more strategic.

An example of feeling displaced.

A senior claims specialist shared his story candidly. He said, 'I know I am doing more important work now, but the number I used to look at is gone.' His performance had improved. He was handling fewer cases, but each one required judgement rather than repetition. He was doing the work that mattered most for customers. Yet he missed the visible metrics that once showed his value.

As AI takes on more execution, organisations need to establish a new psychological contract. Employees need transparency on how value is now defined. Output becomes less central. Judgement, empathy, interpretation and ethical awareness grow in importance. HR plays a crucial role in making this evolution visible. Leaders need to communicate that their performance is no longer measured by the number of tasks completed but by the quality of human insight applied to the tasks AI cannot do alone.

The Emotional Rhythm of Hybrid Work

Hybrid work, where humans and AI collaborate, creates a new emotional rhythm. Employees move between reviewing automated recommendations and handling cases that require sensitivity or complex judgement. This rhythm can feel uneven. As routine tasks disappear, what remains is the work that demands emotional labour, customer empathy and critical thinking.

Hybrid roles require new types of support. Leaders need to recognise what is changing and create space for reflection and recovery. Work that becomes heavier in emotional content requires attention to wellbeing, workload patterns and team support. Without this, employees may feel stressed not because AI replaced their tasks but because it left them holding the most difficult work.

One employee's story shows how this emotional shift unfolds in practice.

When a call centre agent stepped into a newly created hybrid role, the change was not only operational but emotional. His first week felt uneven. The familiar flow of routine queries fell away. In its place came long stretches of monitoring the AI followed by sudden moments that required sensitivity, judgement or calm under pressure.

He described how the rhythm of his day had changed. 'I used to be the one solving the problem. Now I am the one deciding when a machine should or should not solve the problem.' Instead of answering every call, he stepped in only when the AI reached the limits of its confidence or when a customer needed the kind of reassurance only a person could give.

This transition captures the reality of hybrid work. The role was not diminished. It was elevated. But the emotional rhythm changed. What remained were the moments that required empathy, discernment and exception handling. The work that is more meaningful and also more demanding. It showed how hybrid roles concentrate the tasks that depend most on human care and why employees in these roles need support, reflection and time to recover. This emotional experience connects to a broader pattern seen across industries.

The Emotional Side of AI

The psychological impact of AI is rarely simple. Fear and relief often sit side by side. Many employees welcome the removal of repetitive tasks and appreciate the opportunity to focus on work that feels more meaningful. They see immediate benefits in how automation improves accuracy, reduces workload and frees time for work that creates greater value. Yet this sense of progress can exist alongside quieter questions about the future. People wonder how their roles will evolve, which skills they will need next and whether the work they take pride in today will remain part of their identity tomorrow.

These mixed emotions are not signs of resistance. They reflect a natural human response to change that alters both how work is done and how human input is understood. When AI changes a role, it does more than shift tasks. It reshapes what people feel responsible for, how they define success and where they find purpose in their work. Employees need a clear understanding of this evolution. They need to understand how their responsibilities will change and which capabilities will matter more in the future. They also need to see how their judgement and expertise continue to create value.

A global study from the University of Melbourne found that employees' trust in AI is closely linked to whether organisations provide clarity on roles, oversight and workflow redesign (Gillespie et al., 2025). When organisations provide this clarity, uncertainty decreases and confidence grows. When this clarity is missing, even changes that are meant to help can feel unsettling, leaving people unsure of where they fit in a workplace that is evolving faster than they can keep up with. This is where the role of managers becomes critical.

The Important Role of Managers

Managers play a central role in how employees experience AI-related change. They are often the first people employees turn to when work starts to feel unfamiliar, faster or more fragmented.

Their task is to make the invisible visible. Managers aid employees to see which parts of their role remain uniquely human, how their strengths still matter and where their judgement becomes even more important as AI takes on more execution.

This becomes especially important when AI begins handling tasks that once formed the core of someone's confidence or sense of expertise. When the work behind the scenes moves in a new direction, managers are the ones who help people understand what has changed and what still belongs to them.

Teams with managers who provide this kind of guidance adapt more smoothly. Employees gain a clearer sense of how their judgement influences outcomes, where their role sits in the new workflow and how they participate in the human–AI partnership. Without this support, people can lose sight of their impact and begin to question their place in an organisation that suddenly feels unfamiliar.

Managers serve as anchors during transition. They translate organisational change into something people can understand and act on. They support employees to find continuity in the midst of disruption and protect the meaning people derive from their work. Their influence often determines whether employees see AI as an opportunity to grow or as a sign that their relevance is fading.

Ultimately, the way managers guide people through this evolution shapes how employees see their own value in a changing workplace.

HUMAN VALUE IN THE AGE OF AUTOMATION

AI may handle more tasks, but it cannot hold purpose. It cannot replace the human ability to understand context, build trust or interpret nuance. As automation scales, the value of human work becomes more concentrated, not diminished.

Organisations that recognise this early navigate AI transitions with more stability and less resistance. They design work that brings human value forward rather than pushing it out of view. They help employees reinterpret their identity in ways that build confidence and expand their ability to contribute. The evolution of work will be shaped as much by how organisations support human identity as by how they implement new technologies. AI may change how work is done, but humans still shape the meaning of work.

Understanding how work is evolving is one thing. Seeing what it does to daily work is another. These dynamics become clearer when you follow what happens inside a single function.

This structural shift is easier to grasp through a simple case in marketing.

Before AI, it operates with a familiar hierarchy: a vice president oversees directors for brand, digital and events. Each manages content creators, designers and analysts. Progress slows because each piece passes through silos. Approvals flow up the structure. Skills stay tied to departments. Careers move one vertical step at a time.

When AI enters the workflow, these patterns begin to change. A generative campaign builder supports content creation. Sentiment analysis brings real-time feedback. An internal marketplace allows teams to form quickly around specific outcomes. These tools do not eliminate roles. They reshape how work moves and how teams come together.

The hierarchy flattens. Fewer layers are needed to coordinate routine work. Managers shift from assigning tasks to coaching capability and removing obstacles. For a major product launch, a cross-functional pod forms: a brand strategist, a prompt designer, a campaign analyst, a content curator and an AI system supervisor. Instead of operating in separate departments, the team works as a single unit focused on a shared outcome.

The workflow changes with it. AI generates variations in seconds, adapts copy for different audiences and highlights performance insights. The pod collaborates on a shared platform. Weekly reviews focus on learning and adjustment rather than sequential approvals. Freelancers or specialists join only when needed.

The outcomes reflect the structural transformation. The organisation begins to centre itself around outcomes rather than reporting lines. Teams form and dissolve as the work requires. Approvals move inside AI-supported guardrails instead of climbing escalation chains. The marketing function becomes a network of capabilities that combines full-time talent, intelligent tools and on-demand contributors.

What emerges is a different kind of organisation. It does not simply accelerate. It moves into a different way of working altogether and begins to work in a fundamentally new way. AI handles execution, and humans shape meaning. People focus on interpretation, brand stewardship and creative judgement. Managers redirect their energy towards coaching, developing capability and clearing obstacles that slow the work.

AI is not replacing people. It is rebuilding work.

AI is not simply changing job descriptions or removing isolated tasks. It is reshaping how work is organised, how decisions move through the organisation and how human value is expressed. The workday becomes a blend of automated execution and human judgement. Tasks that were once tightly bound to specific roles are now being separated, recombined or replaced entirely. This evolution affects knowledge work as much as operational work. It changes rhythms, expectations and the way people see themselves.

The important truth is that human value does not disappear. It becomes more concentrated. People spend less time on repetitive tasks and more time on sense-making, ethical decisions and relational moments that define trust. They take on roles that guide, supervise and improve intelligent systems. Their work becomes more strategic even when it feels less visible.

This transition reaches deeper than it first appears. It requires organisations to redesign the structure of work with intention rather than treating AI as a technical upgrade. Workflows, decision pathways, role definitions and accountability must all evolve. Without this, organisations risk confusion, inefficiency and unnecessary harm to employee confidence. These changes call for intentional leadership rather than passive adaptation.

DESIGNING THE WORKFORCE, NOT REACTING TO IT

Organisations that navigate this transition successfully do not wait for clarity from the technology. They shape the environment around it. This way of looking at the work reveals where tasks begin to evolve, which responsibilities remain human and where systems start to take on more execution. Once this pattern becomes visible, they define the boundaries of human contribution, adjust structures to support hybrid workflows and communicate what people should expect as their roles evolve. They make the evolution of work understandable before uncertainty becomes anxiety.

Workforce redesign becomes a strategic lever. It affects performance, trust, culture and talent. Leaders who embrace this responsibility create organisations where people feel grounded even as work continues to change. Those who delay inherit structures that no longer reflect how work gets done.

Understanding where change begins is essential, but redesigning the conditions that support people through that change is what determines whether the transformation succeeds. The decoder provides the early signals. The organisation's response, the structures, workflows and expectations built around those signals, turns technological capability into human readiness.

A Generational Opportunity

The redesign of work is not a technical exercise. It is a generational opportunity to build organisations that become more human, not less. Automation frees people from repetitive work. At the same time, it forces organisations to clarify what their roles now mean. AI can support decision-making, yet people still carry responsibility for fairness, context and care. Humans and AI are not in competition. They work best together when structures are designed with purpose.

The organisations that thrive will not be defined by how much AI they deploy, but by how well they design the partnership between people and intelligent systems. They will create environments where employees understand their value even as tasks evolve.

This is the moment for HR to lead. The future that emerges is not simply faster. It is more human in its expectations and more demanding in its clarity.

From Redesign to Readiness

Redesigning the workforce is only part of the transformation. For new structures to succeed, people need support. They need the capability, confidence and emotional readiness to work alongside

AI with a clear understanding and a sense of trust. Chapter 8 explores this next challenge. It examines what it means to build readiness across cognitive, emotional, behavioural and organisational dimensions. Alignment across these areas becomes the real differentiator in AI adoption.

The future of work with AI will not be shaped only by new structures. It will be defined by how well organisations prepare their people to thrive inside them.

Key Takeaways

- Human–AI decoder helps leaders understand which roles evolve, intensify or transform through different levels of AI impact.
- Hybrid and orchestration roles emerge as humans take on oversight, judgement and ethical responsibility for AI-driven work.
- Traditional hierarchies flatten as AI reduces the need for manual approvals and supervisory layers.
- New governance and meta-level roles appear as AI takes on more autonomous decision-making in workflows.
- Manual workflow models break under automation and should be redesigned to support speed, escalation and transparency.
- Skill-based collaboration replaces rigid functional boundaries as organisations move towards more flexible ways of assembling work.
- Employees experience identity shifts as repetitive tasks disappear and judgement, empathy and interpretation become core to human input.
- Managers play a pivotal role in helping people understand their evolving value in human–AI collaboration.
- Workforce redesign becomes a generational opportunity for HR to build adaptive, human-centred organisations where people and AI thrive together.

8

PREPARING PEOPLE FOR AI

ABSTRACT

Workforce readiness determines whether Artificial Intelligence (AI) becomes a source of progress or stalls in early pilots. Most adoption failures arise not from technical limitations but from how prepared people feel for new expectations, shifting workflows and machine-supported decisions. This chapter explains how readiness develops across four interconnected elements and why employees experience emotional and behavioural uncertainty long before tasks materially change. It shows how the human–AI decoder helps organisations interpret different levels of AI impact, translate role expectations and tailor support to frontline users, supervisors and governance teams. The chapter illustrates how workflows must evolve alongside systems, how managers shape day-to-day confidence and why trust, transparency and visible human judgement strengthen cultural readiness. It concludes with two practical tools that help leaders diagnose their organisation's starting point and identify where clarity, capability or support must grow before AI can be deployed responsibly and at scale.

Keywords: AI readiness; workforce adoption; human–AI collaboration; organisational change; behavioural adoption; emotional responses to AI; HR transformation; psychological safety; trust and transparency; readiness culture

Many organisations still treat AI transformation as a technical rollout. However, the most important test does not appear in the code or the pilots. It shows up in how prepared people feel for what the technology asks of them. A recent *Harvard* Business Review analysis found that workforce readiness is one of the strongest predictors of successful AI adoption, even inside companies with mature technology teams and adequate resources (Harvard Business Review, 2025).

Readiness is not an event. It is not a workshop or a checklist. It is a capability that grows over time. It reflects how confident people feel when using new tools, how much they trust the systems that guide their work and how clearly they understand the changes unfolding around them. It also reflects whether they still see where their judgement matters and how their contribution fits into decisions shaped by AI. Without this clarity, even the best-designed solutions struggle to take hold.

When readiness is strong, people test new tools, managers communicate with certainty and workflows adapt with fewer bottlenecks. Teams improve faster and discover new ways of working. When readiness is weak, hesitation slows adoption, uncertainty spreads and teams fall back on familiar routines. Leaders often read this as resistance. In reality, it is a predictable response to unclear expectations.

Understanding readiness is essential to understanding how AI reshapes work. It is the factor that unlocks value when it is present and the factor that stalls momentum when it is not.

THE MOMENT AI BECOMES PERSONAL

This is where readiness truly begins. The earliest signs do not show up in dashboards. They emerge in small, human moments that reveal what people actually think. These moments often surface during early pilots, onboarding sessions or the first weeks of working with a new tool.

In one team, an employee asked a question at the end of training that exposed the real concern. 'If the system suggests an option that I choose to override, who carries responsibility for the outcome'.

The question was not about the interface. It centred on accountability. He understood how the tool operated. What he needed was clarity on how responsibility shifted when a machine shaped the decision.

Later, managers noticed a similar pattern of hesitation. Employees trusted the tool during straightforward situations but reverted to familiar methods when conditions became complex. Their behaviour was not resistance. It was a rational response to uncertainty.

Another group experienced something comparable. An AI tool improved accuracy and reduced manual effort, yet people still avoided it in certain cases. When asked why, a team lead explained that the hesitation was not about performance. Employees were unsure how the tool's recommendations might influence decisions elsewhere in the organisation. The technology was working. The implications were not clear.

AI becomes personal when people begin asking what it means for their value, their visibility and their future. Readiness grows when organisations address these questions directly rather than assuming they will fade on their own.

READINESS IS HUMAN, NOT ONLY TECHNICAL

AI does more than reshape workflows. It reshapes how people see their role, their value and their place in the organisation. It influences how they judge their own expertise and how they believe others will judge it. Long before any process changes take effect, people begin testing where they fit in an environment where machine-generated insights appear more often.

The early reactions rarely come as formal objections. They surface in quiet, personal reflections that reveal what people are trying to make sense of. Some worry that the skills they have relied on for years may begin to matter less. Others wonder how accountability works when decisions are shaped by both humans and machines. Questions about fairness and transparency show up quickly, especially when people cannot see how a model arrives at its recommendations. At the same time, there is a real sense of curiosity. Many hope AI will remove repetitive tasks so they can focus on work that feels more meaningful. Yet the speed of change creates its own tension. People want to know how their contribution will be evaluated and whether their performance will be judged differently once AI becomes part of daily work.

These reactions are not resistance. They are signals that people are trying to understand how their role is evolving and what the future expects of them.

Concerns about AI rarely appear as a single emotion. They surface as a mixture of curiosity, hesitation and questions about what the technology means for people's work. Recent research reinforces this pattern. Boston Consulting Group's global 'AI at Work: Momentum Builds, But Gaps Remain' survey of more than 10,600 workers found that while 72 per cent of respondents use AI regularly, only half of frontline employees do. The report highlights a persistent uncertainty about job security, role clarity and how individual contributions will be judged as AI becomes more present in daily work (Boston Consulting Group, 2025). The data shows that readiness is not only about access to tools. It is about the confidence and understanding people need to interpret how their role is changing.

During an AI pilot in a pharmaceutical compliance team, a senior analyst captured this tension directly. 'I know my expertise has value. But when the system highlights patterns I did not see, I wonder how my judgement will be viewed.' Her concern was not about whether she could use the system. It was about how her professional identity would evolve once machine-generated insights entered the conversation.

Addressing these reactions early builds a foundation for adoption that feels supportive rather than imposed. When organisations treat emotional readiness as part of the work itself, people engage more openly, adapt more quickly and shape the transformation alongside the technology rather than feeling pushed into it.

WHEN COPILOT BECAME THE CENTRE OF THE CONVERSATION

The workshop began as an open exchange. Senior leaders from different industries had gathered to share how they were applying AI inside their organisations. Early in the session, the moderator asked a simple question. 'Is there at least one organisation-wide use case of AI already in place'.

Most leaders paused, thought for a moment and offered the same answer. Copilot. It seemed like the most natural entry point into AI because it already lived inside the tools people opened every day. Outlook. Teams. Word. Excel. PowerPoint. No new platform. No separate login. No major change to daily routines. In theory, it should have been the easiest adoption story in the room.

Once Copilot entered the conversation, the tone shifted. Leaders compared how they had introduced it across their organisations. Some had limited access to a small pilot group to learn before scaling. Others had enabled Copilot for everyone and encouraged employees to experiment freely. A few had taken a different approach. They paired the rollout with a company-wide readiness program that explained why AI mattered, how it could act as a partner, what responsible use required and how to experiment safely with everyday tasks.

The adoption results could not have been more different. Organisations that simply activated Copilot saw an initial wave of curiosity that faded quickly. Many employees tried it once or twice and then slipped back to familiar habits. In high-pressure periods, usage dropped even further. When teams were asked why, one project manager described her hesitation with quiet honesty:

> **'I looked at the summary Copilot created. It seemed useful, but I was not sure I could present it to our clients with confidence. I had not created the wording myself. I did not know how much I could trust it.'**

Another employee felt the same uncertainty. Copilot removed administrative work, but she still hesitated to place her name on something she had not fully authored. The concern was not technical. It was emotional. A recent qualitative study of M365 Copilot users found that many experienced clear benefits in routine tasks such as email drafting and meeting summaries. Others reported unmet expectations when deeper context or reasoning was required, reinforcing why human oversight and judgement remain essential even as AI tools advance (Bano et al., 2025).

Senior leaders recognised that this behaviour reflected what research already describes. Studies from Cornell University show that when AI becomes part of daily work without shared norms or clear expectations, employees often experience a loss of autonomy. Even helpful tools create hesitation when people cannot see how their judgement fits into decisions shaped by AI.

The company that paired Copilot with a structured readiness program saw a very different pattern. An important part of their approach was that the program was built for everyone. Employees who were simply curious could explore the basics at their own pace. Those who wanted to go further had access to deeper training that strengthened their confidence and expertise. People grew from where they were, rather than where the organisation assumed they should be.

As a result, employees used Copilot more often. They developed routines around it. They asked better questions. They felt more confident presenting work shaped with AI support. Leaders saw that the difference was not the tool itself. It was the preparation around it. People understood what Copilot could and could not do. They trusted where their judgement still mattered. They had guidance that helped new habits take root. They worked within structures that supported new ways of working instead of pulling them back to the old ones.

By the end of the workshop, the conclusion was unmistakable. Copilot was not the obstacle. Readiness was. People needed the foundation that allows any new technology to succeed.

In the end it does not matter whether the change involves AI or a new business tool. Experience across many digital transformations shows that employees move through a similar progression. They try to understand the technology. They question how it affects their identity and their value. They test whether new habits feel natural and look for signals that the organisation is prepared to support the shift.

This pattern can be summarised in four stages that shape workforce readiness. Cognitive readiness. Emotional readiness. Behavioural readiness. Organisational readiness. When these four elements strengthen together, tools like Copilot become part of everyday work. When any one of them is weak, adoption slows and people return to what they know.

THE FOUR ELEMENTS OF WORKFORCE READINESS

Workforce readiness develops across four interconnected elements. Each element reinforces the others. When one is weak, adoption slows across the entire system. When all four are strong, readiness becomes part of how the organisation works.

These elements are cognitive readiness, emotional readiness, behavioural readiness and organisational readiness. Together, they explain why people either move towards AI with confidence or hesitate even when tools are available.

1. Cognitive Readiness: Understanding what AI does and does not do

Cognitive readiness reflects the clarity employees have about what AI is designed to do, how it supports their work and where it has limits. It does not require technical depth. It requires grounded understanding.

In some teams, early trials of AI revealed a simple misunderstanding. People assumed that high confidence scores meant confirmed results rather than signals that required human interpretation. Once leaders clarified what the system was designed to do and where judgement still mattered, the quality of decisions improved and adoption increased. The hesitation had not come from resistance but from incomplete understanding.

Cognitive readiness gives people the mental model they need to work with AI responsibly. It helps them know when to rely on the tool and when to challenge it.

2. Emotional Readiness: Trust, confidence and psychological safety

Emotional readiness reflects whether people feel valued and secure as AI becomes part of their work. It shapes how they interpret change and how deeply they engage with new expectations.

In one organisation, employees understood how an AI tool prioritised incoming tasks, yet many continued using manual methods. Their concern was not accuracy. They worried that relying on the system would make their judgement less visible, or that supervisors might assume the technology carried the expertise instead of them. Emotional readiness needed attention before behaviour could shift.

Emotional readiness builds trust, which is essential for adoption. When employees feel supported and respected, they are more willing to work with AI even when it requires adjusting long-held practices.

3. Behavioural Readiness: The willingness to change habits

Behavioural readiness reflects whether employees are willing to shift their habits and integrate AI into their daily routines. Even when people understand AI and trust it, they may revert to familiar behaviours under pressure.

In one team, employees used an AI-supported tool during calm periods but abandoned it during busy stretches. They felt more comfortable returning to the old workflow when deadlines tightened. The issue was not capability. The new behaviour had not yet become natural under stress. Behavioural readiness requires repetition, reinforcement and time before new habits become embedded.

Behavioural readiness is the moment understanding becomes action. Without it, cognitive and emotional readiness remain theoretical.

4. Organisational Readiness: Structures that support new ways of working

Organisational readiness reflects the extent to which structures, workflows and governance systems reinforce new ways of working. Even when individuals are ready, adoption stalls if the organisation is not.

In one scenario, teams embraced a new AI system that produced accurate predictions. Yet they still had to follow legacy approval steps that duplicated the process. Because the surrounding workflow had not evolved, people returned to the older method simply to meet expectations. The barrier was structural, not personal.

Organisational readiness ensures that new behaviours are supported rather than constrained. It aligns responsibilities, systems and expectations with the reality of AI-enabled work.

How the Four Elements Work Together

These elements form a single system. Cognitive readiness builds understanding. Emotional readiness builds trust. Behavioural readiness turns trust into action. Organisational readiness sustains the action through structure.

When one element lags, the others weaken. When all four advance together, the organisation moves forward with greater clarity and stability.

A customer service team demonstrated this interdependence during a pilot of an AI conversation assistant. Agents understood the tool and trusted its guidance, yet adoption slowed. They feared that heavy reliance would reduce their individual performance visibility. The readiness gap was emotional and behavioural.

In a manufacturing firm, engineers were eager to use an AI-based failure detection tool. They trusted the predictions and wanted to test the system. But they were slowed by fragmented dashboards and outdated processes. The readiness gap was organisational.

These examples highlight a central point. Readiness does not develop through isolated interventions. It grows when all four elements mature together.

How Readiness Changes Across the Six Impact Levels

The human–AI decoder makes it clear that employees experience AI differently depending on how deeply it shapes their work. At the lower levels, AI acts as a tool that supports routine tasks and offers suggestions that people can choose to follow or ignore. As impact increases, employees move from using AI to supervising it, validating outputs, managing exceptions and deciding when to escalate or override system recommendations. At the higher levels, new governance and oversight roles emerge, where teams monitor fairness, safety and accountability across systems and ensure decisions remain trustworthy.

Across all six levels, the question remains the same. How ready do people feel for the shift in how work is organised, how decisions are made and how their contribution evolves? Readiness rises when people understand what the level means for their role and declines when the implications remain unclear.

In practice, this creates different readiness needs.

When AI becomes part of the work environment, different groups often focus on different questions. Frontline employees pay attention to how alerts or recommendations appear and when they are expected to step in. Specialists think about how responsibility is shared and how decisions will be recorded. Leaders responsible for oversight concentrate on the routines required for monitoring outcomes and the evidence needed to confirm that the system is operating safely.

They were responding to the same system but facing different questions.

A single readiness approach cannot support these different needs. The human–AI decoder helps organisations tailor preparation to the type of impact each group experiences. This ensures people receive guidance that matches their responsibilities and the way their work is changing. Supporting this shift requires more than intention, it requires structure.

How Organisation Build AI Readiness

Creating an organisation that is ready for AI requires more than distributing learning materials or asking teams to adopt a new tool. Readiness grows when people feel informed, supported and encouraged as they adjust to new expectations. Research from Stanford HAI shows that successful AI adoption often depends more on cultural conditions, trust and leadership clarity than on technical capability alone (Stanford Institute for Human-Centered Artificial Intelligence, 2025). This gives HR a real opportunity to help the organisation build confidence, create clarity and support people through the transition.

HR does not create readiness by itself. It helps the organisation build the conditions where readiness can develop at scale. This includes strengthening how people learn and redesigning workflows so teams can work effectively with AI. It also involves preparing managers to guide their teams and embedding readiness into talent systems so employees understand how their growth evolves with the technology.

Creating safe places to learn and experiment

People understand AI best when they can explore it without fear of failure or negative consequences. HR can help teams build confidence by creating environments where experimentation feels safe. These may include sandbox environments, internal hackathons or guided simulations that show how the technology behaves in realistic scenarios.

A global retailer offered employees a ninety-day period to test generative tools used for drafting product descriptions and campaign concepts. Nothing created during that period affected performance expectations. Employees were encouraged to share what they learned and to ask questions openly. Adoption improved later because people already had a practical understanding of how the tools worked.

Safe experimentation communicates two messages. Learning is expected, and people do not need to be experts before they begin. It reduces fear and increases engagement.

Redesigning workflows for human and AI collaboration

AI adoption slows when organisations attempt to insert new tools into outdated processes. People return to familiar routines when workflows do not match the logic of the technology. HR can help bridge this gap by redesigning workflows so that AI supports human strengths rather than creating extra steps.

This requires practical questions.

'Where does AI add value?'
'Where does human oversight matter most?'
'How should employees escalate issues?'
'How will decisions be documented?'

An organisation observed this pattern when it introduced an AI tool that offered suggestions. Once the workflow made clear that people remained the final decision-makers and the technology served as guidance, trust increased and use became more consistent.

The improvement came not from the tool itself but from the clarity around who held decision authority.

Workflow redesign is a readiness accelerator. It reduces friction and signals that the organisation is actively supporting new ways of working.

Preparing managers to lead through AI

Managers shape how teams interpret change. Employees watch their reactions closely. They pay attention to how managers talk about AI, how they respond to uncertainty and how they help teams navigate early missteps. Managers become the first line of readiness support.

HR can prepare managers by giving them a clear role in the transition. This includes helping them explain why AI is being introduced, supporting them in conversations about concerns and giving them practical tools to help teams learn.

In another case, a company introduced a short program to help managers support their teams as AI entered daily work. Managers learned how to guide conversations calmly, reinforce learning expectations and show that experimentation was part of the process. Teams responded with greater confidence because they felt their leaders were navigating the transition alongside them.

When managers model clarity and steadiness, readiness grows faster.

Embedding readiness into talent and career systems

As AI becomes more integrated into work, organisations need to reflect this shift in their talent and career systems. Employees want to understand how AI influences their growth, how it shapes progression and how new skills are recognised.

Another organisation updated its development and promotion criteria to reflect the growing importance of AI collaboration skills. Employees were expected to use AI for early research, structuring ideas and preparing initial drafts. This signalled that AI was part of long-term capability rather than a temporary initiative. People began to view readiness as an element of their growth, not a compliance task.

Embedding readiness into talent systems sends a strong signal. It tells employees that AI skills are part of their professional identity and that the organisation is committed to supporting them.

THE ROLE OF THE HUMAN–AI DECODER IN SUPPORTING INTEGRATION

AI transformation raises questions about fairness, responsibility and long-term capability that touch every part of the organisation. The human–AI decoder helps translate these questions into clear guidance so that people understand what is changing, how decisions will evolve and where their judgement continues to matter. It provides a shared way to interpret impact and gives leaders a structured approach to supporting teams through the transition.

Using the decoder, organisations can turn AI impact scans into practical expectations for each role, shape change plans that emphasise inclusion and partnership and coordinate with technology, risk and legal teams to ensure that adoption is both safe and clear. The decoder also helps leaders identify early signs of confusion or hesitation so support can be offered before issues deepen.

Orgnisations that succeed with AI invest in workflow redesign, senior leadership clarity and strong organisational practices. These factors consistently correlate with higher value creation, even when technical maturity is similar across companies (McKinsey & Company, 2024a).

Why Different Roles Need Different Readiness Levels

AI does not reshape work the same way across all roles. Employees who use AI tools for routine tasks experience a different type of change than employees who supervise AI output. Governance teams, responsible for oversight and risk management, experience an even deeper level of transformation.

During a healthcare AI tool deployment, these differences appeared clearly. Nurses concentrated on learning system indicators and thresholds. Clinicians focused on how responsibility would be shared and when escalation was necessary. Governance teams concentrated on oversight routines and documentation. These groups faced the same system but encountered different readiness needs.

A single approach to readiness cannot meet the very different expectations people bring to this transition. Teams feel the impact of AI in uneven ways and their needs shift just as unevenly. Using the principles of the human–AI decoder allows organisations to shape readiness around those differences, offering support that matches the level of change each group is actually experiencing.

MAKING READINESS A DAILY PRACTICE

Readiness becomes sustainable when it grows into a cultural expectation rather than a project with a defined end point. Culture shifts when learning is normal, communication is clear and people see how human judgement continues to matter.

Teams adapt more quickly when they have regular opportunities to ask questions, test new tools and reflect on what is working. Short learning moments, open conversations and practical demonstrations help employees stay grounded as AI evolves.

Transparency reinforces this. Employees want to know why AI is being introduced, what it solves and how decisions will change. Clear communication reduces speculation and builds trust.

Readiness also strengthens when organisations show how human judgement improves the quality of AI-supported work. Employees want to know that their expertise remains central. When organisations reinforce this, people feel valued and approach AI with more confidence.

A 2025 analysis from the World Economic Forum notes that trust is a cornerstone of successful and responsible AI adoption (World Economic Forum, 2025c). When transparency, human judgement and clear expectations are visible, readiness becomes part of the culture.

X ***Executive Checklist for Employee AI Readiness*** *For leaders who want a quick sense of how prepared their organisation is to work with AI, the Employee AI readiness checklist in Appendix 9 offers a simple diagnostic. It highlights the essential elements that shape whether people understand AI, feel confident using it and can integrate it into their work. The exercise helps leadership teams identify early gaps in understanding, trust or workflow design. It also supports more focused conversations about where employees may need clarity or support before AI moves into daily operations. Use this tool as a practical companion to this chapter when assessing your starting point and shaping next steps for responsible AI adoption.*

X ***The Employee AI Culture Pulse Survey*** *The pulse survey in Appendix 10 provides a quick way to understand how employees are actually experiencing AI as it enters their day-to-day work. It reveals whether people feel informed, supported and confident, and it surfaces concerns that may not appear in formal updates. Use this exercise when you want a rapid sense of the organisation's cultural temperature, especially during early rollout phases or immediately after introducing a new tool. The survey gives leaders a grounded view of where clarity is strong, where uncertainty is rising and where additional communication or guidance may be needed.*

READINESS IS A LONG-TERM CAPABILITY

Readiness is a long-term capability. Technology will continue to evolve. New AI systems will emerge. Workflows will change. Tasks that feel manual today will be automated tomorrow. In this environment, readiness becomes one of the most durable competitive strengths an organisation can build.

The organisations that thrive will not be the ones with the most advanced systems. They will be the ones where people understand how to work with AI, trust the role it plays and feel confident navigating the transitions that come with it. Readiness is how organisations ensure that people remain central even as technology evolves.

AI does not only require systems. It requires people who feel prepared, valued and capable as their work changes. Readiness is what turns possibility into progress and keeps people at the centre of the future of work.

But readiness alone is not enough. As AI becomes more deeply woven into decisions, workflows and organisational identity, the way we define work and the way we define HR must also evolve. Preparing people for AI is the first step. Building an operating model that allows humans and intelligent systems to work together with clarity, fairness and shared accountability is the next.

This is where the idea of Human-Machine Resources (HMR) begins to take shape. It is a shift from supporting employees in a world influenced by technology to designing an organisation where humans and intelligent systems operate side by side. It moves beyond readiness and into the structures, roles and principles that will guide the future workforce.

Chapter 9 explores this transition. It shows how organisations can build a model where human judgement and machine capability reinforce each other, where talent systems reflect new forms of contribution and where leadership expands from managing people to orchestrating combined human and machine performance. It is the step that turns readiness into long-term capability and prepares the organisation for the era ahead.

Key Takeaways

- Technology delivers value only when people feel ready to use it with confidence.
- Readiness develops across four elements: cognitive, emotional, behavioural and organisational.
- AI reshapes how people understand their role, influence and long-term value.
- Employees often experience curiosity and uncertainty at the same time when AI enters their work.
- Different roles experience AI differently, so readiness must match the level of impact.
- Managers play a critical role in shaping how teams interpret and embrace AI.

- Safe spaces for experimentation accelerate adoption and reduce fear.
- Clear and consistent communication strengthens trust and reduces speculation.
- Organisational systems must evolve to support new behaviours, not constrain them.
- Readiness is a cultural capability that grows over time and determines long-term success.

9

HUMAN–MACHINE RESOURCES

ABSTRACT

Artificial Intelligence (AI) is reshaping how work is organised, how decisions are made and how employees contribute value. This chapter examines the human side of that shift and introduces Human-Machine Resources (HMR) as the next evolution of the people function. It shows how AI enters organisations through small changes that alter tasks, expectations and the psychological experience of work long before structures begin to adapt. The chapter explains how HMR becomes the connector between technology and human experience by translating complexity into clarity, strengthening trust and guiding employees through continuous change. It outlines the core responsibilities of HMR, including role redesign, collaboration models, readiness building, fairness governance and the integration of human and machine contribution into a single workforce system. It also presents an HMR capability maturity model to help leaders understand their starting point and the conditions required to progress towards a more strategic, human-centred approach to AI. HMR emerges as the function that guides organisations through a future where intelligent systems become part of everyday work.

Keywords: Human–Machine Resources; AI workforce transformation; human–AI collaboration; future of work; organisational readiness; workforce design; intelligent systems; leadership in the age of AI; capability maturity; human-centred transformation

AI is changing how work is organised, how decisions are made and how employees contribute value. Across earlier chapters, we have examined how AI reshapes tasks, skills, judgement and workforce design. Chapter 9 brings the focus to leadership. It asks a question that sits at the centre of every transformation:

'Who leads the human side of AI?'

A first glimpse of AI in the workflow reveals how quietly disruption begins.

A claims officer in a global insurance company opened her system on a Monday morning and saw something new. A draft recommendation appeared beside her usual case file. The text was clear, structured and accurate, but she had not asked for it. She remembered an email about a new AI feature the week before, yet it had not explained what she was seeing now. The system had simply begun to contribute.

She paused. She did not know where the suggestion came from or what the system expected of her, and she was unsure who would be responsible if it turned out to be wrong.

Her manager had similar questions. He had been told that AI would improve efficiency, but he had not been guided on how to integrate the system into expectations, routines or escalation paths. Both experienced the same moment of uncertainty.

AI enters organisations quietly. It arrives through tools, features and small changes that appear long before leaders explain how work is shifting. People notice these signals early, often before any formal guidance is given. They sense that expectations are changing and that the familiar ways of working no longer feel as certain. This is why AI cannot be led by one function alone. It requires collaboration between technology, risk, operations, legal, people leaders and every part of the organisation that shapes how work happens.

As the previous chapters have shown, HR has a unique opportunity to support this transformation. It sits at the intersection of people, systems and work design and carries an obligation to help the organisation build confidence, clarity and trust as AI becomes part of daily work. Yet HR cannot play this role without changing itself. It must evolve into Human-Machine Resources (HMR), a function designed to guide the human side of intelligent systems and support the new relationships between people and AI.

WHY HMR MATTERS

The early signals inside organisations reveal why yesterday's structures are no longer enough. AI redefines workflows, decisions and expectations in ways that appear technical on the surface, but are deeply human in practice. People want clarity about what AI means for their role, their judgment and their future. HMR provides the support that helps leaders interpret these shifts together and ensures that people remain central as AI reshapes how work is organised.

The people function has to evolve to guide employees through these changes. HR cannot meet rising expectations with traditional structures. To ensure AI strengthens rather than weakens human contribution, it needs a broader mandate that reflects how work is now created, supported and experienced. With this gap now clear, the next step is to understand what replaces the old model. This gap between technological advancement and human experience is where the next evolution of the people function begins.

Introducing HMR

HMR represents that evolution. It becomes the organisational decoder for AI-driven change. It translates disruption into clarity and readiness, strengthening human contribution. As intelligent systems take on more responsibility, the people function gains a new role: guiding how humans and systems work together in a single workforce.

HMR also strengthens collaboration across the organisation. It does not replace the work of IT, Finance, Operations or Strategy.

It connects them. AI demands shared ownership and HMR ensures that human experience, system behaviour and organisational priorities stay aligned.

This chapter does not present a full operating model. It offers the ideas leaders need to understand why HMR matters and what it enables. Designing the processes, governance structures and capability frameworks needed for a mature HMR function is a substantial effort that would require its own dedicated book. The goal here is to outline the core ideas that define HMR and provide leaders with the foundation they need to understand why this evolution matters.

It offers a practical view of HMR as a strategic function that shapes human and machine collaboration, protects trust and strengthens the human experience of work. With this framing in place, the focus turns to how HMR moves beyond its traditional remit and becomes a source of leadership in an era where intelligent systems play a growing role in daily work.

Why AI Creates a New Opportunity for HR

AI changes work in ways that reach far beyond automation. It influences routines and alters how people collaborate. It also affects the psychological experience of work. Research shows that digital technologies are changing how people communicate, collaborate and make decisions (Hill et al., 2022).

Most HR functions were built for a different era. They were designed for stable job structures, predictable workflows and long cycles of role evolution. AI does not move at that pace. It shifts tasks, responsibilities and decision boundaries faster than traditional HR processes were ever meant to accommodate. The result is a growing gap inside organisations. Employees feel the change before leaders explain it. Automation advances faster than the structures that support human contribution. These gaps slow adoption, weaken trust and create uncertainty about the future of work.

This moment creates a rare opportunity for HR to redefine its place in the enterprise. The traditional model assumed that people performed the work and technology supported them quietly in the background. That world no longer exists. Intelligent systems now influence how work flows, how decisions are made and how fast organisations can move. HR can step forward as the strategic partner that guides how people and AI work together. The questions that leaders struggle with, from redesigning roles to understanding where human judgment remains essential, sit directly within HR's mandate. So do the questions about trust in machine-supported decisions and how to prepare employees for a workforce that evolves with unprecedented speed.

HMR closes the gap between technological possibility and human experience. It gives leaders a support model that helps them understand how AI affects work and guide employees as tasks shift, roles evolve and expectations rise. It is not a technical function. It is a leadership function that strengthens clarity, trust and accountability across the organisation. For HR, this marks the moment where the function can support the future of work with more influence, focus and purpose than ever before.

The Workforce Now Includes Machines

AI is no longer a background utility. It drafts content, proposes decisions, moves work through a sequence of steps and completes tasks from beginning to end. As these systems take on more responsibility, the definition of workforce expands. It now includes intelligent systems that manage first-level processes, models that generate insights and written output, systems that shape or execute decisions and workflows that run without human initiation.

This change does not reduce the importance of people. It shifts human contribution toward areas that depend on judgement, ethics, context, service quality and creativity.

HMR becomes the function that aligns these contributions. It ensures the organisation integrates intelligent systems in ways that strengthen capability and trust and guides recommendations with business leaders so that decisions reflect what is best for people and the organisation through a human-centred view.

FROM WORKFORCE MANAGEMENT TO WORKFORCE SYSTEM LEADERSHIP

HR has always had an important responsibility: supporting people. In an AI-powered organisation, this responsibility widens. HMR supports people and the systems in which they work. It leads the design, governance and integration of human and machine contribution. It navigates the new boundaries between algorithmic and human decision-making. It supports employees when familiar tasks change and when new expectations arise.

The comparison in Fig. 7 shows the transition from HR to HMR in its simplest form.

The shift is not cosmetic. It reflects a deeper change in how organisations operate.

HR manages the humans. HMR leads the workforce, which includes humans and machines.

A workforce system includes people, intelligent systems, workflows, decision paths and the conditions that shape human contribution. It also includes the guidance people need as tasks shift from humans to machines or move into shared space where both work together. HMR does not replace the work of IT. It makes the human side of intelligent systems understandable, trusted and usable.

Why the Organisation Needs HMR Now

Once the workforce includes both people and intelligent systems, organisations face pressures that traditional HR models cannot address. AI does not disrupt organisations through one large event. It disrupts through many small changes that accumulate over time. Tasks become automated. Workflows become orchestrated by intelligent systems. Decisions become influenced by models. Employees encounter new tools that they do not fully understand. Leaders face new responsibilities without clear guidance.

HMR steps in to interpret these changes. As intelligent systems enter daily workflows, the organisation feels the impact in multiple dimensions.

HR Focus	HMR Focus
Manage employees and people processes	Lead workforce of humans and intelligent systems
Apply policies and standards	Design how humans and machines work together
Ensure legal and regulatory compliance	Safeguard fairness, transparency and ethical AI use
Support wellbeing and development	Build readiness for responsible AI use across organisation
Advise leaders on people matters	Guide leaders on shared human–machine decisions
Maintain structures and job architecture	Support identity and purpose in an AI-enabled workforce
Handle employee relations and conflict	Protect psychological safety and trust in AI-enabled work

Fig. 7. Human–Machine Resources (HMR).

Source: Author's Own Creation.

Intelligent Systems Shift How Work Is Created and Performed

Workflows no longer follow fixed steps. Tasks can shift between humans and machines based on context, quality requirements and business rules. Human judgement becomes more valuable, not less, because people must know when to rely on AI and when to redirect.

HMR helps define these boundaries by clarifying when to rely on AI, when to intervene and how accountability is maintained.

Automation Alters the Psychological Experience of Work

As AI takes on more responsibility, employees ask new questions. They want to know how their role will evolve, what skills matter and where their judgement fits. These questions determine engagement and trust.

HMR supports people through this transition by giving them clarity and direction.

Digital Workflows Create New Expectations For Leadership

Leaders have to navigate systems where decisions are shared between humans and algorithms. They need guidance on accountability, escalation and ethical use. They also need support in learning how to manage mixed human and machine teams.

HMR provides this leadership support by clarifying accountability, guiding decision-making and strengthening leaders' ability to manage human–AI collaboration..

Intelligent Systems Reshape Governance

Intelligent systems introduce new risks. Bias, lack of transparency and inconsistent outcomes can undermine trust. Employees need to know that the organisation protects fairness and transparency.

HMR becomes the custodian of responsible AI for the workforce. It works with legal, risk and technology teams to ensure that AI supports human rights, organisational values and regulatory requirements.

Automation Transforms Organisational Identity

As the workforce expands to include intelligent systems, employees need a unifying narrative. They want to understand how their contribution grows, how they remain relevant and how the organisation recognises their impact.

HMR builds that narrative by making clear how humans and AI work together and how human contribution continues to matter.

Humans at the Centre of an Intelligent Workforce

Despite advances in AI, organisations remain human systems. Culture shapes behaviour. Trust shapes resilience. Purpose shapes performance. AI can complement human capability, but it does not replace the need for connection, clarity and identity.

Employees need to understand how to work with AI systems. They need the skills to judge when AI output is reliable and when it requires escalation. They need confidence in their ability to add value in a system where machines support many tasks.

HMR is responsible for building this confidence. It redesigns development pathways. It supports employees as tasks move. It ensures that wellbeing, learning and psychological safety remain at the core of transformation.

The goal is not to defend the human role. The goal is to strengthen human contribution.

HMR'S FUTURE MANDATE

With this foundation in place, we can define what HMR is expected to do. HMR steps into a role that goes beyond traditional people management. It becomes the function that designs how humans and intelligent systems work together. It interprets the impact of AI on roles and workflows and supports leaders as they adjust accountability boundaries. It ensures that employees have the understanding and confidence they need when tasks shift and expectations rise.

HMR helps the organisation lead the human side of AI. It guides leaders in making decisions that balance operational progress with human experience and ensures that the introduction of intelligent systems strengthens trust, capability and clarity across the workforce.

The organisation cannot rely on technical teams alone to guide this transition. Engineers build systems. Product owners define features. Data scientists optimise models. None of these groups specialises in how people experience change, how identity evolves, or how culture responds when technology takes on more responsibility.

HMR fills this gap. It acts as the translator between technology and workforce experience. It makes the implications of AI understandable. It helps people develop the skills and confidence needed to operate alongside intelligent systems. It ensures that wellbeing, fairness and transparency remain central to the transformation.

The mandate of HMR can be summarised through five core responsibilities.

1. Decode AI disruption into human insight

Employees face rapid changes in how their work is structured. Tasks move. Processes automate. Systems generate recommendations that influence decisions. Without explanation, these changes create confusion and weaken trust.

HMR turns disruption into clarity. It shows employees where their judgement matters. It outlines which skills become more important. It connects AI adoption with purpose and contribution.

2. Redesign roles and collaboration models

AI transforms work at task level, which means organisations need a structured way to redesign roles and define how humans and intelligent systems collaborate.

HMR uses the human–AI decoder to guide this process. This helps to identify which responsibilities shift to systems, which remain human and which move into shared space where both contribute. They give leaders a clear foundation for redesigning work in ways that strengthen capability, clarity and trust.

3. Govern trust, fairness and responsibility

AI introduces new expectations. People want to know that systems are used responsibly. They want transparency about how decisions are made. They want assurance that oversight exists.

HMR works with technology, legal and risk teams to define how accountable AI operates in the workforce. It ensures that fairness and transparency are part of everyday practice.

4. Enable readiness and growth
Employees need skills that help them work alongside AI. They also need time to learn and adapt.

HMR supports this learning curve by redesigning development pathways, learning experiences and team practices.

5. Strengthen psychological safety
AI can create uncertainty. Employees may worry about relevance, capability or performance expectations. Leaders may feel unsure about how to manage systems that make recommendations or automate tasks.

HMR ensures that people can ask questions, raise concerns and experiment without fear. It treats psychological safety as a requirement, not an aspiration.

THE EMERGING STRUCTURE OF HMR

This section provides a high-level structural map of how HMR evolves. To see where HR is heading, it helps to first understand the traditional structure it has been built on for decades. For more than two decades, most organisations have relied on a structure shaped by Dave Ulrich's influential book Human Resource Champions (Ulrich, 1997). His model reframed HR from an administrative function into a strategic partner and introduced a design that quickly became the global standard. At its core, this approach organises HR into a small number of distinct roles that separate strategy, specialist expertise and operational delivery.

Most organisations still follow a similar pattern. 'HR Leadership' sets the people strategy and connects HR to the executive agenda. 'HR Business Partners' work directly with leaders and translate business priorities into workforce actions. 'Centres of Expertise' design specialist programs and frameworks in areas such as talent, leadership, compensation, learning and employee relations. 'HR Operations', delivered either in-country or through shared services, handles the employee lifecycle, core transactions and day-to-day support. 'HR Technology & Data' oversees systems, data, workflows and the platforms that support employees and managers. 'Country HR' anchors all of this at the local level, ensuring compliance with national regulations and acting as the first touchpoint for employees.

This traditional structure has been durable because it offers clarity and consistency to deliver people services across complex organisations. It established the operating model that many companies still rely on today as they enter the age of AI.

At first glance, the structure still looks familiar, but every team carries new responsibilities, new roles and new forms of accountability that reflect how profoundly AI shifts the nature of work.

HR REBORN FOR THE AGE OF AI

A new kind of structure is taking shape. It is not a dual system with humans on one side and intelligent machines on the other. Work no longer separates this way. Machines enter the flow of work, decisions and team dynamics, while human roles evolve in response. This creates a single integrated model of contribution. The people function needs to understand capability, culture and system behaviour, along with the boundaries that govern machine participation.

Every part of the structure has to be grounded in responsible AI practice. It must protect equity, support explainability, uphold safety and ensure responsible use. The details of this design require their own dedicated treatment, which we will not cover in detail. They involve entire operating models, role architectures, governance frameworks, development paths and decision systems. The following outlines the new structure and responsibilities shaped by this AI shift.

HMR Workforce Leadership

Workforce Leadership becomes responsible for both people and the intelligent systems that support them. The role shifts from shaping people strategy to shaping how humans and machines contribute together. Workforce Leaders decide where human judgment matters most and where machine capability adds value. They make sure AI systems work safely, operate transparently and uphold fairness and trust. Ethical oversight and responsible stewardship sit at the centre of their mandate.

This shift also changes how Workforce leaders think about their own work. Success is no longer measured only through efficiency or policy compliance. It is measured by the strength of the overall workforce system. That includes employee skills, the behaviour of intelligent systems, clear decision pathways and the level of trust people feel in the environment around them.

HMR Workforce Orchestrator

Workforce Orchestrators take on a clearer role in helping leaders understand how AI impacts work. Their responsibilities move beyond translating business plans into people actions. They explain how intelligent systems shift tasks, responsibilities and decision points. They help leaders see where AI can support work and where human judgment must remain in control. They also help teams navigate the emotional and practical adjustments that come when people and machines operate in the same workflow. In this environment they become the link between organisational strategy and the daily reality of human and machine collaboration.

They also play a central role in shaping AI adoption. Workforce Orchestrators work with the business and IT to identify suitable AI use cases, assess their impact and guide leaders on the workforce implications. They provide recommendations on how roles may change, where new skills are needed and which approach best balances benefit, risk and fairness.

This requires accuracy and confidence. Workforce Orchestrators need to understand how tasks move across the six levels of AI impact and how the human–AI decoder interprets those shifts so they can guide leaders with clarity. They need to detect early signs of change that employees may not yet recognise. They should challenge assumptions when the risks of AI outweigh the benefits. And they need the judgement to know when machine recommendations require human review.

HMR Capability Domains

The capability domains *(previously Centres of Expetise)* bring human and machine considerations into every part of the people function.

Talent teams define the skills needed for AI-ready roles and show where human strengths grow in value as machines handle more execution. Leadership development prepares managers to lead teams shaped by data and autonomous workflows and to intervene when decisions need a human hand. Talent acquisition selects people who can operate confidently in a shared human-machine environment and ensures AI-enabled recruiting tools are used fairly. Total rewards designs models that reflect the combined contribution of humans and intelligent systems.

Workforce intelligence monitors system behaviour, detects unintended bias, tracks shifts in human capability and assesses the combined impact on performance and organisational health. Employee relations becomes the guardian of algorithmic fairness. Machine-supported decisions need to remain transparent, explainable and open to challenge. This approach embeds digital accountability into the organisation's duty of care.

These domains form the backbone of HMR. They help employees navigate change. They help leaders make decisions rooted in human values. They ensure that AI adoption strengthens rather than fragments the organisation.

HMR Workforce Operations and Intelligent Workflows

Workforce Operations becomes responsible for aligning human processes with machine processes. It manages onboarding, pay and transitions. It also oversees system deployment, retraining cycles and the behaviour of AI embedded in workflows.

Automated processes now initiate tasks on their own. Workforce Operations keeps both human and machine workflows reliable, coherent and fair. Equity and transparency become central measures of success.

Employees feel this shift directly in the systems they use and the tasks they perform. Workforce Operations ensures that intelligent systems behave in line with leadership expectations and the broader guidance set by HMR. Once human and machine workflows are stable, the next requirement is to protect the integrity of the systems that operate within them.

Digital HMR and AI Governance

The digital pillar (previously HR Tech & Data) becomes home of system integrity and responsible operation. It establishes the guardrails that keep intelligent systems safe, ethical and consistent. Model stewards monitor performance. AI audit leads test decisions for fairness and accuracy. AI supervisors oversee the daily behaviour of agents and escalate anomalies.

Employee experience technologists ensure that interactions between humans and digital systems remain intuitive and supportive.

This pillar is as essential as talent management or organisational design because it protects the integrity of the machine side of the workforce and keeps it aligned with human values. Without this foundation, even well-designed workflows can break down. Employees lose trust when systems behave unpredictably. Risks increase when oversight is unclear. Digital HMR prevents this erosion by keeping expectations clear and monitoring them with discipline. With global system integrity in place, the focus turns to how these practices land at the local level where employees experience AI most directly.

Country HMR

Country HMR ensures that human and machine collaboration complies with national laws and cultural expectations. It safeguards employee rights, ensures fairness in automated decisions and guarantees that human recourse remains accessible. This is where employees feel the impact of AI most directly and where trust is built or lost.

Country teams manage the most sensitive questions. Employees want to know who is accountable when an automated decision affects their work. They want explanations they can understand and support they can access without hesitation. Country HMR provides that clarity and anchors trust at the local level.

Together these elements form a single system. Workforce Leadership sets direction and defines the values that guide people and intelligent systems. Workforce Orchestrators translate those values into practical decisions. Capability domains shape the skills and behaviours needed for collaboration. Operations keep workflows stable. Digital HMR protects system integrity. Country teams anchor the change locally. Cross-cutting roles connect these elements so the organisation can evolve as the workforce evolves.

This is not HR with upgraded tools. This is HMR. It is a structure built for a workforce where humans and intelligent systems operate together and strengthen one another.

THE ROLE OF HR IN AI ETHICS AND GOVERNANCE

'What happens when intelligent systems begin to make decisions that affect people?'

This question sits at the heart of ethics and governance in an AI-driven world.

It is also becoming increasingly important. Many organisations have created AI ethics boards or councils, yet the field is still young and lacks the transparency and clarity that employees expect. These efforts often sit inside technology or operations functions and focus on ethics within the technology itself. Far less attention is given to the ethical impact on people, which leaves other functions contributing only at the margins.

HMR helps close this gap by working with business leaders to define when technology should support a decision and when a human must take responsibility. It ensures that employees understand how AI is used and that they have clear ways to question or challenge outcomes. It also helps monitor how systems shape day-to-day experiences, identifies unintended bias and works with other functions to address it. The human–AI decoder strengthens this work by translating system behaviour into guidance employees can understand. This human-centred view ensures that AI strengthens work rather than undermining confidence or fairness.

A complete ethics and governance model requires structured processes, shared ownership across functions, dedicated monitoring routines and clear escalation paths. The purpose here is simply to show why ethics and governance must sit at the centre of any AI transformation.

HR SHARED SERVICES IN THE ERA OF INTELLIGENT SYSTEMS

As organisations modernise their operating models, many are revisiting the question of whether HR Shared Services should still be built or expanded. Automation changes the nature of shared services, but it does not remove the need for a centre that protects consistency, quality and fairness.

Intelligent systems decentralise the experience of service because employees can resolve more tasks directly through assistants embedded in the tools they already use. Yet the underlying responsibilities for governance, accuracy, security and workflow integrity still benefit from a coordinated structure. Without this centre, decentralised AI agents may drift towards inconsistent decisions, unmanaged risks or fragmented experiences.

For organisations that are establishing HR Shared Services for the first time, the recommendation is not to abandon the model but to design it for a world where intelligent systems perform most of the transactions. This means building a smaller, more specialised centre with a stronger focus on policy ownership, workflow quality, exception handling and cross-country complexity. The scale of the work changes, but its importance does not.

In this sense, AI does not replace the rationale for HR shared services. It redefines it. The centre becomes the guardian of coherence in a landscape where service delivery feels increasingly decentralised to employees but still relies on shared ownership, trusted governance and human judgement behind the scenes.

This evolution brings HR Shared Services closer to Digital HMR. Together, they form the environment in which AI agents operate and ensure that processes, data and decisions remain safe, fair and transparent. HR shared services becomes a strategic part of HMR, not a processing engine. It supports the organisation as human and machine contributions continue to evolve and helps maintain stability and trust as transactions shift into automated workflows.

HMR DOES NOT REPLACE THE IT FUNCTION

The evolution towards HMR does not mean that HR is absorbing the responsibilities of IT. It means the opposite. AI makes the partnership between HR and IT more important than at any point in recent history. Each function brings a different kind of expertise to the organisation. IT understands system design, architecture, data flows and technical integrity. HR understands people, roles, skills and the conditions under which employees trust and use intelligent systems. AI requires both to work in harmony, which is why a stronger partnership becomes essential as organisations mature.

Some of the new human and machine roles will emerge exactly in this shared space. Skills architects shape the competencies needed for effective human and machine collaboration. Ethics partners monitor how AI influences decisions and whether the outcomes remain fair and transparent. Workflow designers map the handoffs between people and intelligent systems. Readiness coaches support employees as tasks evolve. Human insight partners protect the qualities of judgement, empathy and context that no system can replicate. These roles do not replace IT or overshadow HR. They act as connectors between the two functions and translate between human needs and digital behaviours so that systems strengthen work rather than disrupt it. The roles mentioned here are only at a high level and conceptual, and not all organisations will require each of them in the same form or to the same extent.

A simple example illustrates the point.

Imagine a customer support team adopting an AI assistant that drafts responses and routes queries. IT builds and maintains the system, ensures data security and monitors performance. HR defines how the role of the agent evolves, identifies the skills required, guides employees through the transition and establishes when a human should step in. The cross-cutting HMR roles operate between the two, ensuring the AI behaves ethically, the workflow is coherent and employees feel confident using it. No single function could manage this alone.

In an AI-enabled workplace, neither HR nor IT can succeed in isolation. They coexist, complement one another and shape an environment where people and intelligent systems work together to drive business results. The future belongs to organisations that treat this partnership as a shared leadership responsibility and equip both functions to thrive together.

HOW HMR GUIDES THE ORGANISATION THROUGH AI ADOPTION

HMR becomes the point of stability in a period defined by constant change. It is the function that helps the organisation understand what is happening, why it matters and how people should respond. Without this layer, AI adoption becomes uneven. Some teams adapt, others hold back and employees interpret changes on their own. HMR brings structure to a process that can easily feel disjointed.

Its role begins with translation. Engineers and product owners speak in technical terms that do not map easily to the lived realities of work. Employees need the implications explained in plain language. They want to understand how tasks will shift, how workflows will evolve and what these changes mean for their contribution. HMR provides this clarity before assumptions take over.

HMR also brings visibility to changes that directly affect work. In many organisations, people first encounter AI when a new feature appears in a tool they use every day. They see prompts they have not been prepared for. They feel responsible for outcomes without understanding the intent. HMR anticipates these moments and prepares teams so that the first experience with new capabilities does not create anxiety.

Another part of HMR's role is guiding accountability. When AI generates recommendations or automates steps, leaders must understand their responsibility. They need to know when to review and when to override. They need to understand how to evaluate quality when a system contributes to an outcome. HMR gives leaders the frameworks that make these decisions clear by clarifying when to rely on AI, when to intervene, and how responsibility is assigned.

HMR also keeps adoption aligned with readiness. Technology can move ahead of people if the organisation is not careful. When employees feel unprepared, adoption slows and confidence drops. HMR redesigns learning pathways so employees gain the skills they need to work with AI reliably rather than defensively.

The final element is trust. People want to know that systems are used responsibly and that oversight exists. HMR works with legal, compliance and technology teams to ensure that the organisation earns this trust through behaviour, not through statements. Trust becomes a daily practice rather than a communication campaign.

THE HMR CAPABILITY MATURITY MODEL

Organisations do not arrive in the age of AI at the same starting point. Some still operate HR as a service function focused on efficiency and compliance. Others have begun experimenting with AI-enabled workflows and analytics. A small number have already moved toward redesigning roles and capabilities, as reflected in recent industry shifts toward unlearning and adaptive organisational cultures (BW People, 2006). The HMR Capability Maturity Model helps leaders understand where they are today and what it takes to progress towards a more strategic, human-centred approach to AI. The model that follows gives leaders a way to assess where they stand and what must change as AI reshapes work.

Stage 1: Foundational – HR as Service

In the earliest stage, the people function is primarily administrative. HR focuses on reliability, compliance and basic digitisation. AI appears only in isolated tools, usually through simple automation such as chatbots, workflow routing or document handling. The strategic focus is stability. Leaders want confidence that essential processes run smoothly. The role of HR is to support operations rather than shape the workforce.

Stage 2: Operational – HR as Enabler

The second stage begins when organisations adopt AI more consistently. Tools show up across recruitment, learning, engagement surveys and service delivery. Teams start to use analytics. Workflows become more efficient. HR becomes an enabler of AI use rather than the architect of it. Processes improve, but decisions about how AI affects work and roles remain fragmented. At this stage, HR supports experimentation but does not yet define how AI impacts the workforce.

Stage 3: Transformational – HMR as Workforce Architect
The third stage marks the transition into HMR. HR evolves from managing processes to shaping how work is designed and how people and intelligent systems operate together. The function uses models like human–AI decoder to understand how tasks shift across the impact levels, how accountability boundaries evolve and where human judgement becomes more important as systems take on execution. HR works with IT, Operations, Finance and Strategy to redesign roles, workflows and organisational structures. It begins to guide the workforce through change rather than respond to it, helping leaders apply the decoder to interpret what work is becoming and what people need to succeed within it.

This is the stage where responsible AI practice becomes visible. HR helps leaders evaluate the fairness, transparency and impact of AI and ensures that systems strengthen human contribution.

The HMR Capability Maturity Model is not a measure of technical sophistication. It reflects how well the organisation understands the human implications of AI and how prepared it is to lead people through continuous evolution. Organisations advance when they gain clarity about responsibility, build a shared language for human and machine collaboration and develop the confidence to redesign work at scale.

How Organisations Move to Higher Maturity

Progress through these stages depends on alignment. Organisations move faster when someone clearly owns the human side of AI. When ownership is unclear, technical initiatives advance while the workforce lags behind. Recognising HMR as the anchor for this space reduces friction and gives change a clear direction.

Shared understanding accelerates progress. Teams make better decisions when they use the same language to describe how tasks, roles and decision-making are changing. The human–AI decoder provides that common ground. It is a simple way to make sense of how deeply AI is entering the work and what that means for the people who do it. By breaking the change into clear levels of impact, it turns what can feel emotional or abstract into something concrete that leaders can discuss, compare and act on. Instead of debating opinions, teams can see the same picture and focus on what matters most: how to support people as their work evolves.

Confidence matters as well. Leaders who understand the dynamics of human and machine collaboration create calmer environments. They help employees anticipate change and recognise how their contribution grows as systems take on routine work. HMR strengthens this confidence by providing scenarios, guidance and practical tools rather than abstract principles.

How HMR Supports Employees Through Role Evolution

Employees do not experience AI as a strategic concept. They experience it as changes to their daily routines. Tasks move into systems. AI drafts summaries or recommendations. New workflows replace familiar steps. These shifts raise questions long before leaders address them.

HMR Can provides the clarity employees need. It explains what is changing and why. It focuses on the work employees perform rather than high-level narratives. It helps people understand where their judgment becomes more valuable and where their contribution increases in importance. It also supports practical skill development. Employees do not need deep technical knowledge, but they do need to know how to review AI output, catch errors, escalate decisions and work within mixed human and machine processes.

Beyond skills, HMR supports identity. When tasks shift, people wonder where they fit. HMR reassures employees that their role evolves with the organisation and that human capabilities become more important as intelligent systems take on routine work.

How HMR Strengthens Organisational Trust

Trust determines whether employees adopt AI confidently or reluctantly. They want to know that systems are used responsibly, that decisions are monitored and that fairness is protected. They also want to know who to turn to when a system makes a decision that does not seem right.

HMR strengthens trust through clear communication, consistent oversight and visible ethical safeguards. It ensures that employees understand why AI is used, how it works and what checks exist. It partners with technology, legal and risk teams to address concerns early and openly. Trust grows when employees see that systems are built to support their judgement rather than displace it.

How HMR Enables Human and Machine Collaboration

Human and machine collaboration is practical. It shows up in everyday work as people learn how to interpret system output, escalate decisions and work within new routines. These changes require structure, clarity and time.

HMR designs the environment that makes this collaboration possible. It sets expectations, guides communication, aligns workflows and ensures that transitions do not leave people uncertain or excluded. Collaboration becomes part of organisational capability, influencing quality, productivity and culture. HMR turns it into an intentional practice rather than an improvised one.

PREPARING FOR WHAT COMES NEXT

AI capability will continue to expand and intelligent systems will take on a larger share of routine and analytical work. Expectations for leaders and employees will shift and the pace of change will accelerate. HMR positions the organisation to move through this evolution with stability and foresight. It gives people a structure they can trust and provides leaders with a support model they can rely on as work continues to transform.

HMR is built for a future where AI becomes part of the workforce. The current wave of technological advancement and the attention surrounding it only increase the urgency for HR to evolve. The shift cannot wait until systems are mature or fully understood. By the time machines take on visible roles in daily work, it will be too late for HR to build the capabilities and confidence the organisation needs.

The transition from HR to HMR is already in motion. It does not wait for technology to stabilise or for organisational structures to settle. Readiness emerges from the lived experiences of employees who feel their work change in real time. It is shaped by the pressure leaders face when intelligent systems offer recommendations they must interpret and oversee. It strengthens through the search for clarity and fairness in a period defined by continuous adjustment.

HMR provides this clarity. It gives the organisation a common foundation for understanding how people and intelligent systems work together by defining roles, setting decision boundaries and establishing shared principles for human–AI collaboration. It supports the transition in a way that feels steady and understandable. It shows how human contribution increases in value as systems take on more tasks.

Organisations that treat AI as a technical upgrade will struggle. Those that treat it as a workforce transformation will move faster. They will be better prepared for what comes next. Their employees will trust the direction of change and understand their place within it.

HMR is the function that makes this possible. It becomes the leadership engine that guides the organisation through continuous change and helps people stay confident in a world shaped by intelligent systems. It does this by aligning workforce strategy with AI adoption, defining how roles evolve, and ensuring that decisions, accountability and human contribution remain clear.

In the end, the name matters less than the readiness behind it. Whether organisations call it HMR or something else, the real priority is that HR is equipped to lead the AI transformation. A recent article reinforces this point, showing that Chief HR Officers play a pivotal role in how AI is adopted, governed and integrated into the workforce (Bersin, 2025).

The real transformation is not the rise of intelligent systems, but how people grow and lead alongside them with confidence and purpose.

Key Takeaways

- AI reshapes work in ways that extend beyond technology and require leadership that understands the human impact.
- Employees notice changes before leaders explain them and look for clarity about what these shifts mean for their role.
- HMR becomes the function that interprets AI disruption and translates it into actions people understand.
- The move from HR to HMR reflects a shift from process administration to workforce system leadership.
- Leaders need guidance on how to navigate shared human and machine decision-making.
- Employees need support as tasks shift and as their contribution evolves.
- Trust grows when AI is used responsibly and supported by transparency, consistency and clear accountability.
- Skills rooted in judgement, analysis and human understanding become more valuable as systems take on more execution.
- Human and machine collaboration becomes a defining organisational capability and requires intentional design.
- HMR becomes essential for guiding the organisation through continuous change and helping people stay confident as intelligent systems become part of daily work.

CLOSING NOTE

We are standing at an extraordinary moment in the history of work. Artificial Intelligence (AI) is moving faster than most people imagined and the choices leaders make now will shape how this period is remembered. The systems we build will matter. The principles behind them will matter even more. What will define this era is not the technology itself, but the kind of leadership that guides its use.

The rise of AI brings enormous potential, but it also carries a shared responsibility and raises questions that leaders can no longer ignore. People want to understand how their roles will evolve. They want to know where their judgement still matters and how they can grow as work around them shifts at an unfamiliar pace. They want reassurance that progress will still feel human. These are not questions that can be answered with broad statements or distant plans. They require honesty, presence and care.

The future asks something new of leaders. It asks whether we can guide people through change without losing empathy. It asks whether we can build organisations where work remains meaningful even when machines take on more execution. It asks whether we can protect dignity and fairness at a time when decisions may begin with algorithms long before a human has seen them.

Some concerns will be technical. Most will be human. People will wonder how their strengths will be recognised in a world shaped by both human and machine judgement. They will question who carries responsibility when a system influences a critical choice. They will look for clarity when familiar routines feel less stable than before.

New risks will emerge as AI interprets behaviour, predicts choices or reflects the biases hidden in its data. Organisations will need rules that are clear and transparent. They will need ways to explain how information is used, how digital work is monitored and how errors are addressed. Human connection, fairness and compassion will need to be protected deliberately. Trust will become as important as speed.

Careers will shift as roles evolve faster than structures were designed to change. The skills people need will stretch far beyond technical ability. Critical thinking, creativity, ethical reasoning and the confidence to work with intelligent systems will shape the next generation of talent. None of this is simple. All of it is possible when learning and openness become part of the day-to-day experience rather than something reserved for a select few.

There is a deeper truth beneath all of this. The future of work is not being written by technology. It is being written by the people who decide how technology is used. AI may accelerate tasks, but humans define meaning. AI may expand possibility, but humans decide what those possibilities are for.

The human–AI decoder gives leaders a way to make sense of this moment. It shows where work is shifting, how those shifts affect people and what responsible action looks like. It does not promise certainty. It offers a way to move through uncertainty with clarity, direction and care.

The six levels of AI impact give organisations something they have been missing. They provide a common language and a clear classification that helps leaders talk about AI's impact on the workforce without silence or hesitation. They replace vague concern with grounded conversation. They show how deeply AI is involved in a role and what that involvement means for people. They turn an uncomfortable topic into one that can be explored openly and with purpose.

The evolution of HR to Human–Machine Resources (HMR) has a defining role in the AI transformation. It can help organisations design the systems and structures that support people and clarify responsibilities. It can help leaders navigate complexity and give employees the confidence to understand where they fit as work evolves. When people understand the change, they can shape it.

This closing note is not an ending. It is an invitation. It invites us to approach AI with intention. It invites us to design the future rather than inherit it. It invites us to protect what makes work human and to help people grow as the world accelerates around them.

The responsibility belongs to all of us. If we choose clarity over confusion, fairness over convenience and people over speed, the future of work will not become a story of replacement. It will become a story of renewal and responsibility.

Let us meet that future with courage, curiosity and confidence.

The age of AI has begun. The human side still depends on us.

HOW THE BOOK USES AI AND EXAMPLES

This book uses the term Artificial Intelligence (AI) in a broad and practical way. It includes automation, algorithms, intelligent systems, AI agents and the digital co-workers that are beginning to shape daily work. It refers to any technology that shifts part of the workload from humans to machines. Particularly in Part III, the book speaks more directly about machines to show how these systems influence tasks, roles, team structures and the evolving definition of human work. To keep the reading experience clear, the book treats AI and machines as collective terms and focuses on their combined impact rather than on the differences between individual tools.

The examples throughout the book come from my professional experience and from conversations with peers, practitioners, researchers and technology leaders. They illustrate how the ideas in each chapter appear in real settings and how people navigate the practical realities of AI in their work. Several scenarios are blended or fictionalised to protect privacy and to illustrate patterns that extend beyond any single organisation, project or individual. Where the information is publicly available, the organisations involved have been named. Together, the examples reflect themes that appear across many environments facing similar challenges. Some examples also describe near-future situations that are realistic given the speed of AI development and the direction in which workplace practices are moving.

APPENDIX 1: EXECUTIVE AI AWARENESS PULSE CHECK

PURPOSE

This pulse check offers leaders a fast, structured way to understand how well their organisation grasps the workforce implications of AI. It shows what executives believe and whether they share the same view. This difference often explains why some transformations succeed while others stall.

HOW TO USE THIS EXECUTIVE AI AWARENESS PULSE CHECK

Invite each member of the leadership team to score the statements in the below table on a scale from one to five. The exercise takes less than ten minutes, but the conversations that follow often uncover blind spots that have been hiding in plain sight.

INTERPRETING THE RESULTS

The combined score provides an immediate sense of organisational readiness:

- **0–10 = At Risk:** AI remains abstract or misunderstood; begin with foundational learning and consistent definitions.
- **11–20 = Emerging:** Some alignment exists, but shared language and cross-functional coordination must be strengthened.
- **21–25 = Leading:** The organisation is prepared to move from awareness to structured action with clarity and confidence.

WHY IT MATTERS

Across industries, leadership teams often assume they share a common understanding of AI. In practice, definitions vary, expectations diverge and ethical concerns surface late in the process. The pulse check makes these differences visible. It highlights whether the organisation has agreed on what AI is, how it will reshape roles and which areas are ready for adoption. It also shows where ethical guard-rails still need to be strengthened. It also reveals whether HR has been involved early enough to guide the human side of transformation.

The tool does not replace deep analysis, but it creates the alignment necessary for meaningful dialogue. By beginning with this shared baseline, organisations can move from scattered efforts to coherent strategy.

The pulse check shown in Table A1 turns these insights into a practical tool for leadership teams.

Table A1. Executive AI Awareness Pulse Check.

Statements	Strongly Disagree – 1	Disagree – 2	Neutral – 3	Agree – 4	Strongly Agree – 5
We have a shared definition of what AI is and isn't.					
We've discussed how AI will impact roles in our business.					
We know which areas of the business are most AI-ready.					
We have policies in place for ethical AI usage.					

Table A1. (*Continued*)

Statements	Strongly Disagree – 1	Disagree – 2	Neutral – 3	Agree – 4	Strongly Agree – 5
We've involved HR early in our AI transformation strategy.					

Source: Author's own creation.

Developed as part of the human–AI decoder, this pulse check offers leaders a clear starting point for addressing AI's workforce impact with structure, transparency and a human-centred approach.

APPENDIX 2: RESEARCH ON AI AND WORK

A growing number of international studies and organisational frameworks have examined how AI is reshaping work, skills, jobs and organisational structures. Each takes a different lens, from economic modelling to enterprise readiness and together they contribute to a broader understanding of AI's workforce implications.

One of the earliest and most cited is Frey and Osborne (2013), who estimated the automatability of occupations by analysing whether tasks rely on perception, manipulation, creative intelligence or social intelligence. Their work helped shape the early debate around automation risk and task-level exposure.

The OECD's AI and the Future of Skills project (2021) extends this thinking by comparing human and AI capabilities across cognitive, socio-emotional and technical domains to guide education and training policy. The International Labour Organization (ILO) (2024) adds a global perspective with its index of occupational exposure to generative AI, combining task-level data, expert assessment and predictive modelling to show how different jobs may transform.

From a business perspective, Gartner (2024a) introduced its AI Maturity Model and Roadmap toolkit to help organisations understand how tasks and roles evolve under different levels of autonomy. The World Economic Forum (WEF) (2025b), through its Future of Jobs reports, continues to track global employment trends and emerging skill requirements, offering insight for governments, employers and educators.

At the enterprise level, McKinsey & Company (2023) explores how generative AI affects productivity and workforce redesign, linking task exposure to value creation. IBM's research (2021) focuses on organisational readiness and capability building, while PricewaterhouseCoopers (PwC) (2018) models the economic scale and timing of automation across countries and industries.

Together, these studies form a diverse ecosystem of research. They range from global economic projections to maturity assessments and organisational readiness tools, each offering insight into the relationship between AI, skills and the future of work. The list in Table A2 is not exhaustive, but it reflects some of the most referenced and influential work in the field.

Table A2. Overview of Frameworks and Studies Exploring AI's Impact on Work.

Framework / Study	Primary Focus	Key Insight / Contribution	Human-Centred Emphasis
Frey and Osborne (2013)	Probability of job automation based on task characteristics and cognitive demands	Established an early understanding of automation risk and job susceptibility	Low – focuses on technical feasibility rather than human adaptation
OECD (2021)	Comparison of AI and human capabilities across skill domains to inform policy	Compares cognitive, socio-emotional and technical abilities to support education and skills planning	Moderate – includes human capability domains at a high level
ILO (2024)	Global index of occupational exposure to generative AI	Assesses exposure using task-level data, expert input and predictive models	Moderate – acknowledges worker exposure and equity implications
Gartner (2024a)	Enterprise AI maturity and organisational readiness	Provides structure for assessing AI autonomy and enterprise adoption	Moderate – focuses on change management and operational readiness

Table A2. ***(Continued)***

Framework / Study	**Primary Focus**	**Key Insight / Contribution**	**Human-Centred Emphasis**
WEF (2025b)	Global labour-market trends and reskilling pathways	Tracks employment transitions, emerging skills and workforce shifts	High – emphasises reskilling, inclusion and human capability
McKinsey & Company (2023)	Economic and organisational impact of generative AI	Explores links between task exposure, productivity, value creation and role redesign	High – recognises augmentation and workforce evolution
IBM (2021)	Enterprise readiness and capability development	Highlights learning culture and continuous reskilling as foundations for AI success	High – centred on human capability growth
PwC (2018)	Macroeconomic modelling of automation	Models economic trajectories of automation across sectors and countries	Low – primarily economic perspective with limited human emphasis
AI Workforce Impact Model (Jacober, 2026)	Structured, human-centred framework assessing AI's effect on roles and workforce value	Translates AI impact into actionable insights across tasks, skills, decisions and workforce value	Very High – explicitly human-centred, practical and role focused

Source: Author's own creation.

The human–AI decoder, based on the AI Workforce Impact Model, builds on this foundation. It draws on insights from socio-technical systems theory (Katz & Kahn, 1966), job-redesign research (Hackman & Oldham, 1980) and the literature on skill-biased technological change (Acemoglu & Restrepo, 2018). These traditions emphasise the interaction between people, tasks, technology and structure. The decoder applies this thinking to the era of intelligent systems, offering a practical way to interpret how AI reshapes work at the level where people experience it: the role.

APPENDIX 3: AI WORKFORCE IMPACT MODEL – AIWIM

Despite Artificial Intelligence's (AI's) expanding influence, many organisations continue to face persistent challenges when trying to make sense of its workforce impact. These challenges appear in different forms but tend to cluster around the same themes:

- Limited visibility into how specific roles will be affected
- Uncertainty over whether AI will augment or replace parts of the job
- Inconsistent approaches to reskilling or role evolution
- Fragmented efforts across HR, operations, technology and strategy
- A lack of shared standards to classify workforce disruption.

These challenges are not abstract. They show up in real conversations, delayed decisions, hesitant investments and inconsistent plans. People want to act, but do not have a shared way to interpret what AI is changing.

Analysis from Deloitte confirms these patterns. Most organisations lack clear governance, skills visibility and alignment between functions, which slows decision-making and creates inconsistent approaches to workforce planning. Leaders can often describe the business impact of AI, but struggle to explain what it means for individuals, teams or skill portfolios (Deloitte, 2024).

In many of my own conversations with executives, one sentence repeats itself.

'We know AI is reshaping roles. We just cannot yet explain how.'

Every function sees a different part of the story. Operations sees efficiency. Finance sees cost. HR sees capability gaps. IT sees system integration. Risk sees compliance and governance.

Each perspective is valid. None of them is complete. What organisations need is not more data or more maturity models. They need a shared understanding that connects technological understanding with human transformation and provides a structured way to respond instead of react.

This is the gap the AI Workforce Impact Model (AIWIM) was created to fill. It draws on the author's 20 years of experience leading digital transformation, on conversations with peers and AI experts across industries and on the growing body of research on how intelligent systems are reshaping work.

TERMINOLOGY GUIDE: AIWIM AND THE HUMAN–AI DECODER

AIWIM provides the solid framework underneath, giving the model its structure and depth. The human–AI decoder is the part people interact with. It takes the same foundation and translates it into straightforward language that leaders, policymakers and workers can use in everyday conversations without feeling overwhelmed by technical terms.

In the decoder, impact dimensions are presented as AI impact areas.
Impact assessment is presented as the AI impact scan.
Impact score is expressed as the AI impact index.
Impact levels appear as the six levels of AI impact.
Strategic levers are translated into AI impact actions.
Calibration parameters are introduced in the decoder as influencing factors.

HOW AIWIM GUIDES WORKFORCE TRANSFORMATION

To understand how AI reshapes work, AIWIM follows a practical sequence: Identify, Assess, Classify and Strategise. Each step builds

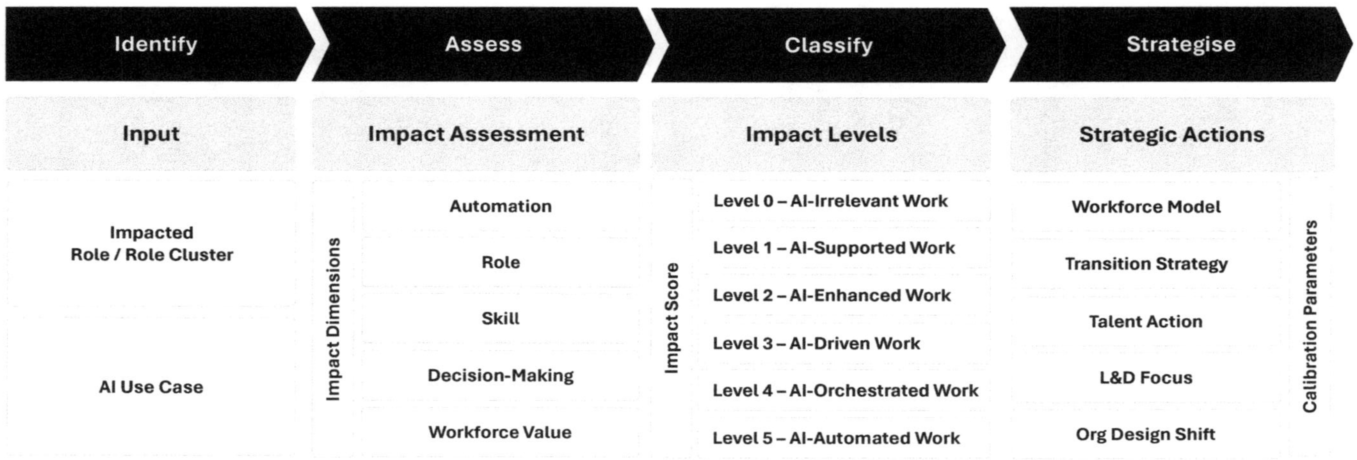

Fig. A1. AI Workforce Impact Model (AIWIM).

Source: Author's Own Creation.

on the last, moving leaders from early signals of change to structured insight and then to meaningful workforce actions.

The model in Fig. A1 provides a common framework to observe disruption, compare roles consistently and turn shifting expectations into clear decisions. Before diving into each phase, we introduce the overall flow.

These four elements form a sequence that can be repeated as technology evolves. They help organisations track how AI changes work today and how it will continue to change it tomorrow.

IDENTIFY

The purpose of this first phase is to identify the role being assessed and the specific AI use case that is influencing the work. This clarifies who is affected and which technology is driving the change. By starting here, the assessment stays anchored in real jobs and real applications rather than abstract concepts, making it clear how AI is shaping the work in practice.

AIWIM begins by pairing two key inputs: the 'Impacted Role or role cluster' being assessed and the 'AI use case' that is impacting the work. Every AI workforce impact assessment starts with these two inputs:

Impacted role (e.g. call centre agent, HR business partner). This refers to the specific position being assessed for the AI workforce impact. Each role has a distinct set of tasks, decision-making responsibilities, required skills and business value; all of which can be affected differently by AI. For example, a call centre agent may experience high levels of automation through generative AI handling routine queries, whereas an HR business partner might see AI augmenting rather than replacing decision support functions. In AIWIM, the terms 'job' and 'role' are used interchangeably, with job referring to the formal position and role describing the function and responsibilities a person performs within it.

AI use case (e.g. virtual assistants, predictive analytics or generative content tools). This refers to the specific application of AI technology being introduced or assessed within the role. Different use cases impact work in different ways. For example, virtual assistants may automate administrative tasks like scheduling or data retrieval, predictive analytics might support decision-making by forecasting trends or risks. Generative content tools can create written responses, reports or creative assets, potentially reshaping knowledge work. Understanding the exact AI use case is essential to accurately assess its impact, as it defines which tasks are affected, what new capabilities are needed and how the human–AI interaction plays out within the role.

AIWIM is designed to focus primarily on individual roles or groups of similar roles. It can be extended to wider areas such as functions, or departments, but this broader use should be approached with care. At that level, the model offers only indicative insights and lacks the granularity needed for precise workforce impact planning. At the current stage of AI development, AIWIM is built to understand how AI affects the person performing the role rather than to model entire systems of interconnected roles. Agentic AI use cases, which can influence several roles at once, are best broken down into smaller and more specific sub-use cases. This helps capture the nuances of impact for each individual more accurately. The same principle applies within a single job. Many roles contain tasks that fall across different levels of automation or augmentation, which is natural because real work rarely fits neatly into a single category. As AI becomes more agentic and begins to blur role boundaries, multi-role collaboration will grow. Even so, AIWIM remains intentionally anchored in the human perspective. It ensures that every discussion starts with the same core questions: what is the human impact and what support does the employee need as their work evolves?

ASSESS

The purpose of this phase is to evaluate how AI is transforming work across five core impact dimensions that capture the depth of its impact. By analysing the impact on AUTOMATION, ROLE, SKILLS, DECISION MAKING and WORKFORCE VALUE, the reader can quantify and compare how AI influences different roles. This structured impact assessment provides a consistent way to measure the extent of change and calculate the impact score required for the classification in the next step. It moves beyond assumptions or isolated observations to offer a clear, evidence-based view of how work is evolving under the influence of AI.

Evaluating Workforce Impact Across the Five Impact Dimensions

AIWIM evaluates workforce transformation through five human-centred impact dimensions. Together, they provide a holistic perspective that helps readers move beyond surface-level assumptions to understand how AI is reshaping work not only in terms of efficiency and automation but also purpose, skill and human meaning. These impact dimensions ensure that workforce planning considers both the technical and emotional aspects of change, giving organisations a fuller picture of how AI affects their people and operations.

These five impact dimensions form a consistent way to examine how AI is reshaping work:

Automation – How much of the task is now done by AI?

This dimension looks at how much of the work previously done by a human is now being handled by AI.

Role – Has the purpose or structure of the role changed?

This dimension assess whether the job itself is fundamentally changing and if the core purpose of the role is being redefined.

Skills – Do people need new or different skills to succeed in this role?

This dimension examines whether the current skills overall still hold value, whether new skills need to be developed, or whether entirely different capabilities are now needed to thrive in the role.

Decision-Making – Who makes the primary decisions for this role?

This dimension asks whether human judgement remains a core part of the job and looks at how decision authority and accountability are shifting between people and machines.

Workforce Value – How has the nature of human contribution changed?

This final dimension focuses on how the human contribution is perceived and valued. Is the role becoming more strategic, relational, or interpretive? Or is its significance diminishing in light of AI's growing capabilities?

By assessing all five impact dimensions, readers gain a balanced, data-informed and human-centred view of AI transformation, important for every subsequent step in the AIWIM process. These dimensions are then applied within the Impact Assessment, where they provide the structure for systematically evaluating the depth and nature of AI's effect on the workforce.

Impact Assessment

The impact assessment is a clear and repeatable way to understand how AI is changing work. It measures the severity of change across the five impact dimensions: Automation, Role, Skills, Decision-Making and Workforce Value. Each dimension is assessed on a 0 to 5 scale, using evidence-based questions that help teams translate early observations into insights that are measurable and comparable. This structured approach allows organisations to judge how AI is influencing work with consistency and ease.

The 0 to 5 scale reflects the severity of change across each dimension.

0 – **No Impact:** No meaningful change observed. Work continues in the same way and responsibilities remain stable.

1 – **Minor Impact:** Small and contained adjustments with limited effect. Some tasks shift slightly, but the overall role remains unchanged.

2 – **Moderate Impact:** Noticeable changes that require adaptation. Parts of the work evolve, and employees adjust responsibilities or develop new skills.

3 – **High Impact:** Major shifts with broader implications. The role changes significantly, responsibilities realign and new capabilities become essential.

4 – **Full Impact:** The core activities are carried out by AI, and people remain involved to manage complexity, ensure quality and provide oversight where judgement or context is still required.

Work is fundamentally altered from end to end. Responsibilities move into a new paradigm, with human contribution focused on purpose setting, ethical direction and long-term guidance rather than operational execution.

The 0 to 5 scale is applied independently across all impact dimensions. Each dimension reflects a distinct aspect of how work changes with AI. The following summaries describe what impact looks like within each one.

Automation
How much of the task execution is done by AI versus humans?

0 – No Impact: All tasks done by humans
1 – Low Impact: AI supports small or repetitive tasks
2 – Moderate Impact: AI completes routine tasks; humans review and refine
3 – High Impact: AI handles most tasks; humans manage exceptions
4 – Full Impact: AI runs core work; humans step in only for complex tasks
5 – Transformational Impact: AI runs the entire workflow and adapts without human involvement.

Role
How much has AI changed the purpose or structure of the role?

0 – No Impact: Role remains the same
1 – Low Impact: Tasks improved or supported by AI; role unchanged
2 – Moderate Impact: Duties shift or expand as AI supports parts of the work
3 – High Impact: Role is redefined; humans supervise AI outputs
4 – Full Impact: Most of the role shifts to AI; humans handle oversight and escalation
5 – Transformational Impact: The original role disappears; humans guide direction and ethics.

Skills
How much has AI changed the skills required to perform the role?

0 – No Impact: No new skills needed
1 – Low Impact: Basic digital or AI skills required
2 – Moderate Impact: New skills needed to collaborate with or oversee AI-supported tasks
3 – High Impact: Significant reskilling needed for AI-driven work

4 – Full Impact: New skills needed to oversee and guide AI
5 – Transformational Impact: Skills shift to system design, ethics and long-term guidance rather than day-to-day work.

Decision-Making
Who makes decisions in the workflow and how?

0 – No Impact: Humans make all decisions
1 – Low Impact: AI provides suggestions; humans decide
2 – Moderate Impact: AI recommends; humans approve or adjust
3 – High Impact: AI makes most decisions; humans handle exceptions
4 – Full Impact: AI decides within set boundaries; humans intervene only for complex judgement
5 – Transformational Impact: AI decides and adapts across the full workflow; humans guide purpose and governance.

Workforce Value
Where does human contribution create value in the workflow?

0 – No Impact: Human value remains unchanged
1 – Low Impact: Human value increases through productivity gains
2 – Moderate Impact: Human value shifts towards creativity, judgement or oversight
3 – High Impact: Human value rises in governance and complex judgement
4 – Full Impact: Human value lies in validating and governing AI managed work.
5 – Transformational Impact: Human value moves to purpose setting, ethics and long-term accountability outside the workflow.

For readers who want to understand how the impact dimensions and questions were shaped please refer to the section 'Inside the five Impact Dimensions' at the end of this appendix.

The impact assessment can be carried out in different formats depending on organisational needs and readiness. It may take the form of a questionnaire, a facilitated workshop or an AI-enabled diagnostic tool. In each case, participants review each impact dimension and agree on the appropriate level of impact severity. Using this structured approach enables organisations to generate a reliable impact score that provides a stable reference point for comparing roles, identifying high-impact areas and prioritising actions.

To calculate the impact score:

Add the five individual impact dimension scores (Automation, Role, Skills, Decision-Making, and Workforce Value)

Divide the total by five, the number of impact dimensions.

$$\text{Impact Score} = \frac{\text{Sum of the Impact Dimensions individual score}}{5}$$

This produces an Impact score, rounded to one decimal place (e.g. 2.8), representing the overall impact level of AI on that specific role.

CLASSIFY

The purpose of this sequence is to translate the impact score from previous phase into a clear classification: the impact level. It converts a numerical value into a shared, easy-to-understand classification of how deeply AI is transforming a role.

Assigning the Impact Level

Once the impact score is calculated, it is mapped to one of six impact levels ranging from 'AI-Irrelevant' to 'AI-Automated Work'.

At the heart of the AIWIM are the impact levels. It is a standardised classification that translates AI disruption into clear, actionable insight. Derived directly from the Impact Score it provides a consistent way to categorise and compare the degree of AI impact across roles, functions and use cases.

Each level represents a different degree of AI involvement and defines how control, decision-making and task execution shift between humans and machines.

At Level 0 – AI-Irrelevant, all tasks and decisions are carried out manually by people with no meaningful AI support.

At Level 1 – AI-Supported Work, AI helps with simple or repetitive tasks, while humans still make all decisions and lead the workflow.

At Level 2 – AI-Enhanced Work marks a step forward: AI takes over structured tasks and provides intelligent recommendations, yet humans continue to steer the process.

At Level 3 – AI-Driven Work, AI performs most of the work and makes routine decisions, with humans shifting into oversight or exception-handling roles.

At Level 4 – AI-Orchestrated Work involves AI systems handling entire workflows, with humans retaining limited strategic oversight.

Finally, at Level 5 – AI-Automated Work describes systems that operate independently, self-govern and even improve themselves over time. Human input is minimal, often limited to ethical oversight or creative direction.

The impact level is more than a label. It acts as a connector within the AIWIM framework linking analysis to action. It defines the balance between human and machine control, the nature of remaining work and the workforce model that emerges.

By mapping each role to one of six impact levels (Levels 0–5), organisations create a common language to classify AI's influence on work. This helps readers evaluate change with clarity, consistency and a shared understanding. These levels provide a common language to evaluate the degree of change affecting roles and to guide the right workforce, talent and leadership responses at each stage.

Each impact level is anchored in a defined numeric range so that roles can be assessed consistently across the organisation.

Level 0, AI-Irrelevant Work, covers scores from **0.0 to 0.5** and reflects roles performed entirely by people with no AI involvement

Level 1, AI-Supported Work, spans **0.6 to 1.5,** where AI supports simple tasks but humans still carry out the core work

Level 2, AI-Enhanced Work, ranges from **1.6 to 2.5** and describes situations where AI performs more routine activities while humans remain in charge

Level 3, AI-Driven Work, covers **2.6 to 3.5** and indicates that AI handles most of the work, with humans stepping in to supervise and intervene

Level 4, AI-Orchestrated Work, spans **3.6 to 4.9** and represents roles where AI runs end-to-end workflows, while humans guide and govern

Level 5, AI-Automated Work, applies to the score of **5.0**, where AI operates independently and improves itself with minimal or no human input.

These ranges provide a shared reference point that turns a numerical score into a clear understanding of how deeply AI is influencing the work.

For readers who want to understand the purpose behind the impact levels and their score ranges, please refer to the section 'Why the Impact Levels matter' at the end of this Appendix.

STRATEGISE

The purpose of the final phase is to turn understanding into action. After identifying which roles are affected, assessing how AI reshapes the work and classifying the depth of that change, leaders reach the point where analysis must become execution. This is where insight becomes direction.

The final phase explains how organisations should respond to AI's workforce impact with clarity, responsibility and foresight. Earlier phases diagnose what is changing. This phase sets out what to do next. It connects analytical insight to practical decisions and ensures that AI adoption strengthens human capability and business performance rather than working against them.

Through the Strategic Levers: Workforce Models, Transition Strategy, Talent Action, Learning and Development Focus and Organisation Design Shift, AIWIM guides organisations in shaping human–machine collaboration in a structured and ethical way. These actions turn the framework from an assessment tool into a transformation roadmap, enabling leaders not only to manage disruption but to lead the human side of AI with purpose and confidence.

Reaching an impact level does not complete the journey. The value of AIWIM lies in translating that insight into meaningful action. This final phase bridges diagnosis and execution by providing strategic levers that help organisations respond to AI-orchestrated change in a consistent and human-centred way.

Workforce Models – Defines how work itself should be structured at each stage of AI maturity. Early levels may rely on traditional teams or digitally supported models, while higher levels evolve into hybrid task environments, supervisory systems or ultimately AI-first operating models where human and machine roles are deeply interwoven.

Transition Strategy – Provides a roadmap for how to move roles from one state to another. This might involve building digital readiness, reshaping jobs for hybrid human–AI collaboration or preparing governance frameworks to ensure ethical oversight. Transition strategy gives clarity on how to guide the workforce through change without leaving people behind.

Talent Action – Specifies the decisions that should be made about impacted employees. Depending on the impact level, this could involve retaining people in place and upskilling them, reskilling and redeploying into new roles or in more disruptive cases, responsibly transitioning or repositioning roles no longer viable. This strategic action ensures talent decisions are intentional, transparent and humane.

L&D Focus – Highlights the most relevant areas for capability building. At lower impact levels this means digital literacy and AI tool proficiency. At higher levels, it shifts to skills in AI collaboration, monitoring, governance, bias detection, ethics or creative innovation. This ensures the workforce grows the right skills at the right pace, aligned with how AI reshapes the role.

Organisation Design Shift – Points to the structural adjustments required for AI to succeed. These could include small changes, such as adding AI oversight roles or larger redesigns, like flattening hierarchies, integrating cross-functional pods or rebuilding entire operating models around AI-first workflows.

Taken together, these strategic levers allow the reader to move beyond theory into practice. They provide a playbook for curated workforce transformation ensuring organisations don't just implement AI, but design responsible, human-centred pathways that protect dignity, preserve value and unlock new opportunities.

In the sections that follow, we will explore each of these strategic levers in more detail. By understanding how each Strategic Action aligns with the different impact levels, organisations can craft tailored, human-centred responses to disruption.

For readers who want to know how the strategic levers were shaped and why they matter, please refer to the section 'Understanding the Strategic Levers' at the end of this Appendix.

Workforce Models

The 'Workforce Models' lever describes how work is structured at each impact level. It reflects how responsibility shifts between humans and intelligent systems as AI matures. Organisations progress from traditional, human-led work, to hybrid environments where humans and AI share tasks, to levels where AI drives most operational activity and humans focus on oversight, guidance and purpose. Each impact level represents a different operating pattern.

At Impact Levels 0 to 2, humans remain central. AI provides support or completes structured tasks, but people make decisions, manage exceptions and carry responsibility. In the mid-range at Levels 3 and 4, AI takes over most execution and routine decision-making. Human value moves towards supervision, exception handling, governance and assurance. At Level 5, AI operates independently and humans shape the ethical foundations, long-term direction and purpose of the system.

Understanding these models helps leaders rethink role architecture, team composition and organisational design. This strategic lever positions AI as a reshaping force that influences how work is performed, who performs it and how human contribution evolves as intelligent systems become part of daily operations.

Impact Level 0 – Maintain Traditional Workforce

Work is performed manually by humans without support from AI or intelligent systems. Tasks rely on human skill, judgement and craft. Processes are stable, predictable and executed from start to finish by people. Productivity depends entirely on human capacity, experience and expertise.

Human–AI relationship
Humans perform, decide and complete the entire process. No system-based automation is present.

What this means for employees
Employees rely on personal skill, judgement and craftsmanship. Their value comes from experience, creativity, interaction and domain knowledge rather than technology.

Impact Level 1 – Build Digitally Supported Workforce

Digital tools and early AI capabilities enhance human productivity. The core role remains human-led. AI supports tasks such as summarising, retrieving data, scheduling or organising information. Humans make every decision and own every step.

Human–AI relationship
AI provides suggestions, shortcuts or simple automations. Humans retain full control and accountability.

What this means for employees
Employees begin to use AI to work faster and reduce administrative load. They remain responsible for all decisions and outcomes.

Impact Level 2 – Move to Hybrid Workforce

AI automates repetitive, rules-based tasks such as data extraction, verification, scanning or first-pass processing. Humans take responsibility for interpretation, reasoning, collaboration and customer engagement. Work becomes a shared effort between humans and AI.

Human–AI relationship
AI completes parts of the work independently. Humans review, approve and finalise outputs to maintain quality and trust.

What this means for employees
Employees shift away from manual execution and towards higher-value contributions. They rely on AI for groundwork and focus on judgement, problem solving and interpersonal elements.

Impact Level 3 – Adopt a Supervisory Workforce

AI performs most operational activities, including routine decisions. Humans move out of day-to-day execution and into supervisory roles. They monitor system outputs, manage exceptions and intervene only when ambiguity, risk or ethical issues appear.

Human–AI relationship
Humans oversee, audit and step in when systems encounter challenges.

What this means for employees
Employees develop oversight skills. They learn to monitor AI performance, spot anomalies, interpret system behaviour and manage risk rather than execute tasks.

Impact Level 4 – Establish Governance Workforce

AI systems run end-to-end workflows with minimal or no human involvement. Humans provide governance, assurance and ethical oversight. Their primary contribution is to ensure compliance, integrity and responsible use.

Human–AI relationship
Humans shape policies and rules that AI must follow and ensure alignment with organisational and regulatory expectations.

What this means for employees
Employees take on governance, audit and assurance responsibilities. Their value lies in expertise on fairness, accountability, risk and compliance.

Impact Level 5 – Develop Meta-Human Workforce

AI operates independently and adapts without ongoing human intervention. Humans contribute at a meta level, focusing on purpose, values and long-term direction. They design ethical frameworks, define boundaries and guide the intent behind the AI systems.

Human–AI relationship
Humans influence AI through system design, principle setting and strategic oversight rather than monitoring tasks.

What this means for employees
Employees focus on ethics, purpose, meaning and societal impact. Their contribution becomes philosophical, strategic and directional rather than operational.

These workforce models levers help leaders anticipate how the balance between humans and intelligent systems will evolve. By mapping roles against AI maturity, organisations gain a clearer view of which human contributions remain essential, which shift towards higher-value work and which may reduce over time. This foresight supports more intentional decisions in organisational design, leadership development and workforce planning. It ensures that people are equipped not only to adapt but to thrive in redefined roles.

The workforce models also show that human value does not disappear as AI advances. It changes. Empathy, judgement, ethical reasoning and contextual awareness become increasingly important at higher impact levels, while repetitive execution tasks steadily transition to machines.

Transition Strategy

The 'Transition Strategy' lever explains how organisations move from understanding AI's impact to taking intentional steps that align roles, skills and structures with AI maturity. It is the practical pathway from insight to action. Rather than reacting to disruption, transition strategy supports a guided and human-centred evolution of work.

Each impact level calls for a different strategic response, from building digital readiness to strengthening governance and eventually shaping the purpose and direction of autonomous AI. Clear transition strategies allow organisations to transform uncertainty into structured progress and ensure that workforce evolution remains ethical, responsible and future-ready.

Impact Level 0 – Build Digital Readiness

At this early stage, the strategy focuses on building digital readiness. Organisations develop basic digital literacy, introduce simple tools and standardise foundational processes. The goal is not to change roles but to create awareness, confidence and early capability.

Human–AI relationship
No meaningful AI involvement. Humans perform all work and use digital tools only to support organisation and structure.

What it means for employees
Employees build digital literacy and confidence. They gain awareness of emerging tools and become more prepared for future AI integration.

Impact Level 1 – Introduce AI Augmentation

Here, the strategy is to introduce AI augmentation. Humans remain fully in control while AI begins to support routine tasks. Organisations train employees to work with co-pilots, assistants and simple automations embedded into existing workflows.

Human–AI relationship
AI supports, suggests and speeds up repetitive tasks, while humans retain ownership of all decisions.

What it means for employees
Employees work more efficiently and begin to see AI as a helpful enabler. They remain fully accountable for outcomes and final judgements.

Impact Level 2 – Drive Role Evolution

Structured tasks shift towards AI, and human work expands into judgement, creativity and contextual interpretation. The transition strategy is role evolution. Roles are redesigned to reflect new boundaries between human contribution and AI execution.

Human–AI relationship
AI handles predictable elements of work. Humans review, interpret and shape outputs.

What it means for employees
Employees move into hybrid roles. Their work emphasises human strengths such as empathy, creativity and critical thinking, supported by AI for repetitive tasks.

Impact Level 3 – Integrate AI into Workforce

AI performs most operational tasks and routine decisions. Transition Strategy becomes workforce integration. Employees shift into oversight, orchestration and supervisory responsibilities. They manage exceptions, monitor system performance and ensure alignment with ethical standards.

Human–AI relationship
AI executes. Humans oversee, audit and intervene when risk, ambiguity or exceptions appear.

What it means for employees
Employees develop skills in system monitoring, anomaly detection and escalation handling. Their value lies in supervision rather than execution.

Impact Level 4 – Strengthen AI Governance & Oversight

AI manages end-to-end workflows autonomously. Transition Strategy shifts towards governance and oversight. Organisations establish robust policies, ethical guardrails and compliance structures. Human roles focus on accountability, transparency and ethical assurance.

Human–AI relationship
AI operates independently. Humans define rules, boundaries and governance frameworks.

What it means for employees
Employees move into roles that safeguard trust and integrity. They focus on fairness, accountability, compliance and responsible use of AI.

Impact Level 5 – Lead Ethically & Strategically with AI

AI adapts with minimal human involvement. Transition Strategy becomes ethical and strategic leadership. Humans shape AI's purpose, boundaries and societal contribution. Their focus moves to long-term direction, ethical frameworks and purpose-setting.

Human–AI relationship
AI self-optimises and operates autonomously. Humans guide the mission, principles and design philosophy behind the systems.

What it means for employees
Employees contribute at the highest strategic level. Their roles emphasise ethics, purpose, societal impact and long-term direction rather than operational engagement.

Each transition strategy lever aligns with a specific level of AI maturity and guides how organisations evolve. The goal is not only to integrate advanced technology but to do so in a way that protects human value, strengthens organisational integrity and prepares people for the capabilities that matter most. When thoughtfully applied, transition strategies transform disruption into structured progress. They replace uncertainty with opportunity and enable organisations to reinvent with purpose and clarity as AI continues to mature.

Talent Action

AI's impact is not abstract. It affects people directly. Every automation, augmentation or workflow redesign influences how work is performed and how employees experience their roles. As tasks shift and responsibilities evolve, HR and business leaders must decide how to support employees fairly and responsibly. The talent action lever provides that structure. It gives leaders a clear way to determine what happens to people when roles change.

Talent actions operate along a spectrum. At the early impact levels, the focus is retaining employees and strengthening their skills. As AI becomes more capable, the emphasis moves towards reskilling, transitioning into oversight roles, redeploying into closely related areas or, at higher Levels, repositioning people into strategic or ethical functions. Grounding these actions in AI maturity ensures that change happens intentionally and with respect for employees.

Impact Level 0 – Retain

AI does not influence the role. Employees perform work in the usual way with stable tasks and predictable processes. Performance continues to rely on experience and consistency.

Human–AI relationship
Humans perform all tasks. AI is not part of the workflow.

What it means for employees
Employees remain in place and develop through existing pathways. Responsibilities and skill expectations do not change.

Impact Level 1 – Retain & Upskill

AI appears in small, supportive forms such as scheduling tools, summarisation or simple automations. The role remains human-led, although digital fluency becomes part of everyday performance.

Human–AI relationship
AI supports minor tasks. Humans keep full control and decision-making authority.

What it means for employees
Employees stay in their roles but build confidence using AI tools responsibly. Upskilling focuses on digital awareness and basic AI literacy.

Impact Level 2 – Reskill within role

AI begins handling structured, rules-based tasks such as transaction processing or document review. The human role shifts towards interpretation, collaboration and higher-value problem-solving.

Human–AI relationship
AI executes predictable components. Humans refine, validate and complete the work.

What it means for employees
Employees reskill within their roles to perform hybrid responsibilities. They learn how to interpret AI outputs, manage exceptions and focus on tasks that require judgement and empathy.

Impact Level 3 – Transition & Reskill

AI performs most operational work and many routine decisions. Human contribution moves into supervisoryand orchestration focused toles. Employees step into new responsibilities that ensure system accuracy, trust and alignment with organisational standards.

Human–AI relationship
AI executes. Humans oversee, audit and intervene when judgement or escalation is required.

What it means for employees
Employees transition into oversight roles and receive reskilling to supervise AI-orchestrated workflows. They focus on monitoring accuracy, managing exceptions and ensuring responsible system behaviour.

Impact Level 4 – Redeploy or Phase Out

AI manages end-to-end workflows with minimal human involvement. Traditional roles fade while new ones appear in governance, compliance and system assurance. Redeployment becomes essential for employees whose roles no longer exist.

Human–AI relationship
AI governs the workflow. Humans contribute through policy oversight, governance and quality assurance.

What it means for employees
Employees move into related roles where their skills can transfer. If no suitable pathway exists, the organisation provides responsible, structured transitions that preserve dignity and support future employability.

Impact Level 5 – Reposition

AI-Automated environments eliminate execution roles entirely. Human contribution moves into strategic, ethical and creative responsibilities that shape organisational direction and long-term system behaviour.

Human–AI relationship
AI operates independently. Humans guide purpose, ethics, trust and long-term decisions.

What it means for employees
Employees are repositioned into roles that influence strategy, ethical use of AI and organisational direction. Their contribution becomes focused on shaping principles rather than managing daily tasks.

The 'Talent Action' lever ensures that workforce transformation is deliberate and human centred. Instead of allowing roles to drift as AI matures, organisations guide employees through reskilling, transition, redeployment or repositioning in a clear and structured way. These actions protect trust, preserve dignity and help people grow into new responsibilities. When applied thoughtfully, Talent Actions turn disruption into opportunity and support the development of a resilient and capable workforce.

Learning & Development Focus

In an AI-augmented world, the ability to learn, unlearn and relearn faster than change itself becomes the ultimate differentiator (Toffler, 1970). As technology reshapes tasks and decisions, organisations must realign their learning priorities with the maturity of AI adoption.

The 'L&D Focus' lever helps leaders determine where learning investment should be directed at each Impact Level. Early stages emphasise digital literacy and tool familiarity. As AI assumes more operational responsibility, learning shifts towards oversight, critical judgement and ethical assurance. At the highest levels of AI maturity, development focuses on creativity, systems thinking and purpose-driven leadership, where human capability extends far beyond what machines can replicate.

By aligning L&D Focus with the reality of AI's role in work, organisations create a confident, adaptive workforce capable of contributing unique and irreplaceable value at every stage of transformation.

Impact Level 0 – Build Digital Skills

There is little or no AI involvement. The L&D Focus is to introduce foundational digital skills and build employee comfort with basic platforms. Training covers email systems, collaboration tools and standardised workflow applications. The goal is to create confidence in digital environments before AI becomes more visible.

Human–AI relationship
No AI contribution. Humans use basic digital tools to organise and execute work.

What it means for employees
Employees gain familiarity with digital systems. They build the comfort and confidence needed for future AI-supported tasks.

Impact Level 1 – Learn AI Tools

AI tools begin to support routine tasks. L&D priorities focus on teaching employees how to use AI-enhanced systems, simple automations and digital assistants. Responsible usage, data handling and human accountability become key themes.

Human–AI relationship
AI supports productivity. Humans remain fully accountable for decisions and outcomes.

What it means for employees
Employees learn to integrate AI into daily work, improve efficiency and use digital tools responsibly.

Impact Level 2 – Work Effectively with AI

AI automates structured and predictable tasks. Learning shifts towards effective teaming with AI. Employees build skills in contextual reasoning, decision framing, adaptive thinking and problem solving. They focus on adding human value where AI stops.

Human–AI relationship
AI executes defined tasks. Humans interpret, refine and complete the work.

What it means for employees
Employees learn how to use AI insights, make sound decisions and contribute judgement, empathy and situational awareness.

Impact Level 3 – Oversee AI systems

AI performs most repetitive work and routine decisions. Humans transition into supervisory and escalation roles. L&D must develop skills in AI monitoring, anomaly detection, exception handling and ethical assurance.

Human–AI relationship
AI drives the workflow. Humans oversee, validate and step in when necessary.

What it means for employees
Employees learn how to supervise AI outcomes, guide system behaviour and manage exceptions with sound judgement.

Impact Level 4 – Manage AI Responsibly

AI manages end-to-end workflows autonomously. L&D focuses on teaching employees how to manage AI responsibly by building expertise in ethics, compliance, risk assessment and transparency. Employees must interpret audit trails, assess systemic risks and ensure AI alignment with business objectives.

Human–AI relationship
AI operates independently. Humans maintain governance, compliance and alignment with organisational values.

What it means for employees
Employees build fluency in ethical AI use, compliance frameworks and risk management, contributing to responsible oversight.

Impact Level 5 – Guide AI Purposefully

AI systems adapt and operate with minimal human intervention. Learning focuses on creativity, systems thinking, future-oriented design and ethical leadership. Employees contribute to shaping AI's vision, societal role and long-term purpose.

Human–AI relationship
AI self-optimises. Humans influence purpose, values and high-level design.

What it means for employees
Employees develop the ability to guide AI strategically, design ethical frameworks and shape long-term direction and societal impact.

The L&D Focus Lever ensures that the workforce does more than keep up with technology. It prepares people to interpret, oversee and shape AI as it matures. Learning in the age of AI is continuous and expanding. It builds technical fluency where needed, but also strengthens human capabilities such as ethical judgement, creative thinking and resilience. By matching development priorities to AI maturity, organisations help employees thrive alongside intelligent systems and lead with confidence in a rapidly evolving world.

Organisation Design Shift

As AI reshapes the nature of work, organisations must rethink how they are structured to support that work effectively. AI influences not only individual roles but also the architecture of teams, workflows, reporting lines and governance mechanisms. Hierarchies built around manual execution begin to shift towards more dynamic, AI-integrated structures where decision rights, accountability and value creation evolve. The organisation design shift lever in AIWIM helps leaders identify when to maintain stability, when to embed light automation and when more substantial redesign is needed. These shifts may include redefining roles, streamlining structures, forming AI-enabled pods or creating new roles such as AI ethics officers, algorithmic auditors or risk monitors. Over time, organisations move from traditional hierarchies to AI-native operating models.

Impact Level 0 – Maintain Traditional Structures

AI has no direct impact on work processes. Organisations maintain existing team structures, reporting lines and workflows. Leadership focuses on continuity, development and stability without introducing structural disruption.

Human–AI relationship
Humans perform all work. No AI involvement in process design or execution.

What it means for employees
Employees continue operating in familiar structures with unchanged reporting lines and progression pathways.

Impact Level 1 – Automate Basic Workflows

AI tools support simple tasks such as scheduling, reminders or document summarisation. Automation is introduced into existing workflows to improve efficiency without altering organisational design. A practical example is Microsoft Copilot, which automates repetitive tasks like drafting emails, summarising documents or generating presentations in Word, Excel and Outlook (Microsoft, 2023b). This improves productivity without structural change.

Human–AI relationship
AI assists with routine tasks but does not influence team structure or accountability.

What it means for employees
Employees experience greater efficiency but remain in the same roles and structures. Workflows feel lighter but unchanged.

Impact Level 2 – Redefine Roles

AI begins performing structured, rules-based tasks. Organisations rethink responsibilities and redesign workflows so humans and AI can work side by side. Teams may be reorganised to reflect hybrid roles and new collaboration points between people and intelligent systems.

Human–AI relationship
AI handles predictable tasks. Humans focus on interpretation, collaboration, problem solving and relationship-driven work.

What it means for employees
Employees adapt to new responsibilities, clearer accountability boundaries and redesigned workflows that integrate AI.

Impact Level 3 – Streamline Structures

As AI takes over most execution, traditional hierarchies built around task ownership lose relevance. Organisations streamline structures, reduce layers and focus on supervisory and escalation roles. New positions emerge to oversee AI outputs, ensure quality, manage exceptions and uphold ethical standards.

Human–AI relationship
AI executes most operational tasks. Humans supervise, escalate and ensure ethical and accurate outcomes.

What it means for employees
Employees move into oversight and monitoring roles. Reporting lines may change as layers are simplified and structures become leaner.

Impact Level 4 – Establish Governance Bodies

AI autonomously manages entire workflows. Operational layers shrink while governance, compliance and assurance become central.

Organisations formalise AI governance structures with cross-functional oversight teams responsible for compliance, risk and ethical assurance.

Human–AI relationship
AI operates independently. Humans establish rules, monitor risks and ensure alignment with organisational and societal expectations.

What it means for employees
Employees shift into governance, risk, compliance and assurance roles. Operational redundancies are consolidated or redeployed.

Impact Level 5 – Rebuild Around AI-First Models

AI becomes the core engine of the enterprise. Organisations rebuild around AI-first models, with structures designed for adaptability, decentralisation and continuous co-evolution with intelligent systems. Human responsibilities shift to purpose setting, ethical direction, system visioning and long-term accountability. This aligns with Daugherty and Wilson's (2018) view of AI-native enterprises, where human–machine collaboration serves as the organising principle of value creation.

Human–AI relationship
AI self-optimises and drives operations. Humans guide principles, purpose, ethics and long-term direction.

What it means for employees
Employees move into meta-level roles focused on ethics, societal alignment, innovation and system oversight. Traditional operational work disappears.

The organisation design shift ensures that structures evolve in step with the work they support. Without structural alignment, organisations risk inefficiency, role confusion and weakened accountability. By adapting reporting lines, decision rights and team architecture to AI-enabled workflows, leaders unlock efficiency and protect trust and human value. This strategic action serves as a compass for structural evolution, guiding enterprises towards adaptive, responsible and future-fit operating models as AI integration deepens.

In strategise, the focus moves from analysis to execution through the strategic levers that translate AIWIM insights into concrete action. Beyond these structural levers, leadership mindset and organisational culture determine how effectively AIWIM outcomes translate into practice. Leaders who demonstrate transparency, experimentation and psychological safety accelerate adoption by fostering a culture in which AI and people learn together. Embedding this cultural readiness turns strategic intent into everyday behaviour.

SUMMARY OF STRATEGIC LEVERS BY IMPACT LEVEL

The strategic levers translate clear, actionable responses for each impact level to outline the strategic direction of the AIWIM. Each level presents five elements:

Workforce Model, Transition Strategy, Talent Action, Learning and Development Focus, and Organisation Design Shift.

Level 0 – AI-Irrelevant
Workforce Model: Maintain Traditional Workforce
Transition Strategy: Build Digital Readiness
Talent Action: Retain
Learning and Development Focus: Build Digital Skills
Organisation Design Shift: Maintain Traditional Structures

Level 1 – AI-Supported Work
Workforce Model: Build Digitally Supported Workforce
Transition Strategy: Introduce AI Augmentation
Talent Action: Retain and Upskill
Learning and Development Focus: Learn AI Tools
Organisation Design Shift: Automate Basic Workflows

Level 2 – AI-Enhanced Work
Workforce Model: Move to Hybrid Workforce
Transition Strategy: Drive Role Evolution
Talent Action: Reskill Within Role
Learning and Development Focus: Work Effectively with AI
Organisation Design Shift: Redefine Roles

Level 3 – AI-Driven Work
Workforce Model: Adopt a Supervisory Workforce Model
Transition Strategy: Integrate AI into Workforce
Talent Action: Transition and Reskill
Learning and Development Focus: Oversee AI Systems
Organisation Design Shift: Streamline Structures

Level 4 – AI-Orchestrated Work
Workforce Model: Establish Governance Workforce
Transition Strategy: Strengthen AI Governance and Oversight
Talent Action: Redeploy or Phase Out
Learning and Development Focus: Manage AI Responsibly
Organisation Design Shift: Establish Governance Bodies

Level 5 – AI-Automated Work
Workforce Model: Develop Meta-Human Workforce
Transition Strategy: Lead Ethically and Strategically with AI
Talent Action: Reposition
Learning and Development Focus: Guide AI Purposefully
Organisation Design Shift: Rebuild Around AI-First Models.

As impact levels progress from 0 to 5, the strategic levers evolve from maintaining continuity to enabling deep transformation. At the lower levels, where AI has little influence, organisations focus on digital readiness, basic upskilling and embedding light-touch automation into existing structures. The 'Workforce Model' remains largely traditional or digitally supported, with minimal changes to role architecture.

At the mid-levels, where AI begins to automate structured tasks or drive operational execution, the emphasis shifts to role evolution, human–AI task blending and the creation of 'Hybrid' or 'Supervisory' workforce models. 'Transition Strategy' at this stage guide employees into new responsibilities that require judgement, oversight and adaptive thinking. Talent actions involve reskilling in-role or redeploying into oversight functions. 'L&D' Focus expands to include collaboration with AI, exception handling and governance. 'Organisation Design Shift' start to flatten, embedding AI oversight roles directly into team structures.

At the highest levels of AI maturity where systems manage end-to-end workflows or operate autonomously the focus shifts to governance, integrity, and leadership. The strategic levers call for establishing cross-functional governance bodies and embedding new roles such as AI ethics officers, compliance leads and algorithmic risk monitors within the enterprise. 'Talent Actions' at this impact level involve redeploying employees into governance and assurance roles or managing responsible transitions from legacy positions that automation has replaced. 'L&D Focus' pivot towards policy, ethics, system design and strategic leadership, preparing people to guide AI's purpose and societal impact. 'Organisation Design Shift' evolve into an AI-native, decentralised and adaptive model, where humans are repositioned into meta-level roles that define long-term system vision, values, and direction.

Taken together, these Strategic Levers: Workforce Models, Transition Strategy, Talent Action, L&D Focus and Organisation Design Shift, provide a structured, scalable pathway for workforce transformation. They ensure that organisations respond proportionately to the degree of disruption: preserving stability where impact is low, redesigning roles and learning where impact is moderate and embedding governance or leadership where AI becomes the dominant driver of work. By anchoring workforce decisions in these strategic levers, leaders can manage AI disruption in a way that is responsible, future-fit and aligned with both business needs and human value.

Ongoing application of AIWIM across diverse industries will generate the empirical evidence needed to validate and refine its scoring scales, ensuring continuous academic and practical relevance as organisational contexts evolve.

ADDITIONAL CALIBRATION PARAMETERS

In addition to the strategic levers, there are several calibration parameters that can help refine how organisations apply AIWIM in practice. Calibration parameters are typically applied after Step 5: Strategise, to refine prioritisation and execution planning. While the model provides a structured and consistent way to assess AI disruption, not all roles with the same score will require identical actions. These additional parameters such as headcount size, reskilling time, employee readiness and business criticality allow HR and business leaders to tailor their workforce strategies with greater nuance and operational relevance. They ensure that AI transformation efforts remain strategic, humane and scalable.

These parameters also serve as feedback mechanisms, enabling organisations to recalibrate AIWIM assessments over time as technologies, roles and cultural readiness evolve. This reflexive element ensures that the framework remains a living system that learns from its own application.

While the AIWIM impact level provides a structured classification of how AI affects the workforce, it doesn't operate in isolation. The calibration parameters add critical context to the AIWIM score, helping leaders prioritise actions, allocate resources and manage transformation risk. When layered over AIWIM, these factors enable more precise, human-centred workforce planning.

A closer look at the calibration parameters helps explain how the model is applied.

Headcount Exposure

This input measures the number of employees in roles impacted by AI. High headcount indicates high disruption potential or opportunity, especially when paired with high AIWIM scores. These roles should be prioritised for intervention due to their potential impact on the organisation's cost, productivity or employee base.

→ *Helps identify roles where AI's workforce impact will be most significant at scale*

Skill Transferability

This assesses how easily current skills in a role can be applied to new or adjacent roles. Low transferability means higher transition costs and effort, making the role harder to redesign or redeploy. Use this input to fine-tune talent actions like deciding whether to reskill, redesign or phase out a role.

→ *Helps decide whether to invest in reskilling or prepare for role phase-out through skill mobility*

Time to Reskill

This measures the estimated time and effort required to prepare someone for a new role after AI disruption. It affects the pace, feasibility and cost of transformation. Use this to shape L&D programs and to sequence workforce rollout plans effectively, especially when matched with the AIWIM score.

→ *Helps pace your transformation roadmap by identifying realistic reskilling timelines*

Employee Readiness

This reflects employees' openness, confidence and mindset towards AI adoption. High resistance can slow down change even for technically feasible roles. Use this input to guide communication, leadership alignment and change management planning, especially for roles with mid-range AIWIM scores (Levels 1 to 3).

→ *Helps anticipate resistance and design supportive change interventions*

Organisational Dependency

This input considers how critical a role or process is to business continuity. Some high-impact roles may be tightly linked to operations and not easily replaced. These roles should be flagged for additional oversight, phased rollout or built-in human fallback layers.

→ *Helps transformation plans not unintentionally disrupting mission-critical functions*

Ethical Intelligence

This parameter builds on the concept of moral intelligence, the capacity to apply universal human principles to guide actions and decisions (Lennick & Kiel, 2011). It assesses how responsibly AI-enabled roles operate within ethical, transparent and socially aligned boundaries, gauging whether decision-making systems, data use and human oversight reflect fairness, accountability and integrity. Including ethical intelligence as a calibration factor ensures that workforce strategies reinforce trust, uphold values and safeguard organisational reputation as AI adoption scales.

→ *Helps ensure that AI transformation aligns with organisational values, ethical standards and societal expectations.*

APPLYING AIWIM AS A CONTINUOUS LEARNING PROCESS

While the AIWIM is presented as a sequential process, in practice it functions as a continuous learning system. Each cycle of application generates new data, behavioural insight and organisational feedback that can be reused to refine subsequent assessments. When embedded within annual workforce planning or transformation reviews, AIWIM becomes a living mechanism for organisational learning rather than a one-off diagnostic.

The calibration parameters introduced earlier act as sensors within this loop. They capture evolving indicators such as readiness, cultural sentiment and the speed of role adaptation. These feedback signals allow leaders to recalibrate priorities, redistribute resources and adjust learning strategies in line with technological maturity and workforce sentiment. By integrating these signals, organisations convert observation into foresight.

Sustaining AIWIM as a learning system also depends on leadership behaviour. Transparency, psychological safety and sponsorship from senior leaders enable employees to participate openly in assessments and to view AIWIM as a framework for collaboration, not control. This trust is essential for surfacing the nuanced human data, the perceptions, motivations and ethical concerns that quantitative measures alone cannot capture.

Over time, this adaptive approach transforms AIWIM from an assessment method into a shared governance practice between humans and intelligent systems. It encourages continual dialogue about how work evolves, how value is created and how ethics are preserved. By viewing AIWIM as a continuous loop rather than a linear project, organisations shift their focus from adopting AI to learning with it. This mindset defines capability for sustainable, human-centred transformation.

These recommendations offer a high-level guide for aligning AI's workforce impact with thoughtful and human-centred action. They help organisations connect the dots between understanding what is changing and deciding how to respond. The aim is to keep decisions proactive, consistent and grounded in a simple and adaptable framework. Each path reflects the level of disruption a workforce is experiencing, yet every organisation will need to tailor its approach to its own context, culture and readiness.

The AIWIM provides the structure needed to navigate complex change while keeping people at the centre. It is robust enough to support enterprise-wide transformation and flexible enough to be applied to a single role. The most effective place to begin is wherever the impact is most visible. Use the model to bridge insight and execution, one role, one use case and one decision at a time.

The following sections provide additional detail on the specific elements of AIWIM, explaining how each component works, why it matters and how it supports a clearer and more structured understanding of AI's impact on work.

INSIDE THE FIVE IMPACT DIMENSIONS

Leaders often look for a single indicator of transformation, such as automation rates or efficiency gains. The impact assessment shows why this is not enough. AI's influence spreads across different parts of a role, and each part must be understood to form a complete picture of how work is changing. The combined use of the assessment questions and the scoring scale helps teams see these layers clearly and evaluate them in a consistent and repeatable way.

A role with moderate automation but significant shifts in decision-making may require a very different organisational response from a role with high automation but minimal change in human value. The same is true for skills. A small adjustment in tools can require substantial reskilling if it changes how employees collaborate with AI or how judgement is applied in daily work.

The five dimensions prevent oversimplification. They ensure that organisations recognise the nuances of change, protect the aspects of work that remain uniquely human and prepare people for the responsibilities that emerge as intelligent systems become more capable. They also connect the visible and invisible layers of transformation so that leaders can make decisions that are grounded, human-centred and aligned with the realities of the role.

These dimensions also create the basis for the next stage of the model. Once each dimension has been assessed and scored, the results can be converted into a clear and standardised view of the overall impact. This becomes the foundation for classification and the decisions that follow in workforce planning, reskilling and job redesign.

How These Five Dimensions Were Chosen

The five dimensions are grounded in research and practical observation. Studies across organisational science, labour economics and technology adoption show that technological change follows consistent patterns. It automates tasks, reshapes roles, shifts skill demands, reallocates decision rights and alters how human contribution is valued. These pathways have remained constant from early mechanisation and digitalisation through to generative and agentic AI.

The dimensions allow organisations to examine change holistically rather than react to individual use cases. They combine structural elements, such as tasks and roles, with cognitive elements, such as skills, decisions and value. This balance ensures that assessments remain rigorous and human-centred. By integrating research findings, real-world data and lived organisational experience, AIWIM turns broad concepts into a practical framework for workforce analysis.

The following sections outline each dimension in detail including the related AI impact scan questions.

Automation – The substitution of human task execution

The Automation dimension measures how far AI systems now perform tasks previously done by humans. It draws on the concept of technological substitution (Autor et al., 2003) and distinguishes between support, partial replacement and full automation.

Automation ranges from simple assistance to autonomous workflows. It includes visible automation such as chatbots and robotic process automation, as well as invisible automation such as algorithmic predictions or workflow triggers.

This dimension quantifies task substitution and highlights new oversight duties that arise when systems take on more operational responsibility.

Role – Redefinition of role purpose and structure

The role dimension examines how AI reshapes the purpose, boundaries and structure of a role. Research in organisational design shows that technology influences both what people do and why they do it (Hackman & Oldham, 1980).

AI may enlarge, enrich, merge or eliminate roles. As systems take over repetitive work, human roles shift towards oversight, exception handling or orchestration. In more advanced stages, roles consolidate or disappear where automation replaces operational needs.

Skills – Transformation of Capability Requirements

The skills dimension tracks how capability requirements evolve with AI adoption. It builds on research into skill-biased technological change, including the work of Acemoglu and Restrepo (2018), which shows that AI complements cognitive and socio-emotional skills while reducing the need for routine work.

Skills change typically takes three forms:

- Reinforcement of existing skills
- Adaptation of skills to work with AI
- Emergence of new digital, analytical or human-centred capabilities.

The dimension also reflects the rise of collaboration skills such as interpreting AI outputs, monitoring performance, ensuring fairness and resolving ethical issues. It helps organisations align learning and development efforts with new work demands.

Decision-Making – Redistribution of authority and accountability

The decision-making dimension measures how AI changes who makes decisions, how they are made and where accountability sits. It draws on research into decision automation (Ransbotham et al., 2021).

Early-stage AI supports human judgement through insights and recommendations. Mature systems make operational decisions within predefined boundaries, such as approving transactions or triaging service requests. This dimension clarifies how much autonomy the system holds and how governance maintains accountability.

Workforce Value – Reconfiguration of human contribution
The workforce value dimension captures how the role and perception of human contribution change as AI becomes embedded in work. Research on meaning and motivation (Grant, 2007) shows that contribution is shaped not only by productivity but also by purpose and recognition.

As AI takes on analytical or transactional tasks, human effort often shifts towards strategic, creative or relational work. This dimension assesses whether AI elevates or diminishes human contribution and helps organisations ensure that adoption strengthens inclusion, recognition and purpose.

How the Five Impact Dimensions Work Together

Each dimension captures a specific aspect of workforce transformation, but their interaction is what ultimately reshapes work. Automation changes role structure. Role changes affect skill needs. Skills shifts influence who decides. Together they redefine the value people bring.

The dimensions create a coherent and evidence-based framework that helps organisations identify current impact, anticipate what comes next and align workforce strategy with technological change. AIWIM's multidimensional structure ensures assessments remain holistic and repeatable.

Alternative Impact Dimension Considered

Several additional dimensions were explored during the development of AIWIM. These included Organisational Performance, Culture and Change Readiness, Technology Maturity, Ethics and Governance, Collaboration and Employee Wellbeing. They were excluded because they either overlap with the five selected dimensions or describe organisational context rather than workforce-level change.

Ethical intelligence appears today as a calibration parameter rather than a formal impact dimension. It may become a full dimension in future versions of AIWIM as organisational use of autonomous systems increases.

WHY THE IMPACT LEVELS MATTER

The six AIWIM impact levels describe how AI reshapes the relationship between humans and work. They translate the combined results of the five impact dimensions into a single classification that shows how far a role has moved from human control to machine autonomy.

Where the impact dimensions describe how AI changes the elements of work, the impact levels show how far those changes reshape a role. The six levels give readers a clear reference point for discussing AI's workforce impact across functions, industries and regions. They make it possible to compare roles, identify priorities for transformation and ensure that AI adoption remains grounded in the human experience rather than in technical terminology.

The impact levels were shaped by real organisational transitions. They mirror the points at which AI capability begins to change the purpose, skills and decision rights of a role. These turning points reveal how the balance between people and systems shifts as AI becomes more capable.

How the Six Impact Levels Were Designed

Each level reflects an observable shift in behaviour or structure. Together, the six levels create a continuous narrative of change from AI-irrelevant to AI-automated work while keeping focus on how people continue to contribute value.

Level 0 – AI-irrelevant

All work is performed by humans without AI support. Judgement, creativity and execution rely entirely on human capability.

Technology may help communication or logistics but does not change the substance of the work. This level acts as the baseline against which all other levels are measured.

Level 1 – AI-supported work

AI supports discrete, low-complexity tasks. Examples include predictive text or simple chatbots. These tools help efficiency but do not change accountability or job purpose. Humans decide when to use AI and remain responsible for all outcomes

---

Level 2 – AI-enhanced work

AI handles structured or data-intensive tasks such as document processing, pattern recognition or early-stage analysis. Collaboration between humans and AI becomes routine. People still make final decisions and interpret AI outputs. Skill requirements begin to shift, though the role remains largely intact.

Level 3 – AI-driven work

AI performs most operational tasks and makes rule-based decisions. Humans intervene only when ambiguity or judgement is needed. The human role shifts from doing the work to overseeing the work. This is the first significant redefinition of role purpose.

Level 4 – AI-orchestrated work

AI operates autonomously across end-to-end workflows. The system integrates data sources, applies logic and delivers outcomes with minimal human involvement. Humans act as governors, auditors and custodians of policy. Decision rights have largely moved to the system, and human involvement focuses on oversight and alignment with organisational values.

Level 5 – AI-automated work

AI works independently and is capable of ongoing optimisation and self-correction. Human involvement is limited to defining boundaries, ethical principles and strategic intent. AI has absorbed the operational domain and the human role becomes one of leadership, trust-building and direction-setting.

Why Six Levels

Six levels capture the full journey from human to autonomous work while keeping the model clear and usable. Fewer levels would blur important differences, and more would add complexity that makes the model harder to apply in practice. Level 5 is not yet common in real workplaces, but advancing agentic and self-learning systems suggest it may become achievable in the future.

Key reasons include:

Completeness of transformation: Six levels provide a complete view of how work changes, from fully human tasks to autonomous systems. This structure captures the full arc of transformation without losing important distinctions.

Behavioural realism: Each level reflects a recognisable behavioural shift. Work moves from using tools to collaborating with systems, to supervising them, then governing them and finally directing their purpose.

Natural midpoint: The split between three augmentation levels and three autonomy levels mirrors how organisations experience role evolution.

Alignment with established autonomy scales: Six levels map to well-known autonomy frameworks in fields such as transport and robotics while staying focused on workforce change.

This structure ensures that the model is intuitive for practitioners yet grounded in observable organisational behaviour.

IMPACT-LEVEL RANGES

Each Impact Level correlates with a numerical range calculated from the average of the five Impact Dimensions. These ranges convert qualitative observations into a measurable framework that is consistent and easy to use.

Score ranges

Level 0: 0.0–0.5
Level 1: 0.6–1.5

Level 2: 1.6–2.5
Level 3: 2.6–3.5
Level 4: 3.6–4.9
Level 5: 5.0

Why These Ranges

The impact score ranges provide a structured and consistent way to translate the results of the impact scan into one of six impact levels. These levels describe how deeply AI is reshaping a role and give organisations a shared and reliable scale for comparison. The ranges are not arbitrary. They reflect the logic of the scoring system, which evaluates five impact simensions on a scale from 0 to 5. Each range creates a clear threshold between levels and prevents misclassification as AI becomes more embedded in work.

Scores from 0.0 to 0.5 represent roles with no meaningful AI impact. Scores from 0.6 to 1.5 reflect early moments where AI assists work but does not alter how it is carried out. The next range, 1.6 to 2.5, captures roles where AI enhances routine tasks while humans remain fully in control. Together, these levels describe work where AI is present but not dominant.

Scores from 2.6 to 3.5 mark a significant shift. This is the point where AI becomes a central part of the workflow and begins to influence how work is structured, decided and delivered. At this stage, humans move into a supervisory position while AI leads the operational flow.

The next range, 3.6 to 4.9, is intentionally broad. It reflects roles where AI runs most of the workflow and humans step in only for complex, sensitive or unusual cases. Level 4 represents a mature AI-orchestrated environment in which human involvement still matters, but the nature of that involvement is strategic rather than operational.

The final level has a unique structure. Level 5 applies only when the impact score reaches 5.0. This is possible only when every dimension is scored at the highest level. Level 5 is therefore rare and corresponds to roles where AI performs the entire workflow independently and adapts without human involvement. Human contribution shifts to purpose setting, ethics, governance and long-term direction. By reserving Level 5 for a perfect score, the model avoids accidental or premature classification of roles as AI-Automated and preserves the clear distinction between advanced AI-orchestrated work and true autonomy.

The ranges are designed to create clear interpretive distance between levels. Each band spans roughly one point on the scale, with a small buffer that prevents overlap and keeps boundaries crisp. This structure mirrors the inflection points observed in real roles. Analysis consistently shows two decisive transitions: around 2.6, where work moves from human-led to AI-led, and around 3.6, where workflows become AI-orchestrated with minimal supervision. These cut-offs reflect how organisations experience autonomy in practice.

The ranges follow a non-linear pattern. Early levels cover broader intervals because early change happens gradually. The upper levels narrow because each increase in autonomy brings a sharper rise in impact, risk and the need for governance. The scoring also remains simple to use at scale. Rounded boundaries such as 0.5, 1.5, 2.5, 3.5 and 4.9 allow rapid classification without complex calculation, which supports consistency across large assessments.

Taken together, these ranges keep the model stable, intuitive and proportionate. They reflect real shifts in human contribution and give organisations a practical and trustworthy guide for understanding how AI is changing work.

Guardrails for AI-Based Simulations of AIWIM

When an AI model is used to simulate human–AI decoder classifications, specific guardrails are needed to prevent inflated or inaccurate Level assignments. These safeguards ensure that simulated scoring remains conservative and reflects the real thresholds of autonomy in work.

Level 4 should only be assigned when the average impact score reaches at least 3.6 and both automation and decision-making score 4 or higher. This ensures that AI is genuinely running the core workflow and that humans are involved only for complex or unusual cases.

Level 5 should remain reserved for a perfect score of 5.0 and require all five dimensions to score at the highest level, including a 5 in both automation and decision-making. This reflects true end-to-end autonomy where AI performs the full workflow independently and human involvement is limited to purpose, ethics and long-term direction.

These guardrails keep simulated results accurate, stable and resistant to over-classification. They can be relaxed in facilitated workshops or exploratory sessions where the purpose is insight, discussion or alignment rather than strict quantitative precision.

A Model That Will Evolve

The score ranges and thresholds reflect the current state of AI capability. As agentic, multimodal and self-learning systems advance, these cut-offs may need adjustment. Future versions of AIWIM will continue to track how autonomy changes the nature of work and may expand to include new forms of machine-to-machine coordination, emerging governance patterns and evolving human oversight.

The goal remains the same: keep the model accurate, practical and centred on the real experience of people working with intelligent systems.

OVERVIEW OF COMPARATIVE FRAMEWORKS EXPLORING CLASSIFICATIONS

AIWIM's six-level classification builds upon the author's research and practical observations of how human oversight evolves as systems gain autonomy. While many existing classifications focus on AI capability and system maturity, few address the human aspect how work, roles and decision-making evolve alongside increasing automation. To close this gap, the six AIWIM levels draw on regulatory, technical and organisational frameworks and reinterpret them from a workforce perspective. This turns system-focused classifications into a practical, human-centred view of how work transforms as AI matures. Below are three examples of such classification models.

OECD AI Capability Indicators

OECD research categorises AI capability into five levels across nine human-ability domains like language, perception or reasoning (OECD, 2025). These range from narrow pattern recognition to adaptive, self-improving systems. AIWIM converts this technical maturity scale into its human equivalent, demonstrating how increasing AI capability translates into progressive workforce redesign from augmentation to autonomy.

Gartner AI Maturity Model

Gartner's five-stage model (Awareness, Active, Operational, Systemic, Transformational) describes how organisations embed AI into culture and process (Gartner, 2024). As firms reach Systemic and Transformational stages, their roles increasingly span AIWIM Levels 3 to 5. This highlights AIWIM's role as the operational lens within enterprise maturity, connecting corporate readiness to role-level impact.

Common 'Levels of AI Usages' Lists

These widely used 'levels of AI usage' lists outline simple stages of adoption, often from basic awareness to more advanced applications, and are commonly applied without a structured framework or deeper definitions. They describe how much people use AI tools, not how work itself changes. AIWIM fills that gap by focusing on workforce impact and showing how roles, skills and decision-making evolve as AI takes on more responsibility.

UNDERSTANDING THE STRATEGIC LEVERS

The five strategic levers connect analysis to execution. They guide leaders in translating AIWIM insights into decisions that support people, strengthen the organisation and maintain performance through technological change.

These actions draw from the author's experience in workforce transformation and from discussions with HR leaders, executives and practitioners. They are informed by organisational design theory, change management and human-capital analytics. Together, they offer a practical, people-centred approach for managing workforce change in the age of AI.

How These Strategic Levers Were Developed

The five actions were chosen because they address the most critical areas where AI reshapes work. They translate what the model reveals about changing tasks, roles, skills, decisions and value into clear areas of response.

Each strategic lever balances two needs. It protects the person affected by change by supporting employability, confidence and trust. It strengthens the organisation by ensuring clarity, accountability and sustained value creation. Together, they help leaders act responsibly as AI alters workflows and workforce expectations.

The sections below outline each strategic lever in detail.

Supporting the Impacted Person

Learning & Development (L&D) Focus

Learning is the first and most direct response to disruption. As AI accelerates change, organisations need learning environments that refresh skills continuously and support both digital capability and enduring human strengths such as creativity, ethics and judgement (World Economic Forum, 2025).

This action gives employees confidence that they can grow with the technology rather than fall behind it. It is supported by research on learning in the flow of work, which emphasises embedding development within daily tasks (Bersin, 2018).

A strong learning strategy includes broad AI literacy, ongoing micro-learning and opportunities to develop human skills that increase in value as automation expands.

Talent Action

Talent action ensures that AI-orchestrated workforce changes are handled with fairness and transparency. It recognises that technological disruption is also a human transition.

This action guides decisions about role evolution, reskilling inside and outside of the role, redeployment and, when necessary, responsible transitions. It protects dignity and employability and ensures that trust is not lost as work changes. It aligns talent decisions with organisational needs without compromising values.

Supporting the Organisation

Workforce Models

Workforce model design defines how work is structured as AI capability grows. It reflects the principle from organisational theory that structure shapes behaviour (Katz & Kahn, 1966).

This action helps leaders determine which tasks stay human-led, which become AI-led and where collaboration is required. It supports hybrid teams that supervise and guide AI systems. It also encourages operating models where human and machine contributions are designed to complement one another.

Transition Strategy

AI adoption requires a clear and responsible path from current to future state. Transition strategy defines how transformation unfolds, how it is communicated and how people are supported through the change.

This action maintains psychological safety and reduces uncertainty. It ensures readiness assessments precede rollout, encourages cross-functional adoption teams and embeds ethical and feedback checkpoints into implementation. Clear communication helps employees understand the purpose of the change and feel supported throughout.

Organisation Design Shift

As AI matures, organisational architecture must evolve. Organisation design shift ensures that reporting lines, governance structures and decision rights adapt in line with AI capability, drawing on principles described in organisational design research (Galbraith, 2012).

This action recognises that technology evolves faster than hierarchy. It helps organisations update governance for human–AI collaboration, adopt metrics that reflect new forms of value creation and build structures capable of sustaining innovation.

Why These Strategic Levers Matter

These actions translate AI insight into decisions that shape how people and organisations respond to change. They bring together individual and organisational responsibilities and provide practical starting points for planning and execution. They are grounded in research, field experience and conversations with leaders managing real workforce transitions.

The strategic levers focus on responsible implementation. They help organisations ensure that learning, workforce moves, task and team design, change planning and structural alignment support both performance and people. As AI capability and workforce systems evolve, additional actions may emerge. Any additions must remain aligned with the core structure of AIWIM and its approach to assessing workforce impact.

Their purpose is to support informed decision-making, encourage human-centred interpretation of change and help organisations design an AI-enabled future that honours both progress and people.

APPENDIX 4: INFLUENCING FACTORS CHECK

PURPOSE

The influencing factors check is used together with the human–AI decoder to refine workforce planning and talent decisions. It adds important context that the level of AI impact alone cannot capture. For each role or role cluster, respond to the questions below using a simple scale or yes/no. The results spark the right discussions about how work is changing and help shape decisions on sequencing, reskilling timelines, redesign priorities, change plans and governance.

HOW TO USE THE QUESTIONNAIRE

1. Apply the influencing factors check to roles that the human–AI decoder classifies at Impact Levels 3, 4 or 5.
2. Combine the check results with the decoder's level of AI impact to create heatmaps or matrices that guide priorities.
3. Use the results to decide which roles should transition first, where reskilling or redesign is most urgent, how much support employees will need and which areas require governance or fallback plans.

Influencing factors do not replace AI impact actions. They refine interpretation so that decisions remain balanced, human-centred and grounded in both impact and context.

1. HEADCOUNT EXPOSURE

To identify roles where AI will have the greatest impact at scale by measuring how many employees are in the role and whether it sits in high-volume or high-cost operations.

Questions

1. How many employees are in this role or role cluster?
   ☐ 1–10 ☐ 11–50 ☐ 51–100
   ☐ 100+ [according to your organisation]

2. What percentage of the workforce does this represent?
   ☐ <5% ☐ 5–15% ☐ 15–30% ☐ >30%

3. Is this role part of high-volume or high-cost operations?
   ☐ Yes ☐ No

2. SKILL TRANSFERABILITY

To determine how easily people in this role can move to adjacent or new roles, helping decide whether the best action is reskilling, redesign or responsible transition.

Questions

4. How easily can this role's skills move to other roles?
   ☐ High ☐ Moderate ☐ Low

5. Would moving to a new role require a full career pivot?
   ☐ Yes ☐ No

3. TIME TO RESKILL

To guide the pace and sequencing of transformation by estimating how long it would take to prepare someone for the next logical role and whether the organisation is ready to support that learning.

Questions

6. What is the estimated duration to reskill this role to its next logical future role?
   ☐ <1 month ☐ 1–3 months ☐ 3–6 months
   ☐ 6–12+ months

7. Are there existing L&D programs or academies in place to support this?
   ☐ Yes ☐ No

---

4. EMPLOYEE READINESS

To assess how confident and prepared employees feel about working with AI so that communication, training and change-management efforts can be tailored to their needs.

Questions

8. How confident are employees about working with AI tools?
   ☐ Very confident ☐ Somewhat confident ☐ Uncertain
   ☐ Resistant

9. Do employees see AI as a threat to their jobs?
   ☐ Yes ☐ No ☐ Mixed

10. Has the role been included in AI communication or training so far?
    ☐ Yes ☐ No

---

5. ORGANISATIONAL DEPENDENCY

To flag roles that are essential for trust, continuity, compliance or safety and therefore require staged rollout, fallback layers or tighter oversight before automation.

Questions

11. Is this role involved in core compliance, financial or legal processes?
    ☐ Yes ☐ No

12. Can AI replace this role without loss of trust or accountability?
    ☐ Yes ☐ No ☐ Unclear
13. Would AI failure in this role lead to customer or operational risk?
    ☐ High ☐ Medium ☐ Low

---

6. ETHICAL INTELLIGENCE

To evaluate whether AI-enabled tasks in the role operate within ethical and socially aligned boundaries covering fairness, accountability, transparency and human oversight.

Questions

14. Does the role involve decisions requiring fairness or bias monitoring?
    ☐ Yes ☐ No
15. Are AI decisions explainable to employees, customers or regulators?
    ☐ Yes ☐ No
16. Is human oversight clearly defined?
    ☐ Yes ☐ No

APPENDIX 5: HUMAN–AI DECODER PLAYBOOK

PURPOSE

The Human–AI Decoder Playbook gives leaders and teams a simple way to understand how AI is reshaping a role and what they should do next. It follows the decoder's three guiding questions. How is AI changing the work? How big is the impact? How should we respond? These steps turn early signals of disruption into clear, human-centred decisions that can be used in workshops, planning sessions or leadership discussions.

HOW TO USE THIS PLAYBOOK

- Analyse how AI is changing the work using the AI impact scan
- Determine how big the impact is mapping to one of the six levels of AI impact
- Define how the organisation should respond using the AI impact actions and influencing factors.

GUIDING QUESTION 1: HOW IS AI CHANGING THE WORK?

Begin by defining the AI use case and the affected role.

Describe what the AI system is intended to do, the tasks it performs and the problem it solves. Keep the description focused on the capability rather than the technology itself.

____

____

____

____

Describe the role today. Capture its purpose, the core tasks it performs and the responsibilities people hold. This keeps the assessment anchored in the real work.

____

____

____

____

This establishes a clear factual baseline so that all later scoring reflects the actual work and not assumptions about the technology.

Run the AI Impact Scan

Using the AI impact scan questions review how the role is changing across the five dimensions. Score each from 0 to 5, where 0 means no change and 4 means complete transformation.

Automation
How much of the task execution is done by AI versus humans?

0 – No Impact: All tasks done by humans
1 – Low Impact: AI supports small or repetitive tasks
2 – Moderate Impact: AI completes routine tasks; humans review and refine
3 – High Impact: AI handles most tasks; humans manage exceptions
4 – Full Impact: AI runs core work; humans step in only for complex tasks
5 – Transformational Impact: AI runs the entire workflow and adapts without human involvement

Score: ______

Role

How much has AI changed the purpose or structure of the role?

0 – No Impact: Role remains the same
1 – Low Impact: Tasks improved or supported by AI; role unchanged
2 – Moderate Impact: Duties shift or expand as AI supports parts of the work
3 – High Impact: Role is redefined; humans supervise AI outputs
4 – Full Impact: Most of the role shifts to AI; humans handle oversight and escalation
5 – Transformational Impact: The original role disappears; humans guide direction and ethics

Score: ______

Skills

How much has AI changed the skills required to perform the role?

0 – No Impact: No new skills needed
1 – Low Impact: Basic digital or AI skills required
2 – Moderate Impact: New skills needed to collaborate with or oversee AI-supported tasks
3 – High Impact: Significant reskilling needed for AI-driven work
4 – Full Impact: New skills needed to oversee and guide AI
5 – Transformational Impact: Skills shift to system design, ethics and long-term guidance rather than day-to-day work

Score: ______

Decision-Making

Who makes decisions in the workflow and how?

0 – No Impact: Humans make all decisions
1 – Low Impact: AI provides suggestions; humans decide
2 – Moderate Impact: AI recommends; humans approve or adjust

3 – High Impact: AI makes most decisions; humans handle exceptions
4 – Full Impact: AI decides within set boundaries; humans intervene only for complex judgement
5 – Transformational Impact: AI decides and adapts across the full workflow; humans guide purpose and governance

Score: ______

Workforce Value
Where does human contribution create value in the workflow?

0 – No Impact: Human value remains unchanged.
1 – Low Impact: Human value increases through productivity gains.
2 – Moderate Impact: Human value shifts towards creativity, judgement or oversight.
3 – High Impact: Human value rises in governance and complex judgement.
4 – Full Impact: Human value lies in validating and governing AI managed work.
5 – Transformational Impact: Human value moves to purpose setting, ethics and long-term accountability outside the workflow.

Score: ______

Add the five scores to obtain a total.

Total Score: ______

This reveals what is changing and creates the foundation for the next question.

GUIDING QUESTION 2: HOW BIG IS THE IMPACT?

Match to the Six Levels of AI Impact

First, divide the total score by five to calculate the AI impact index.

AI Impact Index: Total Score ÷ 5 = ______

Next, map the AI impact index to one of the six levels of AI impact, which show how far the role has shifted from human to AI work.

Level 0 – AI-Irrelevant Work
AI Impact Index: 0.0 to 0.5

Level 1 – AI-Supported Work
AI Impact Index 0.6 to 1.5

Level 2 – AI-Enhanced Work
AI Impact Index 1.6 to 2.5

Level 3 – AI-Driven Work
AI Impact Index 2.6 to 3.5

Level 4 – AI-Orchestrated Work
AI Impact Index 3.6 to 4.9

Level 5 – AI-Automated Work
AI Impact Index 5.0

Level of AI Impact:______

This shows how big the AI Impact is and prepares the ground for deciding what to do next.

GUIDING QUESTION 3: HOW SHOULD WE RESPOND?

Define the AI Impact Actions

Now define the activities that will support the role's transition.

Based on the AI impact level, select the AI impact action that guides how the role should evolve. Each level points to a different set of priorities across workforce design, transition planning, talent decisions, learning needs and organisational structure.

At **Level 0**, work remains fully human-led. The focus is on maintaining traditional structures, building basic digital readiness and retaining people in their current roles.

At **Level 1**, AI begins to assist the work. Organisations shift towards digitally supported workflows, introduce early AI augmentation into daily routines and focus on helping people learn the tools. Talent decisions centre on retaining and upskilling.

At **Level 2,** work becomes hybrid. Tasks move between humans and machines, roles start to evolve and employees learn how to collaborate effectively with AI. Reskilling within the role becomes more prominent, and teams begin rethinking how work should be shared.

At **Level 3,** work becomes AI-led. People supervise and guide AI systems rather than perform most tasks themselves. Talent actions focus on transition and reskilling, learning shifts towards overseeing AI-driven work and organisations often simplify structures to support new workflows.

At **Level 4,** AI drives end-to-end workflows. Human involvement moves into governance and oversight. Talent decisions may include redeployment or responsible phase-out, learning priorities shift to responsible AI management and organisations begin establishing governance bodies to ensure trust, fairness and accountability.

At **Level 5,** work reaches full autonomy. Human contribution centres on ethical and strategic leadership while AI handles execution and optimisation. Talent actions often involve repositioning or phase-out. Learning focuses on guiding AI purposefully, and organisations may rebuild around AI-first models to support long-term operating needs.

When selecting the AI impact actions, also check the influencing factors, which help refine the decision:

Headcount Exposure: How many people are affected

Skill Transferability: How mobile are the skills

Time to Reskill: How long will transitions take

Employee Readiness: How open are people to AI

Organisational Dependency: How critical is the role for continuity

Ethical Intelligence: How ethically sensitive are the tasks

These help confirm that the planned action is realistic and responsible.

Summarise the chosen AI impact action here:

The Human-AI Decoder Playbook gives you a structured way to see how AI is changing work, understand the scale of that change and respond in a way that protects people and strengthens the organisation.

APPENDIX 6: AI IMPACT × SCALE HEATMAP

PURPOSE

The AI Impact × Scale Heatmap helps organisations decide where to focus their efforts as AI reshapes work. It brings together two essential factors: how deeply a role is affected by AI and how many people are impacted. By visualising these two dimensions, the heatmap enables leaders to see which roles require immediate attention, where reskilling or redesign should begin and where governance or communication efforts will matter most. It turns the insights of the human–AI decoder into clear transformation priorities that can be understood by technical and non-technical readers alike.

The example below, drawn from the Call Centre Agent scenario in Chapter 4, illustrates how the heatmap highlights the roles that carry both significant impact and significant scale, helping teams move from analysis to action with confidence.

HOW TO USE THE AI IMPACT × SCALE HEATMAP

The heatmap in Fig. A2 prioritises decisions by showing where high-impact roles affect large groups of employees. It shows where redesign, reskilling, governance or communication should begin and ensures that the organisation focuses first on the roles that matter most for people and performance.

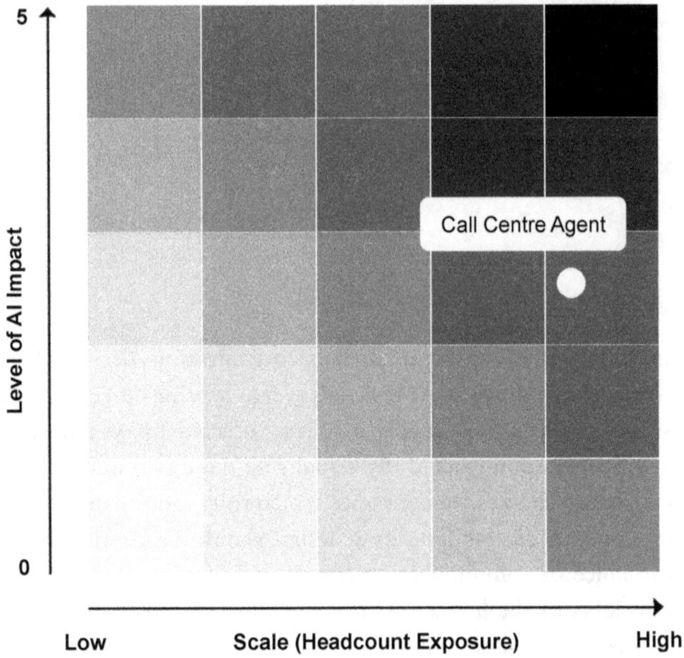

Fig. A2. AI Impact × Scale Heatmap.

Source: Author's Own Creation.

CALL CENTRE AGENT EXAMPLE

- **Impact Score:** 2.8 (Level 3)
- **Headcount Exposure:** 1,200 employees (High Scale)

Placement: Medium–High Impact/High Scale

Interpretation:
Generative AI significantly reshapes the call centre function at scale. While routine customer interactions are increasingly handled by AI, the high headcount exposure means the overall workforce impact is substantial. Organisations must assess whether automation will reduce workload or enable higher interaction volumes and expanded service offerings. Human agents shift towards supervision, escalation handling and more complex, empathy-driven interactions, but the scale of change requires careful workforce

planning, reskilling and clear transition strategies to manage potential displacement and evolving role expectations.

Strategic Guidance:

- Launch targeted reskilling programmes that build oversight, judgement and exception management skills
- Communicate clear career pathways so employees understand how their roles evolve and where they can grow
- Develop metrics that track human–AI collaboration and show where additional human involvement improves outcomes.
- Assess how AI affects interaction volumes and service demand to determine whether automation reduces workload or enables growth.
- Develop workforce transition plans that address redeployment, role redesign and capacity shifts at scale.

APPENDIX 7: AI ROLE IMPACT MAPPING

PURPOSE

This template helps assess how AI is likely to influence specific roles within a team or function. It supports decisions on workforce redesign, talent actions and organisation structure shifts by giving leaders a clear view of how work may evolve.

HOW TO USE THIS ROLE MAPPING TEMPLATE

1. Select the roles to analyse based on importance or expected AI impact.
2. Capture how each role works today to create a clear and factual snapshot.
3. Discuss the findings together to surface judgement needs, risks and opportunities.
4. Use the human–AI decoder to assign an AI Impact Level from 0 to 5.
5. Identify the talent implications for reskilling, redesign, redeployment or transition.
6. Compare results across roles to identify patterns, clusters or shared themes.
7. Feed the insights into workforce planning, including skills, AI pilots and organisational design.

MAPPING TEMPLATE

This template works best when several roles are reviewed together in a workshop or working session. Each role or role cluster is recorded on its own line in a worksheet or digital form. The aim is to create a simple and comparable set of observations that support broader planning.

For each role, document the following information clearly and factually:

- **Role name** such as Underwriter or Marketing Analyst
- **Primary tasks,** describing day-to-day work such as data validation or customer communication
- **Current AI use,** including any tools already in place such as chatbots, CV parsers or sentiment analytics
- **Potential AI use cases,** based on tools available today such as summarisation, document classification or pattern recognition
- **Human judgement required,** indicating whether intuitive, emotional or contextual judgement is high, medium or low
- **Risk of AI error,** describing the consequences if AI makes a mistake, from minor rework to significant regulatory impact
- **Estimated Impact Level,** using the human–AI decoder scale from Level 0 to Level 5.

SCORING AND DISCUSSION

Begin by listing the core tasks of each role and assessing its current level of digital maturity. Focus on realistic AI opportunities based on tools that are proven today rather than on speculative or distant possibilities.

Then, evaluate how much human judgement the role requires and how serious the consequences would be if AI makes an error. This reveals which roles are likely to remain human-led, which may evolve into hybrid or orchestration patterns and which could be redesigned or automated over time.

Use the human–AI decoder to classify the degree of disruption. Roles at Impact Levels 0 to 2 usually experience limited change. Roles at Level 3 often shift towards hybrid models where people guide or supervise AI systems. Roles at Levels 4 and 5 may require deeper redesign, repurposing or full automation, depending on the organisation's context and risk tolerance.

HOW TO USE THE RESULTS

Once the roles are mapped and classified, review them side by side. Group them by impact level to determine where learning, role redesign or reskilling should be prioritised. Look for roles that may evolve into hybrid or orchestration patterns as AI capability grows. Use these insights to direct AI pilots towards areas with mid to high levels of impact. Finally, integrate these findings into your broader workforce planning, skills development and organisational design so the organisation moves in a coordinated way rather than through isolated initiatives.

APPENDIX 8: EMERGING AI ROLES

AI is creating new forms of work as organisations learn how to integrate intelligent systems into daily operations. Many of the roles outlined here already appear in the job market, while others reflect early signals of what companies will soon require as AI becomes more capable. Their responsibilities will continue to evolve as organisations mature, industries adapt and human–machine collaboration deepens.

Each role description includes a short summary, core responsibilities and the skills needed to perform the work. They are based on real job descriptions, emerging practices and observations from AI deployments across sectors. Some have even been shaped with the help of AI tools, reflecting how AI is now part of the process of defining the work itself. Role descriptions reflect patterns from real job postings and industry practices. The role titles and examples are illustrative.

AI/ML AUDIT LEAD

Job Summary

As an AI/ML Audit Lead, you will be responsible for the evaluation, oversight and continuous assurance of AI/ML systems across the enterprise. You will help assess risks, verify controls, and ensure AI systems comply with governance, regulatory and ethical standards. Partnering with internal audit, risk, compliance and engineering teams, you will provide independent challenge and recommend improvements to safeguard AI-driven initiatives.

Key Responsibilities

- Plan and execute audit engagements of AI/ML model deployments, including scoping, testing and reporting of control effectiveness.
- Partner with data science, ML engineering, compliance and business stakeholders to assess design and operating effectiveness of AI controls (e.g. model monitoring, drift detection, bias mitigation).
- Document and present audit findings, including root-cause analysis, risk impact and actionable recommendations.
- Develop, maintain and improve an AI audit framework, methodology and toolkit (including automation opportunities) aligned with industry best-practice.
- Stay abreast of emerging AI/ML regulations, standards (e.g. transparency, fairness), and technology trends; advise stakeholders on implications.
- Support continuous monitoring of model performance, controls and governance mechanisms on a scheduled basis.
- Promote a culture of model risk awareness and responsible AI among audit, business and technology teams.

Required Qualifications, Capabilities & Skills

- Bachelor's degree (or equivalent) in Computer Science, Data Analytics, Information Systems, Risk or Related Field.
- Professional audit qualification (e.g. CISA, CISSP, CIA) or significant experience in internal/technology audit.
- Demonstrated experience auditing technology, data and/or ML systems; familiarity with ML lifecycle, model risk, and model governance. (See e.g. 'Senior Audit Manager – AI Technical Enablement' posting) Citi Careers
- Strong analytical and problem-solving skills, able to evaluate the probability and impact of control weaknesses in AI/ML contexts.

- Good communication skills-able to translate technical risks into business language and present clearly to senior stakeholders.
- Self-motivated, collaborative and able to challenge without disrupting the business.
- Comfortable working in dynamic environments with evolving technology and controls.

HEAD OF COMPUTER VISION & AI SOLUTIONS

Job Summary

As Head of Computer Vision & AI Solutions, you will lead the strategy, research and deployment of computer vision and AI capabilities across the organisation. You will shape high-impact initiatives, build and mentor cross-functional teams, drive innovation and take research into production scale. Reporting to senior leadership, you will influence product roadmaps and ensure AI-driven vision solutions create business value.

Key Responsibilities

- Define and execute the comprehensive R&D and deployment strategy for computer vision/image/video analytics aligned with business objectives.
- Lead, mentor and grow a team of researchers, engineers and data scientists specialising in computer vision, deep learning and AI.
- Identify new frontier research areas (e.g. reinforcement learning for vision, multimodal perception, real-time analytics) and foster partnerships with academia and industry.
- Guide translation of research prototypes into scalable production systems, working with product, engineering and operations teams.
- Establish architectural standards, tool-chains and frameworks (e.g. TensorFlow, PyTorch, OpenCV) for vision applications.

- Oversee performance metrics, reliability, robustness, explainability and scalability of vision solutions.
- Represent the organisation in conferences, publish research work and enhance visibility in the AI community.

Required Qualifications, Capabilities & Skills

- Ph.D. or equivalent experience in Computer Science, Artificial Intelligence, Machine Learning or a related domain.
- 8–10+ years of experience in AI/ML research and development with a track record of leading successful projects (see e.g. current 'Head of Computer Vision' postings). LinkedIn+2Jobstreet+2.
- Deep expertise in machine learning algorithms, computer vision, image/video processing and related frameworks (TensorFlow, PyTorch, OpenCV).
- Proven leadership and mentorship skills, including building and managing high-performing teams.
- Experience deploying AI/vision solutions into production, with attention to scalability, performance and reliability.
- Strong programming skills (Python, C++ or similar) and ability to influence across technical & business domains.
- Excellent spoken and written English; ability to articulate strategy, vision and technical insight to diverse audiences.

AI CUSTOMER SUCCESS LEAD – AI/SAAS PLATFORM

Job Summary

As an AI Customer Success Lead for our AI/SaaS platform, you will be the primary interface for enterprise customers adopting AI-driven solutions. You will guide onboarding, adoption, continuous value realisation and expansion. Embedded in the customer journey, you ensure the AI solutions are responsibly and effectively integrated, promote loyalty and drive product evolution based on user feedback and governance considerations.

Key Responsibilities

- Serve as the trusted advisor and strategic partner for customers using AI solutions, understanding their business goals and aligning AI capabilities accordingly.
- Manage the onboarding, implementation and adoption lifecycle of the AI/SaaS product, including training, change management and continual value delivery.
- Monitor product usage, performance, customer feedback and success metrics (e.g. adoption rate, renewals, customer satisfaction, ROI).
- Identify risks, governance or ethical issues in customer deployments of AI and work with product & engineering teams to mitigate and communicate them.
- Collaborate with Product, Engineering, Data Science and Sales teams to convey customer needs, drive product enhancements and prioritise expansions.
- Develop and deliver training and enablement materials (technical and non-technical) and promote best practices for reliable and ethical AI use.
- Lead customer business reviews, renewal and upsell opportunities, and ensure satisfaction, retention and growth.

Required Qualifications, Capabilities & Skills

- Bachelor's degree in Business, Computer Science, AI/ML or a related field. MBA or advanced degree is a plus.
- 5+ years of experience in Customer Success, Account Management, Solutions Consulting or AI-focused roles.
- Experience working with AI platforms, machine learning applications or SaaS products (see current postings e.g. 'AI Customer Success' in Singapore). jobcube.sg+2Foundit+2.

- Strong communication and relationship-management skills; ability to translate complex AI concepts for business stakeholders.
- Strategic mindset, customer-first outlook, strong problem-solving abilities and root-cause analysis for AI-driven systems.
- Familiarity with AI governance, bias mitigation, ethical AI deployment.
- Proficiency with CRM and AI/SaaS tool-stacks (e.g. Salesforce, OpenAI/HuggingFace integrations) is a plus.
- Data-driven decision-making and ability to track and report success metrics.

AI SYSTEMS GOVERNANCE & MONITORING LEAD

Job Summary

As the AI Systems Governance & Monitoring Lead, you will oversee the performance, trustworthiness, compliance and ethical deployment of AI systems in enterprise operations. You will partner with technical, business and risk teams to ensure AI models behave as intended, remain fair and robust, and support transparent and auditable decision-making.

Key Responsibilities

- Monitor AI system outputs, behaviours and performance in near real-time; detect anomalies, model drift, bias or degradation and oversee remediation.
- Collaborate with data scientists, ML engineers, risk management, compliance and business units to evaluate model behaviour, performance and governance.
- Ensure AI solutions are explainable and auditable: implement dashboards, logs, and controls for transparency and oversight.
- Develop and enforce policies and governance frameworks for responsible AI usage, aligned with industry standards and regulatory requirements.

- Conduct regular assessments and audits of deployed AI systems to identify ethical, fairness or compliance risks and propose mitigation plans.
- Provide training, support and awareness programs to staff across disciplines on AI operations, ethics, governance and risk mitigation.
- Maintain documentation, dashboards and reports to support compliance, model-risk management and senior leadership oversight.

Required Qualifications, Capabilities & Skills

- Bachelor's degree in Computer Science, Data Analytics, Ethics, Governance or a related field.
- Experience in monitoring AI/ML systems, data analytics, model governance or risk/compliance roles.
- Strong understanding of AI technologies, their applications in business contexts and model lifecycle monitoring (e.g. model drift, bias detection).
- Familiarity with regulatory frameworks, ethical guidelines and governance frameworks for AI.
- Excellent analytical, problem-solving and communication skills.
- Ability to work cross-functionally across departments and engage diverse stakeholders.
- Proficiency with data analytics/monitoring tools (e.g. SQL, Python, Power BI) for dashboards and reporting.
- Knowledge of explainable AI (XAI) principles, algorithmic fairness, bias assessment and audit readiness.
- Critical thinking and sound decision-making under uncertainty and evolving risks.

APPENDIX 9: EXECUTIVE CHECKLIST FOR EMPLOYEE AI READINESS

PURPOSE

This checklist helps leadership teams understand whether the conditions for responsible AI adoption are strong enough to support scale. It diagnoses how ready your organisation is to adopt AI responsibly and at scale.

HOW TO USE THIS AI READINESS CHECKLIST

Use the checklist as a quick diagnostic, not a full assessment. Review each item with your leadership team or project group and mark what is already in place. The goal is not to achieve a perfect score. It is to identify where employees may need more clarity, support or structure before AI becomes part of everyday work. The checklist works best when repeated over time as the organisation learns and matures.

AI readiness checklist

1. **Cognitive Readiness**
   - ☐ Employees understand what AI is and how it affects their roles
   - ☐ Learning materials explain AI tools in accessible, non-technical ways

2. **Emotional Readiness**
   - ☐ Leaders are trained to address fear and resistance to AI
   - ☐ Communication emphasises augmentation, not replacement
   - ☐ Success stories of human–AI collaboration are shared
3. **Behavioural Readiness**
   - ☐ Employees have opportunities to experiment with AI in low-risk settings
   - ☐ AI tools are integrated into daily workflows, not bolted on
   - ☐ Adoption is supported by nudges, coaching, or peer support
4. **Organisational Readiness**
   - ☐ Policies are in place for AI ethics, fairness, and transparency
   - ☐ Roles and job structures are being redesigned to support AI–human collaboration
   - ☐ Readiness is recognised in performance and learning systems

HOW TO USE THE RESULTS

If fewer than eight items are checked, the organisation may need to strengthen its foundation before scaling AI. Use any gaps to identify where employees require clearer communication, stronger support or more time to build confidence. The aim is not speed. It is to ensure that people understand the change and feel ready for what comes next.

APPENDIX 10: EMPLOYEE AI CULTURE PULSE SURVEY

PURPOSE

This survey is designed to help leaders understand how people are experiencing AI in real time and where additional guidance may be needed. It measures how employees perceive, experience and emotionally respond to the growing presence of AI in their work. The survey helps identify where trust, clarity or engagement gaps may exist.

HOW TO USE THIS EMPLOYEE AI PULSE SURVEY

This pulse survey is designed to be a quick temperature check rather than a full diagnostic.

Use it to understand how employees are feeling as AI becomes part of their daily work. Run it anonymously, keep the format simple and repeat it at key milestones so you can track shifts in clarity, confidence and trust over time. The results will help identify where employees may need more communication, support or training before AI tools scale more broadly.

AI Culture Pulse Survey
(Response Scale: 1 = Strongly disagree, 5 = Strongly agree)**

Clarity

- I understand what AI tools are being used in our organisation.
- I know how AI affects my role or could change it in the future.

Trust

- I believe our organisation uses AI responsibly and ethically.
- I trust the outputs or decisions generated by AI tools in my work area.

Confidence

- I feel confident using AI-enabled tools or systems.
- I feel safe speaking up if I notice something wrong with an AI system.
- I feel confident working alongside AI tools.

Support

- My manager supports me in learning how to use AI.
- I know where to go if I have questions about an AI tool we use.

Mindset

- I believe AI can help me do my job better.

FORMAT AND INTEGRATION

This survey works best as a short pulse of 10 questions, answered anonymously using a simple one-to-five scale. It is typically run with a representative sample of employees rather than the entire workforce, which keeps it light while still offering an accurate view of how people are experiencing AI. The pulse becomes even more valuable when paired with short interviews or focus groups that reveal the stories behind the numbers. They can also be included into broader engagement surveys, allowing long-term patterns to emerge and ensuring that AI readiness becomes part of the organisation's regular rhythm rather than a one-off exercise.

HOW TO USE THE RESULTS

The results offer a quick picture of where your organisation is steady and where it may need support. If answers cluster below the midpoint 3, it often signals that people need more clarity or reassurance before AI becomes part of their daily work. Patterns matter. Differences between functions, locations or job types can reveal pockets of uncertainty or resistance that might otherwise go unnoticed. The survey becomes even more valuable when repeated after major shifts, such as a new AI tool, a restructure or a communication campaign, because it shows whether confidence and understanding are rising or slipping over time.

EXAMPLE INSIGHTS THAT MIGHT SURFACE

The survey can highlight gaps that are not obvious from the outside. A finance team may feel confident using AI tools but remain unsure about the accuracy of the output, which points to a need for more transparency and explainability. Frontline roles, especially in logistics or operations, may express uncertainty about how AI will affect their jobs, showing the need for clearer communication and targeted upskilling. These insights help leaders decide where to focus attention and where people need more support.

ABOUT THE AUTHOR

Mario Jacober is Regional Head of HR Operations & Technology, APAC, based in Singapore at Zurich Insurance Company, a leading global multi-line insurer operating in more than 200 countries and territories. For more than two decades, he has stood at the intersection of people, technology and transformation. In his senior HR role, he helps define how people evolve and thrive as Artificial Intelligence reshapes the nature of work. His career has taken him into major organisational change, from redesigning skills and structures to guiding leaders through transitions that affect both performance and identity. His work reflects a simple belief. Technology can move quickly, but people must remain the anchor. Mario is committed to giving back to the community and helping young professionals build confidence in a changing world. He serves as Member of the Board of the Swiss Chamber of Commerce in Singapore, where he oversees the People and Skills Committee and is President of the Board at the Swiss School in Singapore. Beyond his professional life, he successfully completed the Dakar Classic Rally in 2022, an experience that reflects the same courage, curiosity and endurance he brings to his work. For more information, visit mario.jacober.com.

REFERENCES

Abrill, D. (2025, September 25). AI is taking on live translations. But jobs and meaning are getting lost. *Washington Post*. https://www.washingtonpost.com/business/2025/09/26/ai-translation-jobs/

Accenture. (2025). *AI and Robots. The economics of reinventing work and the workforce*. https://www.accenture.com/content/dam/accenture/final/capabilities/strategy-and-consulting/strategy/document/Accenture-Humans-AI-Robots.pdf

Acemoglu and Restrepo. (2018). *Artificial intelligence, automation and work*. https://www.nber.org/system/files/working_papers/w24196/w24196.pdf

Afreen. (2025). *Systematic literature review on bias mitigation in generative AI*. Springer. https://link.springer.com/article/10.1007/s43681-025-00721-9

Autor, D. H., Levy, F., & Murnane, R. J. (2003). The skill content of recent technological change: An empirical exploration. *The Quarterly Journal of Economics*, November 2003. https://economics.mit.edu/sites/default/files/publications/theskillcontent2003.pdf

AWS. (2025). *What is Generative AI?* https://aws.amazon.com/what-is/generative-ai

Bain & Company. (2025). *Building the foundation for Agentic AI*. https://www.bain.com/insights/building-the-foundation-for-agentic-ai-technology-report-2025

Bano M., Zowghi, D., Whittle, J., Zhu, L., Reeson, A., Martin, R., & Parsons, J. (2025). *A qualitative study of user perception of M365 AI Copilot*. https://arxiv.org/abs/2503.17661

Beauchene, V., Duranton, S., Kalra, N., & Martin, D. (2025). *AI at work: Momentum builds, but gaps remain.* Boston Consulting Group. https://www.bcg.com/publications/2025/ai-at-work-momentum-builds-but-gaps-remain

Bersin, J. (2018). *A new paradigm for corporate training: Learning in the flow of work*. Deloitte Insights. https://joshbersin.com/2018/06/a-new-paradigm-for-corporate-training-learning-in-the-flow-of-work/

Bersin, J. (2025). The pivotal role of chief HR officer in AI transformation. *Josh Bersin.* https://joshbersin.com/2025/10/the-pivotal-role-of-chief-hr-officer-in-ai-transformation

Bloomberg News. (2025). Klarna turns from AI to real person customer service. *Bloomberg.* https://www.bloomberg.com/news/articles/2025-05-08/klarna-turns-from-ai-to-real-person-customer-service

Boston Consulting Group. (2025). *AI at work: Momentum builds, but gaps remain.* https://www.bcg.com/publications/2025/ai-at-work-momentum-builds-but-gaps-remain

Brynjolfsson & McAfee. (2014). *The Second Machine Age.* W. W. Norton. https://wwnorton.com/books/9780393239355

BW People. (2026). *Microsoft HR reset pushes unlearn and adapt culture.* BW People. https://www.bwpeople.in/article/microsoft-hr-reset-pushes-unlearn-and-adapt-culture-599618

Coachvox AI. (2025). *AI coaching platform for leadership and personal development.* Coachvox Ltd. https://www.coachvox.ai

Daugherty and Wilson. (2018). *Human + machine: Reimagining work in the age of AI.* Harvard Business Review Press.

Deloitte. (2021). *Does your company need a Chief AI Ethics Officer, an AI Ethicist, AI Ethics Council, or all three?* https://www.deloitte.com/us/en/services/consulting/articles/ai-ethicist-and-ai-bias.html

Deloitte. (2024). *State of AI in the enterprise: Generative AI special report.* Deloitte Insights. https://www.deloitte.com/az/en/issues/generative-ai/state-of-generative-ai-in-enterprise.html

Deloitte. (2025a). AI trends 2025: Adoption barriers and updated predictions. *Deloitte Insights.* https://www.deloitte.com/us/en/services/consulting/blogs/ai-adoption-challenges-ai-trends.html

Deloitte. (2025b). *Autonomous generative AI agents: Under development.* https://www.deloitte.com/us/en/insights/industry/technology/technology-media-and-telecom-predictions/2025/autonomous-generative-ai-agents-still-under-development.html

Dewan, N. (2025, May 18). After firing 700 employees for AI, Swedish company admits their mistake and plans to rehire humans. What went wrong? *Economic Times.* https://economictimes.indiatimes.com/magazines/panache/after-firing-700-employees-for-ai-swedish-company-admits-their-mistake-and-plans-to-rehire-humans-what-happened/articleshow/121252776.cms?from=mdr#

European Commission. (2024). *Artificial Intelligence Act: The world's first rules on AI.* https://digital-strategy.ec.europa.eu/en/policies/regulatory-framework-ai

European Union. (2024). *Regulation (EU) 2024/1689 of the European Parliament and of the Council.* https://eur-lex.europa.eu/eli/reg/2024/1689/oj/eng

Feigenbaum. (1988). *Knowledge engineering for the 1980s.* https://purl.stanford.edu/jj871ws1405

Frey & Osborne. (2013). *The future of employment: How susceptible are jobs to computerisation?* University of Oxford. https://oms-www.files.svdcdn.com/production/downloads/academic/The_Future_of_Employment.pdf

Galbraith. (2012). *Designing organizations: Strategy, structure, and process at the business unit and enterprise levels.* Jossey-Bass.

Gartner. (2024a). *Gartner AI maturity model & roadmap toolkit.* Gartner Research. https://www.gartner.com/en/chief-information-officer/research/ai-maturity-model-toolkit

Gartner. (2024b). *Hype cycle for AI.* https://www.gartner.com/en/documents/5505695

Gartner. (2025). *AI in HR: Evolve to an AI-infused HR operating model.* https://www.gartner.com/en/human-resources/topics/artificial-intelligence-in-hr

Gendy & Patel. (2024). Advancements in computer vision: A comprehensive survey of image processing and interdisciplinary applications. *Academic Journal of Science and Technology*. https://www.researchgate.net/publication/386389283_Advancements_in_Computer_Vision_A_Comprehensive_Survey_of_Image_Processing_and_Interdisciplinary_Applications/link/675008d0a7fbc259f1ab1542/download

Gillespie, N., Lockey, S., Ward, T., Macdade, A., & Hassed, G. (2025). *Trust, attitudes and use of artificial intelligence: A global study 2025*. The University of Melbourne & KPMG International. https://assets.kpmg.com/content/dam/kpmgsites/ae/pdf/trust-attitudes-and-use-of-ai-global-report.pdf.coredownload.inline.pdf

Google. (2025a). *AI-enabled imaging and diagnostics previously thought impossible*. Google Health. https://health.google/imaging-and-diagnostics/

Google. (2025b). *Our history*. https://www.google.com/intl/en_us/search/howsearchworks/our-history

Grant. (2007). *Relational job design and the motivation to make a prosocial difference*. Academy of Management Review. https://selfdeterminationtheory.org/SDT/documents/2007_Grant_AMR.pdf

Hackman & Oldham. (1980). *Work redesign*. Addison-Wesley.

Harvard Business Review. (2020). *A practical guide to building ethical AI*. https://hbr.org/2020/10/a-practical-guide-to-building-ethical-ai

Harvard Business Review. (2025). *Overcoming the organizational barriers to AI adoption*. https://hbr.org/2025/11/overcoming-the-organizational-barriers-to-ai-adoption

Hemmer, P., Schemmer, M., Kühl, N., Vössing, M., & Satzger, G. (2025). Complementarity in human-AI collaboration. *Journal of Human-AI Interaction*. https://www.tandfonline.com/doi/epdf/10.1080/0960085X.2025.2475962?needAccess=true

Hill L. A., Le Cam, A., Menon, S., & Tedards, E. (2022). *Digital transformation: A new roadmap for success*. Harvard Business School Working Knowledge. https://www.library.hbs.edu/working-knowledge/leading-in-the-digital-era-a-new-roadmap-for-success

IBM. (2021). *The enterprise guide to closing the skills gap*. https://www.ibm.com/downloads/documents/us-en/10a99803f8afda48

IBM. (2024a). *The history of artificial intelligence*. https://www.ibm.com/think/topics/history-of-artificial-intelligence

IBM. (2024b). *What is machine learning?* https://www.ibm.com/think/topics/machine-learning?mhsrc=ibmsearch_a&mhq=Whatismachinelearn ingquestB

IBM. (2024c). *What is NLP (natural language processing)?* https://www.ibm.com/think/topics/natural-language-processing

IBM. (2025a). *The 5 biggest AI adoption challenges for 2025*. IBM Institute for Business Value. https://www.ibm.com/think/insights/ai-adoption-challenges

IBM. (2025b). *Understanding the different types of artificial intelligence*. https://www.ibm.com/think/topics/artificial-intelligence-types

IBM Research. (2024). *Neuro-symbolic AI*. https://research.ibm.com/topics/neuro-symbolic-ai

Icertis, Inc. (2025). *Icertis Contract Intelligence (CLM) platform*. Icertis. https://www.icertis.com

Inge, C. (2025, April 14). *AI will shape the future of marketing*. Harvard Division of Continuing Education. https://professional.dce.harvard.edu/blog/ai-will-shape-the-future-of-marketing

International Labour Organization (ILO). (2024). *Generative AI and jobs: A refined global index of occupational exposure*. https://www.ilo.org/publications/generative-ai-and-jobs-refined-global-index-occupational-exposure

Ironclad, Inc. (2025). *Ironclad AI contract lifecycle management platform*. Ironclad. https://ironcladapp.com

Jacober, M. (2026). *AI workforce impact model (AIWIM). The human-AI decoder – Leading the human side of AI to drive business results*. Emerald Publishing.

J.P. Morgan Global Research. (2025). *Is AI already impacting job growth.* https://www.jpmorgan.com/insights/global-research/artificial-intelligence/ai-impact-job-growth

Katz & Kahn. (1966). *The social psychology of organizations.* Wiley.

Kramer, R. S. S., Jones, A. L., Fitousi, D., & Tree, J. J. (2025). *AI-generated images of familiar faces are indistinguishable from real photographs.* https://link.springer.com/article/10.1186/s41235-025-00683-w

LawGeex. (2025). *LawGeex AI contract review automation platform.* LawGeex. https://www.lawgeex.com"

Lennick & Kiel. (2011). *Moral intelligence: Enhancing business performance & leadership Success 2.0.* Pearson Education.

LinkedIn Learning. (2025). *Workplace Learning Report 2025.* https://learning.linkedin.com/content/dam/me/learning/en-us/images/lls-workplace-learning-report/2025/full-page/pdfs/LinkedIn-Workplace-Learning-Report-2025.pdf

Lisondra, M., Benhabib, B., & Nejat, G. (2025). *Embodied AI with foundation models for mobile service robots: A systematic review.* Cornell University. https://arxiv.org/pdf/2505.20503

Liu & David. (2025). AI simulation by digital twins: Systematic survey of the state of the art and a reference framework. https://arxiv.org/pdf/2506.06580

McKinsey & Company. (2023). *The economic potential of generative AI.* https://www.mckinsey.com/~/media/mckinsey/business%20functions/mckinsey%20digital/our%20insights/the%20economic%20potential%20of%20generative%20ai%20the%20next%20productivity%20frontier/the-economic-potential-of-generative-ai-the-next-productivity-frontier.pdf

McKinsey & Company. (2024a). *The state of AI in 2025: Agents, innovation, and transformation.* https://www.mckinsey.com/capabilities/quantumblack/our-insights/the-state-of-ai"

McKinsey & Company. (2024b). *What is artificial general intelligence (AGI)?* https://www.mckinsey.com/featured-insights/mckinsey-explainers/what-is-artificial-general-intelligence-agi

McKinsey & Company. (2024c). *What is generative AI?* https://www.mckinsey.com/featured-insights/mckinsey-explainers/what-is-generative-ai

McKinsey & Company. (2025a). *JPMorgan Chase's Derek Waldron on Building an AI-First Bank Culture*. https://www.mckinsey.com/industries/financial-services/our-insights/jpmorgan-chases-derek-waldron-on-building-an-ai-first-bank-culture

McKinsey & Company. (2025b). *Superagency in the workplace: Empowering people to unlock AI's full potential*. https://www.mckinsey.com/industries/financial-services/our-insights/jpmorgan-chases-derek-waldron-on-building-an-ai-first-bank-culture

McKinsey & Company. (2025c). *McKinsey Technology Trends Outlook 2025*. https://www.mckinsey.com/capabilities/tech-and-ai/our-insights/the-top-trends-in-tech

McKinsey & Company. (2025d). *The state of AI: How organizations are rewiring to capture value*. https://www.mckinsey.com/capabilities/quantumblack/our-insights/the-state-of-ai

Merriam-Webster. (2025). *Artificial Intelligence*. https://www.merriam-webster.com/dictionary/artificial%20intelligence

Microsoft. (2023a). *Gone-but-not-forgotten: A look back at discontinued Microsoft products*. https://www.microsoft.com/en-us/microsoft-365-life-hacks/stories/gone-but-not-forgotten-m365-features

Microsoft. (2023b). *Microsoft 365 Copilot*. Microsoft. https://www.microsoft.com/en-us/microsoft-365-copilot

MIT Technology Review. (2024). *The four most basic elements in machine cognition*. https://direct.mit.edu/dint/article/6/2/297/123379/The-Four-Most-Basic-Elements-In-Machine-Cognition

MIT Technology Review. (2025). *The road to AGI*. https://wp.technologyreview.com/wp-content/uploads/2025/09/MITTR_ArmEBrief_V12_final-v13.pdf

Mitchell. (2021). *Why AI is harder than we think*. Santa Fe Institute. https://arxiv.org/pdf/2104.12871

Mu, G., Zhang, Y., Yan, Z., Yu, Q., & Wang, Q. (2025). Recent advancements in wearable sensors: integration with machine learning for human–machine interaction. *RSC Advances*. https://pubs.rsc.org/en/content/articlepdf/2025/ra/d5ra00167f

Nanyang Technological University Business School. (2025). *How to develop continuous learners: Building a culture of adaptability*. https://www.ntu.edu.sg/business/news-events/news/story-detail/how-to-develop-continuous-learners–building-a-culture-of-adaptability

OECD. (2021). *AI and the future of skills, Volume 1: Capabilities and assessments, educational research and innovation*. OECD Publishing. https://www.oecd.org/en/publications/ai-and-the-future-of-skills-volume-1_5ee71f34-en.html

OECD. (2025). *Introducing the OECD AI capability indicators*. OECD Publishing. https://www.oecd.org/content/dam/oecd/en/publications/reports/2025/06/introducing-the-oecd-ai-capability-indicators_7c0731f0/be745f04-en.pdf

Olufunmilayo, O., Okon, S. U., Olaniyi, O. O., Samuel-Okon, A. D., & Asonze, C. U. (2024). Exploring the concept of explainable AI and developing information governance standards for enhancing trust and transparency in handling customer data. *Journal of Engineering Research and Reports*. https://journaljerr.com/index.php/JERR/article/view/1206/2396

Opentools.ai. (2025, July 6). *UK High Court Judge warns lawyers: Fabricating cases with AI could lead to sanctions*. https://opentools.ai/news/uk-high-court-judge-warns-lawyers-fabricating-cases-with-ai-could-lead-to-sanctions

Pearl & Mackenzie. (2024). *The new science of cause and effect: Causal models for AI and human reasoning*. MIT Press.

PricewaterhouseCoopers (PwC). (2018). *Will robots really steal our jobs?* PwC Global. https://www.pwc.com/gx/en/issues/analytics/assets/pwc-ai-analysis-sizing-the-prize-report.pdf

PricewaterhouseCoopers (PwC). (2025a). *Global AI jobs barometer 2025*. https://www.pwc.com/gx/en/issues/artificial-intelligence/ai-jobs-barometer.html

PricewaterhouseCoopers (PwC). (2025b). Global workforce hopes and fears survey 2025. *PwC*. https://www.pwc.com/gx/en/issues/workforce/hopes-and-fears.html

PricewaterhouseCoopers (PwC). (2025c). *PwC's AI agent survey*. https://www.pwc.com/us/en/tech-effect/ai-analytics/ai-agent-survey.html

PricewaterhouseCoopers (PwC). (2025d). *Global AI jobs barometer: Empowering people in the age of AI*. PwC Research Insights. https://www.pwc.com/gx/en/news-room/press-releases/2025/ai-linked-to-a-fourfold-increase-in-productivity-growth.html

Ransbotham, S., Khodabandeh, S., Kiron, D., Candelon, F., Chu, M., & LaFountain, B. (2021). *Expanding AI impact with organizational learning Oct 2020 - MIT – Sloan*. https://www.scribd.com/document/808624736/expanding-ai-impact-with-organizational-learning-oct-2020-MIT-Sloan

Richter, J. D. (2025, August 18). *How AI is transforming the legal profession*. Thomson Reuters. https://legal.thomsonreuters.com/blog/how-ai-is-transforming-the-legal-profession

Riedl & De Cremer. (2025). *AI for collective intelligence*. https://journals.sagepub.com/doi/10.1177/26339137251328909

Roth, E. (2025, August 13). *Reconfiguring work: Change management in the age of gen AI*. McKinsey & Company. https://www.mckinsey.com/capabilities/quantumblack/our-insights/reconfiguring-work-change-management-in-the-age-of-gen-ai

Russell & Norvig. (2022). *Artificial intelligence: A modern approach* (4th ed.). Pearson Education.

Schwab. (2016). *The Fourth Industrial Revolution*. World Economic Forum. https://www.weforum.org/about/the-fourth-industrial-revolution-by-klaus-schwab

Shahbandi. (2025). AI chatbots vs. human customer service: Impact on consumer satisfaction and purchase decisions. *International Business & Economics Studies*. https://www.scholink.org/ojs/index.php/ibes/article/view/56028

Stanford AI Index. (2025). *Artificial Intelligence Index Report 2025*. https://hai.stanford.edu/assets/files/hai_ai_index_report_2025.pdf

Stanford Institute for Human-Centered Artificial Intelligence. (2025). *AI index report 2025*. Stanford University. https://hai.stanford.edu/ai-index/2025-ai-index-report

Toffler. (1970). *Future shock*. Random House.

Tupsakhare. (2025). Intelligent automation: Integrating AI and RPA for smarter processes. *International Journal on Science and Technology*. https://www.ijsat.org/papers/2025/1/2833.pdf"

Ulrich. (1997). *Human resource champions: The next agenda for adding value and delivering results*. Harvard Business School Press.

Wilson & Daugherty. (2024). Designing AI systems with human–machine teams. *MIT Sloan Management Review*. https://sloanreview.mit.edu/article/designing-ai-systems-with-human-machine-teams/

World Economic Forum (WEF). (2024, January 3). *To truly harness AI we must close the AI skills gap*. WEF. https://www.weforum.org/stories/2024/01/to-truly-harness-ai-we-must-close-the-ai-skills-gap

World Economic Forum (WEF). (2025). *The future of jobs report 2025*. WEF. https://www.weforum.org/publications/the-future-of-jobs-report-2025/

World Economic Forum (WEF). (2025a). *Future of jobs report 2025*. https://reports.weforum.org/docs/WEF_Future_of_Jobs_Report_2025.pdf

World Economic Forum (WEF). (2025b). *The future of jobs report 2025*. WEF. https://www.weforum.org/publications/the-future-of-jobs-report-2025/

World Economic Forum (WEF). (2025c). *The trust imperative: 5 levers for scaling AI responsibly*. https://www.weforum.org/stories/2025/01/the-trust-imperative-5-levers-for-scaling-ai-responsibly

World Economic Forum (WEF). (2025d). *A practical guide to implementing and scaling new tools*. World Economic Forum in collaboration with PwC. https://www.weforum.org/stories/2024/11/generative-ai-work-implementation-scaling/

World Health Organization. (2023). *Ethics and governance of artificial intelligence for health: Guidance for policy-makers*. WHO. https://www.who.int/publications/i/item/9789240084759

XPENG. (2025). *XPENG unveils P5 humanoid robot with enhanced mobility and expanded capabilities*. https://www.xpeng.com/news/019a56f54fe99a2a0a8d8a0282e402b7

Zhao, F., Zeng, Y., Wang, Y., Lu, E., Yang, Y., Wang, L., Liu, C., Liang, Y., Zhao, X., Han, B., Tong, H., Liang, Y. Liang, D., Sun, K., Chen, B., & Fan, J. (2025). *Super co-alignment of human and AI for Sustainable Symbiotic Society*. Cornell University. https://arxiv.org/abs/2504.17404

www.ingramcontent.com/pod-product-compliance
Lightning Source LLC
Chambersburg PA
CBHW061737140826
49883CB00030B/327
* 9 7 8 1 8 0 6 8 6 8 9 2 6 *